HOSTAGE

Other books by the Author:

Non-Fiction
Afghanistan: A History of Conflict
Afghanistan: Key to a Continent
Fathercare: A Handbook for Single Fathers
Flashpoint Afghanistan – A Guide for Sixth Formers
Modern Iceland
Nimbus: Technology Serving the Arts
The Science of Winning Squash
The Third Man: A Biography of William Murdoch
Three Tomorrows: A Comparative Study of Russian, American and British Science Fiction

Fiction
The Queen of Spades: An Afghan Adventure
The Survivors

HOSTAGE

The History, Facts & Reasoning Behind Hostage Taking

John C. Griffiths

First published in 2003 by
André Deutsch Ltd
An imprint of the
Carlton Publishing Group
20 Mortimer Street
London W1T 3JW

A catalogue record for this book is available from the British Library

ISBN 0 233 00034 8

The publishers would like to thank the following sources for their kind permission to
reproduce the pictures in this book:

Page 1: Top: John Meagher/Hulton-Deutsch Collection/CORBIS; Bottom: Topham;
Page 2: Top: Bettmann/CORBIS; Middle: Stringer/Gettyimages; Bottom: PA Photos/EPA;
Page 3: Top: Sipa Press/Rex Features; Bottom: Bettman/CORBIS; Page 4: Sipa Press/Rex
Features; Page 5: Top: David Rubinger/CORBIS; Bottom: AFP/Gettyimages; Page 6: Top:
Fabian Cevallos/CORBIS SYGMA; Bottom: F Zabci/Rex Features; Page 7: Top: PA
Photos/Adam Butler; Bottom: PA Photos/Barry Batchelor; Page 8: Top: Itar-Tass/Rex
Features; Bottom: Denisov Anton/Rex Features

Every effort has been made to acknowledge correctly and contact the source and/or
copyright holder of each picture, and André Deutsch Ltd apologizes for any unintentional
errors or omissions which will be corrected in future editions of this book.

Printed and bound in Great Britain
by Mackays

Contents

For Penelope

Acknowledgements

Many people have helped me in the research for this book.
A few, who have no objection, are acknowledged in the footnotes,
and I hope the others will accept my sincere thanks anonymously.

Chapter One

A Short History of Political Hostage-Taking

The holding of hostages as a means of coercing an enemy or an ally into complying with your will is at least as old as the recorded history of human conflict. In Homer and the Old Testament, in Herodotus and Thucydides, in Holinshed and the Venerable Bede, accounts of the leverage afforded by the control of hostages abound. While the practice may have developed differently at different times and in quite separate cultures, the underlying idea remains the same. On their very first contact with Europeans, the natives of the West Indies and South America left hostages aboard the ships of the early explorers without even having to be asked to do so, but in China and other parts of the Far East in the same period, prisoners of war were either put to death or used as slaves rather than being held hostage as a means of exerting pressure on the enemy. In our own time, however, China has been one of the more sophisticated hostage-takers.

Nominally, the oldest record of hostage-taking can be found in Ireland where the Mound of the Hostages, the Duma na n Giall, dates to about the middle of the third millennium BC – the name, however, may have been attached much later. The patriarch Abraham probably has a more authentic claim, at least to having been the first successful rescuer of hostages, in around 2000 BC. The story is told in Genesis[1] of how, when his nephew Lot was taken hostage, Abraham…

> … led forth his trained men, born in his house, three hundred and eighteen, and pursued as far as Dan. And he divided himself against them by night, he and his servants, and smote them, and pursued them unto Hobah, which is on the left hand of

7

Damascus. And he brought back all the goods, and also brought again his brother Lot, and his goods, and the women also, and the people.

Sometime in the 13th or 14th century BC Athens was sending hostages in tribute to the Minoan kingdom in Crete, an event mythologized in the story of Theseus and the Minotaur and the seven maids and seven youths that had to be sent annually to Knossos. Whether Theseus' great adventure actually took place on 6 April 1400 BC is another matter, however.[2]

The oldest contemporary documentary record of hostage-taking and exchange is one dated 1269 BC in which Ramses II of Egypt and the Hittite ruler, Hattusilis III, agreed to exchange each other's traitorous fugitives. By the fifth century BC the exchange of hostages as sureties for the loyalty or neutrality of potentially hostile states in times of war was a well-established practice. The Persians, recruiting for their armies in the Aegean islands in 490 BC, insisted on being given children as hostages. If their request was denied, they would destroy the recalcitrant city. Similar exchanges took place during the Peloponnesian wars (460 to 445 BC and 431 to 404 BC) and seem to have kept the potential enemies of both Sparta and Athens in check, at least while the outcome of the war was undecided.[3] In his play *Lysistrata*, Euripedes has the eponymous heroine making hostages of the young Athenian wives, a dramatic device no doubt inspired by the experience of contemporary practice among the Greek city states during the Peloponnesian wars.[4]

A hundred years later, Alexander the Great was doing the same thing, sending hostages back to Macedonia, recruiting them into his armies or, in the case of the wife, mother and children of the defeated King Darius, making them a part of his entourage and treating them royally.[5]

The Romans, ever quick to learn from the Greeks, were also prudent hostage-takers. In 197 BC they suppressed a revolt by a confederacy of Spanish tribes and took hostages from each of those involved to ensure that there was no recurrence. During the Roman occupation of Britain similar tactics were employed and were presumably becoming universal if the name of the Irish hero Nial of the Nine Hostages in the fourth century AD is indicative of the times.

However, by the end of the first millennium AD, the two streams of hostage-taking clearly overlapped, giving and exchanging or simply taking being utilized according to the distribution of power between the parties. It has been argued that the exchange of marital hostages grew both as a result of a recognition of the cost of blood feuds and tribal wars between neighbours and the instinctive recognition that the genetic problems of incest within small tribal and family groups were best solved by "marrying out".[6] By 1100 AD, the Saracens were taking leading crusaders as hostages – such as Count Bohemond of Taranto – and the trade had soon become a wholesale and ruthless one. On one occasion, the Crusaders beheaded 2,700 Turks on the feast of the

Assumption of the Blessed Virgin Mary, giving thanks for this act of vengeance while remembering those Christians slain in battle.[7] These were not casual acts of cruelty, rather more a calculated policy, as a gruesome passage from the following account[8] demonstrates.

> Saladin had not arranged for the return of the Holy Cross. Instead, he neglected the hostages who were held as security for its return. He hoped, indeed, that by using the Holy Cross he could gain much greater concessions in negotiation. Saladin, meanwhile, was sending gifts and messengers to the King, gaining time by false and clever words. He fulfilled none of his promises, but by an increasing use of graceful and ambiguous words he attempted for a long time to keep the King from making up his mind … Later, indeed, after the time limit had more than passed, King Richard determined that Saladin had hardened his heart and cared no longer about ransoming the hostages. He assembled a council of the greater men among the people and they decided that they would wait in vain no longer, but that they would behead the captives. They decided, however, to set apart some of the greater and more noble men on the chance that they might be ransomed or exchanged for some other Christian captives.

Richard himself was to become a hostage to Duke Leopold of Austria in 1193 and even if the songs of Blondin may have cheered him up they did not improve his temper over the matter of the long delay by his brother John and the English nobles in assembling a ransom for him: "Sad and full of shame will be their plight if long I languish here."[9] Since the enormous ransom demanded did not seem to be forthcoming, the Emperor Henry VI settled for a part-payment and various political concessions. A more important consequence, perhaps, was that when the barons compelled Richard's successor, King John, to sign Magna Carta in 1215, it specifically contained a number of clauses dealing with the taking and holding of hostages. The three clauses state:

41.   All merchants may safely and securely go out of England, and come into England, and delay and pass through England, as well by land as by water, for the purpose of buying and selling, free from all evil taxes, subject to the ancient and right customs – save in time of war, and if they are of the land at war against us. And if such be found in our land at the beginning of the war, they shall be held, without harm to their bodies and goods, until it shall be known to us or our chief justice how the merchants of our land are to be treated who shall, at that time, be found in the land at war against us. And if ours shall be safe there, the others shall be safe in our land.

58.   We shall straightway return the son of Llewelin and all the Welsh hostages, and the charters delivered to us as surety for the peace.

59.   We shall act towards Alexander, king of the Scots, regarding the restoration of his sisters, and his hostages, and his liberties and his lawful right, as we shall act

> towards our other barons of England; unless it ought to be otherwise according
> to the charters which we hold from William, his father, the former king of the
> Scots. And this shall be done through judgement of his peers in our court.

The latter clause was a reference to the treaty made between England and
Scotland in 1174 in an attempt to regularize an increasingly anarchic situation.
France and Savoy signed a similar treaty in 1303. In the 17th century, Hugo
Grotius was to make the first attempt to codify all these piecemeal agreements
into a coherent international law that culminated in the 1979 United Nations
Hostage Convention.

The practice of hostage-taking was no less common on the outer fringes of
Europe. It is clear from *Beowulf* that truces and peace treaties were secured in
Scandinavian countries both by the taking of oaths and the more reliable giving
of hostages well before the early 11th century when the poem was written. The
story itself appears to take place in the sixth century. The appearance in names
of *gisl*, *gils* or *gisli* in the Icelandic sagas may indicate the nominee's status, or
that of a forbear* who at some time might have been taken as a hostage. In
Grimnismal a hero's horse enjoys this title – presumably a valuable or favourite
steed that had been given as security at an earlier stage. Being a hostage was
nothing to be ashamed of in the Europe of the Middle Ages, as hostages of both
sexes were usually adopted as members of the tribe or family holding them and
many of the men would even fight on their captor's behalf, though their lives
could still be forfeited if things went wrong.

One of the best known, and certainly one of the most romantic, of hostage
tales is that of the legendary Burgundian hostages Walther and Hildigunde,
who, in the fifth century AD, were sent as children to the court of Attila the
Hun. When they grew up they fell in love, ran away and lived happily ever
after![10] Even better known was Barbarossa, who, in 1158, forced the city of
Milan to make considerable concessions to him by taking 300 of its citizens
hostage.

Little changed over the next three or four hundred years. The Ottoman
sultans forced the rulers of their numerous satrapies to send family members to
Byzantium as a guarantee of subservience; Elizabeth I's generals in Ireland
during Tyrone's rebellion took and hanged hostages; when Emperor Charles V
was taken hostage, two of his sons were sent in his place and a treaty with
England's Henry VIII was sealed by despatching four gentlemen of the
bedchamber and four pages to the English court.[11] England's Charles I set up
a hostage redemption fund in the 1640s which was usually called on to secure
the release of wealthy heiresses from what amounted to criminal kidnappings.

---

* *In the way that we have Smiths, Bakers and Taylors etc.*

This is one of the few occasions where the taking of a female, rather than a male, hostage was preferred.

Then, in 1683, almost unnoticed at the time, an event occurred that would, in due course, mark a new phase in hostage-taking – the role played not by a regional power, but by a global one.

A young Dutch immigrant, Joost Jansen van Meteren, arrived on the shores of America on 12 April 1662. The following year, on 10 June, Minnisink Indians attacked and burned the village in which he had settled and took a number of women and children hostage, young Joost and his mother among them. Ten weeks later, on 5 September 1683, Captain Martin Krieger and a squad of soldiers from New Amsterdam rescued 23 hostages. From the late 18th century onwards, America, rapidly emerging as a global force to be reckoned with and which would eventually become the most powerful nation in the history of mankind, increasingly featured in incidents of hostage-taking. The first embryonic manifestation of that power took place between the end of the 18th and the beginning of the 19th century.

From 1784 to 1815 the four westernmost states on the north African shore of the Mediterranean – Algeria, Morocco, Tunisia and what is now Libya – indulged vicariously in state-sponsored terrorism – a tradition that was sustained by some of them in the latter part of the 20th century. The notorious Barbary pirates were encouraged and protected by the rulers of the countries in which they were based, as they took a handsome cut from the money the corsairs seized or extorted. With the navies of the world's two great powers, Britain and France, tied up in the prolonged and bitter war that would last until 1812, America had no option but to send envoys to negotiate the release of the 700 or so American sailors who had been taken from 36 merchant ships and one naval vessel during the course of the 30-year war. The majority of them were held for long periods in the most degrading and brutal conditions and it is amazing that only a small percentage of them died. Nevertheless, by the end of the 19th century, America had paid out more than $1 million in cash and naval stores to redeem its citizens. Jefferson and Adams skilfully played upon the injured pride of a narrow majority of congressmen to secure the funds to build up America's then almost non-existent navy.[12] They could never have envisaged the day when a single US carrier force would dispose of more firepower than the rest of the world's navies put together. However, the crucial factor in ending the Barbary corsairs' reign of terror and putting an end to their depredations remained the still-mighty British navy. Yet even the modest participation of American warships in the Barbary coast operation nurtured the belief in the overriding importance of securing the nation's honour that was to become a hallmark of subsequent US foreign policy.

As communications across the Atlantic were so slow, the protection of that honour was largely dependent on the decisions made by the commanders who were on the spot – it was a responsibility they seemed to relish. Jefferson's declaration of his "determination to prefer war in all cases to tribute under any form and under any people whatsoever" simply endorsed that fact and was just the first of many examples of presidential rhetoric that were to cost some American hostages their lives. Not until the early 1900s would the United States face another challenge to its honour overseas. In the intervening years, hostage-taking became a highly domestic United States pastime.

On 23 September 1858, a Colonel G. Wright of the 9th Infantry signed a treaty with the Spokane Indians following their defeat in a punitive attack. The relevant clauses are typical victor's terms.

Article 3. The chiefs and headmen of the Spokane Indians, for and on behalf of the whole nation, promise and agree to deliver to the officers in command of the United States troops the men who commenced the attack upon Lieutenant Colonel Steptoe contrary to the orders of their chiefs, and further to deliver as aforesaid at least one chief and four men with their families as hostages for their future good conduct.

Article 4. The chiefs and headmen of the Spokane nation of Indians promise, for and on behalf of the whole tribe, that all white persons shall at all times and places pass through their country unmolested, and further, that no Indians hostile to the United States shall be allowed to pass through or remain in their country.

Article 5. The foregoing conditions being fully complied with by the Spokane nation, the officer in command of the United States troops promises that no war shall be made upon the Spokanes, and further, that the men delivered up, whether as prisoners or hostages, shall in no ways be injured, and shall, within the period of one year, be restored to their nation.

Brigadier Clarke of the 6th Infantry, the general commanding officer, objected vigorously to the "leniency" of Article 5, but grudgingly conceded that it was too late to do anything about it. History does not seem to record whether or not the Spokanes got their hostages back in due course.

Not surprisingly, once the Civil War broke out there was some fierce and unscrupulous tit-for-tatting with regard to the taking and treatment of hostages. The crews of two Confederate privateers were captured and all 50 men were condemned to death for piracy by the Union in 1861. Since privateering was deemed legal in time of war, the indignant Confederates immediately turned 50 prisoners in their jail in Charleston into hostages under sentence of death. When two Confederate soldiers were executed for spying, two Union prisoners were promptly sentenced to death. The Union riposted by threatening to hang General Lee's son if the sentences were carried out.

The practice of using hostages as human shields was not unknown either. The Confederates placed 50 Union captives in the civilian part of Charleston to deter Union gunboats from bombarding the area; in return, the Union placed 50 Confederate prisoners on the selfsame gunboats to protect them from the fire of the Charleston forts. In all these instances, both the Confederates and the Union backed down and the prisoners were exchanged. However, not all Civil War hostages escaped with their lives. When General Grant executed seven Southern guerrillas, their commander, Colonel Mosby, ordered his Union prisoners to select seven of their own number and executed them in retaliation. In all these cases, the distinction between hostages and prisoners of war was a fine one.

In an attempt to bring some order to these exchanges, President Lincoln drew up general order number 100 and issued it on 24 April 1863. Articles 54 to 56 make interesting reading.

Article 54.	A hostage is a person accepted as a pledge for the fulfilment of an agreement concluded between belligerents during the war, or in consequence of a war. Hostages are rare in the present age.
Article 55.	If a hostage is accepted, he is treated like a prisoner of war, according to rank and condition, as circumstances may admit.
Article 56.	A prisoner of war is subject to no punishment for being a public enemy, nor is any revenge wreaked upon him by the intentional infliction of any suffering, or disgrace, by cruel imprisonment, want of food, by mutilation, death, or any other barbarity.

Meanwhile the imperial powers of "Old Europe" were going about the business of dealing with the hostage-taking of their citizens in their usual high-handed way. In 1868, Field Marshall Napier undertook one of the most remarkable military campaigns of the century – and all to rescue a handful of hostages (Irish, French, German and English, including Rassam, the British envoy) from the volatile and unbalanced Emperor Theodore of Ethiopa who had taken them. Britannia had decided that her pride and honour were at stake and that no cost was too high to demonstrate that this was not an Empire to be trifled with. Napier commanded a combined military and auxiliary force of 32,000 men together with their supplies, ammunition and transport. They were conveyed to the coast of East Africa in 280 ships where a harbour and a 700-foot pier had been carved from the barren shore to receive them. Two water desalinization plants were constructed for men and beasts, though even these proved inadequate in the extreme heat. A railway was laid to take the army on the first part of its expedition and roads were built through some extraordinarily difficult terrain into the heart of Ethiopia. Eventually Napier caught up with Theodore and his courageous and not ill-armed force at the mountain-city fortress of Magdala. There, at the cost of only a couple of score of wounded redcoats, he inflicted a heavy defeat and many casualties on the Ethiopians and so secured the release of all the hostages unharmed before marching home again to be received with great acclaim and a peerage. Britain, like America in recent times, had demonstrated that you do not trifle with the world's only superpower.[13]

In the heyday of the British Empire in the 19th century, its native people, overwhelmed by Britain's rarely defeated military machine, extended their inter-tribal practice of hostage-taking to the vulnerable among their conquerors. The Afghans were past masters at this. For example, contrary to the popular misconception that Dr Brydon was the sole survivor of the British retreat from Kabul in 1842, several tribal chiefs held some 40 hostages between them, mostly women and children, who were well treated and released when it became apparent that the Lion was about to bite the jackal that had twisted its tail so painfully.*

In the 19th century, the Belgians, then still an imperial power, also began to develop further the idea of codifying the rules governing the taking and holding of hostages on which Grotius had embarked. The French and American Revolutions and the general scepticism fostered by the Enlightenment were challenging the concept that hereditary monarchs, and indeed Republican governments, could act as they pleased. If this divine right was unjustified, then some acts of rebellion and the challenging of governmental authority in certain circumstances, could be construed neither as treason nor as a crime. In 1833, Belgium enacted a law exempting political prisoners from extradition and this exclusion was widely accepted throughout Europe by the end of the 19th century. As we have seen earlier, this was a complete reversal of the historic concept that such offenders were precisely the ones who should be extradited. Such revolutionary ideas clearly made the heads of many European countries nervous and again many followed Belgium's lead of 1855 in deciding that: "No act shall be considered a political crime or connected with such a crime if it is an attack upon the person of the head of a foreign government or of the members of his family, when this attack takes the form of either murder, assassination or poisoning."[14]

In 1901 came the next significant challenge to the authority and the political thinking of the United States, arguably already the world's foremost economic and military power, if not yet widely acknowledged as such. The seizure by Macedonian nationalist brigands of the American missionary Ellen Stone in September presented Teddy Roosevelt with a considerable dilemma which was

* See the author's Afghanistan: A History of Conflict, André Deutsch, 2001, p31.

encapsulated in a memo to his Assistant Secretary of State: "Every missionary, every trader in wild lands, should know and is inexcusable for not knowing that the American government had no power to pay the ransom of anyone who is captured by brigands or savages ... But it is impossible to adopt this standard about women."

How could an excessively evangelical nation allow one of its evangelists, and a woman at that, to languish in captivity, as Stone did for nearly six months? Had the captive been a man, Roosevelt would no doubt have said: "Tough. You got yourself into this mess you get yourself out," but as the *Houston Post* made clear, such a laissez-faire attitude to the predicament of a female hostage could not be tolerated:

> This affair of Miss Stone has taxed the patience of the American people until it is about to be exhausted ... We have a President who boasts himself to be strenuous, but who has been playing the role of the faineant, a do-nothing who lets himself and the country be made a mock of by a handful of foreign brigands ... A few warships in the harbors of the countries at fault and a couple of regiments of American regulars would do the trick.

And, as Roosevelt knew, cost a great deal of money and risk war with the still by no means insignificant Ottoman Empire. However, simply to pay the ransom of 25,000 Turkish pounds demanded – no very great sum – would have shown the President to be a wimp and his government ineffectual.

Roosevelt got round the problem cunningly. On the one hand, he instructed his cabinet to make a rousing declaration that "never again will we sanction the payment of a ransom", while on the other he ensured that the ransom was paid under the apparent umbrella of public subscription, though eventually the US government reimbursed the subscribers. Other American missionaries in the Balkans were furious at what they saw as an open invitation to kidnap them, too. Nor was the *Houston Post* appeased:

> Why was the protection afforded to Miss Stone limited to vain protests and fruitless negotiations? Is an American citizen abroad to be taken care of only by letter writing? Or are the army and navy of the United States to be used only when there is a motive of gain and Mr Roosevelt's rich tropical islands are in question?

This was a little harsh, but there does seem to be more than a little truth in Mark Twain's crack that Roosevelt "would go to Halifax for half a chance to show off and to Hell for a whole one"- a failing not unknown to subsequent American Presidents.

In May 1904, conveniently only two months before the Republican Convention, another opportunity arose for Roosevelt to polish up his tough-guy image. With the connivance of the Sultan, a Moroccan tribal chieftan called Raisuli had seized the American envoy, Perdicaris, and his stepson and demanded both a ransom and political concessions from his own Sultan for their release. Roosevelt's scriptwriters coined another ringing phrase on 22 June: "The government wants Perdicaris alive or Raisuli dead!" The president had already despatched a naval squadron to the Moroccan coast to back up his threat, but in a secret protocol the marines were told neither to land nor to seize the Moroccan customs house. As Raisuli had previously cut the throat of the local envoy sent to relay the consequences if Perdicaris were not released, Roosevelt, with the Convention imminent, had second thoughts. A ransom of $70,000 was paid and both Perdicaris and his stepson were released. It would never have done to have an American citizen in durance vile during a presidential nomination contest![15] This pattern of tough public posturing and behind-the-scenes concessions was to be followed up often over the next 100 years.

While the German use of hostages in the First World War was nothing like as extensive as it was to become in the Second World War, it was, nevertheless, an openly declared means for controlling the population of a conquered territory. In Liège, for example, the bishop, mayor, sheriff and a number of other prominent citizens were held as unequivocal surety for the city's docile compliance with its occupier's demands, as a proclamation to the public makes clear:

> Every aggression committed against the German troops by any persons other than soldiers in uniform, not only exposes the guilty person to be immediately shot, but will also entail the severest reprisals against all the inhabitants and especially against those natives of Liège who have been detained as hostages in the citadel of Liège by the Commandant of the German troops.[16]

The success of the Russian Revolution and the rather half-hearted intervention of the Allies on the side of the White Russians resulted in the retaliatory seizing of American and British hostages, among them the British consul, the Scots literateur and adventurer, R. Bruce Lockhart. In return for the release of the captives, the communists demanded food and medical supplies and diplomatic recognition of the new regime. The first they quickly obtained, but the second only grudgingly and long after the hostages had been released.*

Between the two World Wars the public and the media were intrigued mostly by criminal kidnappings – the first-ever skyjacking in Peru in 1931 and the kidnapping of the child of the aviation pioneer Lindbergh in 1932, for instance.

The Second World War saw both the wholesale involvement of civilian populations and, as Germany's forces became uncomfortably stretched, the

---

The UK in 1924, France in 1932 and the USA in 1933.

ever-increasing taking of hostages, particularly in France,[17] Greece, the Netherlands, Poland and the former Yugoslavia, as a means of trying to free German troops tied down by the need to counter partisans and guerrillas. However, what is more significant than the scale of these actions is the fact that for the first time the senior officers responsible for the taking and frequent killing of such hostages were held to account for their actions by due judicial process.

At the Nuremberg trials following the Allied victory, several high-ranking Nazi officers pleaded *Kriegsraeson geht vor Kriegsmanier* (military necessity) as justification for the taking or killing of hostages. The Tribunal (instituted by the victors, naturally) went along with them in principle, while condemning the Nazi interpretation and application of that principle. It concurred with the defendants that:

> ... the taking and shooting of hostages in order to guarantee the peaceful conduct in the future of the populations of occupied territories, may in certain circumstances be legal under international law [and that] ... as a last resort, hostages and prisoners may be shot in accordance with international custom and practice.

In the case of General List, a field officer commanding in Greece and Yugoslavia, the Tribunal agreed that:

> He was authorized to pacify the country with military force; he was entitled to punish those who attacked his troops or sabotaged his transportation and communication lines as *francs tireurs*; he was entitled to take precautions against those suspected of participation in the resistance movement, such as registration, limitations of movement, curfew regulations and other measures hereinbefore set forth in this opinion. As a last resort, hostages and reprisal prisoners may be shot in accordance with international custom and practice.

The judges representing the four occupying powers – America, Russia, Britain and France – added that:

> If adequate troops were not available, or if the lawful measures against the population failed in their purpose, the occupant could limit its operations or withdraw from the country in whole or in part, but no right existed to pursue a policy in violation of International Law.

In a biting rider they observed:

> The taking of reprisals against the civilian population by killing members thereof in retaliation for hostile acts against the armed forces or military operations of the

occupant seems to have been originated by Germany in modern times. It has been invoked by Germany in the Franco-Prussian War, the First World War and in the Second World War. No other nation has resorted to the killing of members of the civilian population to secure peace and order in so far as our investigation has revealed.

The judges spelled out clearly the circumstances in which they considered it might be permissible to execute hostages:

(i)   the step should be taken only "as a last resort" and only after regulations such as those elaborated by the Tribunal had first been enforced;

(ii)   the hostages may not be taken or executed as a matter of military expediency;

(iii)   the population generally must be a party "either actively or passively", to the offences whose cessation is aimed at;

(iv)   it must have proved impossible to find the actual perpetrators of the offences complained of;

(v)   a proclamation must be made "giving the names and addresses of hostages taken, notifying the population that upon the recurrence of stated acts of war treason the hostages will be shot";

(vi)   the number of hostages shot must not exceed in severity the offences the shooting is designed to deter.

The Tribunal decided that articles 46, 47 and 50 for the protection of civilians in the Hague Convention of 1907 on the conduct of war did not the permit killing of innocent inhabitants for purposes of revenge or the satisfaction of a lust to kill. This view was in close accord and clearly influenced by both the *British Manual of Military Law* and the *United States Basic Field Manual (Rules of Land Warfare)*. Both sets of rules make a clear distinction between the legal execution of hostages and the taking of reprisals. The officers at Nuremberg were inevitably convicted in what seems to have been as much a moral as a legal judgement.

Moreover, apart from the general absurdity of having rules of war that are, in any case, more honoured in the breach than the observance by all sides, the taking and executing of hostages in wartime is usually an ineffectual practice. Though some individuals with relatives or close friends in enemy hands may have been deterred from resistance, the majority of the community at large, including many of those close to the captives, clearly were not, as is evidenced by the scale of partisan resistance throughout occupied Europe.[18] This leads us to the central question of exactly who is a hostage and what is the distinction between a hostage and a prisoner. I shall address this in the next chapter.

    Perhaps the Nuremberg trials had provided a salutary warning to would-be hostage-takers that they could no longer necessarily seize their captives with impunity. Perhaps mankind, even the dissident, were weary of violence after a war that had unleashed terrifying forces and affected nearly every corner of the globe, however remote. Whatever the reason, the incidence of political hostage-taking was relatively low for nearly a quarter of a century afterwards, even during, or perhaps because of, the Cold War, as it had been after the First World War. One author[19] has argued that the truly mad doctrine of Mutually Assured Destruction was itself a form of hostage-taking on an unprecedented scale in that whole continents were held under threat of reprisal.

In the immediate post-war period, the Jews in Palestine forced the weary British to withdraw and create for them the independent state of Israel by terrorist tactics, including the taking and killing of hostages. In due course, the dispossessed Palestinians would use much the same tactics against Israel to try to regain a homeland for themselves. Those who live by the sword ... Americans soon replaced the British as the most popular target of the political hostage-taker. Several US missionaries were held by the advancing Communist armies as they drove Chiang Kai-Shek out of China in 1948. In February 1958, a nine-man US helicopter crew that came down in East Germany was seized by the Russians and used as a pawn in the Soviet campaign to gain diplomatic recognition for its satellite. In Cuba, in June of the same year, 30 US marines were seized by Castro's guerrillas. In all these cases a combination of tough talk and minor concessions resulted in the release of the hostages after a few weeks in captivity. In 1961, a Portuguese cruise liner was taken over by Portuguese rebels – a foretaste of the *Achille Lauro* affair – and its 600 passengers and crew were eventually released in Brazil. The 1960s also saw a gradual increase in the frequency of political kidnappings in Latin America.

Then, on 22 July 1968, another of those watershed events occurred that have marked a change in the volume and tempo of hostage-taking. On that day, the Popular Front for the Liberation of Palestine (PFLP) carried out the first and only skyjacking of an Israeli commercial airliner. The El Al plane was seized in an attempt to focus world public opinion ...

> ... on the plight of the dispossessed Palestinians who rightly regarded the Israelis as the principal cause of their misfortunes, the PFLP held the 32 Jewish passengers hostage for five weeks during which time it aroused the conscience of the world and awakened the media and world opinion much more – and more effectively – than 20 years of pleading at the UN."[20]

Using helicopter gunships on 29 December to destroy 13 commercial aircraft belonging to various Arab airlines which were parked at Beirut's International Airport, the Israelis responded to the hijacking and a subsequent airport shooting with that robust eye-for-an-eye, to-hell-with-international-law attitude which became the leitmotif of its anti-terrorist policy.

The Palestinians' daring coup marked a new phase in political hostage-taking that reached a sustained climax in the 1970s before gradually diminishing in intensity over the next 20 years. However, over the three millennia prior to 1945, all the elements of a modern hostage-taking incident had emerged: that leverage depends on the importance and or the number of hostages; that some two-thirds of political hostages are randomly seized; that while rescue attempts may be good for national pride, they are often fatal to the hostages; that the giving of kin is better replaced by the forceful seizure of complete strangers.

Whether captors or coerced come out the better in the period from 1945 to 2002 will be the subject of the remainder of the first part of this book.

Chapter Two

Introduction

"Give me somewhere to stand and I will move the earth."
Archimedes referring to the principle of leverage in the third century BC.

I n this study of political hostage-taking, I shall take account of all four functions of Archimedes' hypothesis, but so that the reader can gauge the values I attribute to each I must first define my terms. Except where I am quoting others I shall try to avoid such prejudicial nomenclature as "terrorist" or "victim". The use of such terms tends to illustrate the bias of the commentator rather than the status of the people involved in an incident. To the German army of occupation in France during the Second World War the maquis were terrorists, to Vichy they were an embarrassment, but to the majority of Frenchmen they were heroes and freedom fighters, as many an American newspaper article attested. But when the boot was on the other foot and the Vietcong were employing much the same tactics as the maquis against American occupying troops, there was no doubting their terrorist status as far as the American press was concerned. The takers or holders of hostages I shall call "captors" or "hostage-takers"; those taken, "captives" or "hostages"; and the authorities whose actions, policies or opinions are threatened, the "coerced". The relationship between these three principal actors in any hostage incident can vary enormously. The tensions created by such relationships have been a matter of fascination to playwrights, novelists and even composers, from Shakespeare to Brendan Behan, from Dostoevsky to Thomas Keneally, from Janacek to John Adams. The exploration of these relationships and an assessment of the effectiveness of political hostage-taking, or seizure, as an instrument for achieving political change constitute the principal subject matter of this book.

What is meant by political hostage-taking? Like many questions of definition this one can most easily be answered by first eliminating what it is not. Thus, when I have cleared the decks of 98 per cent of all hostage incidents, I shall be left with those whose motivation is predominantly political and the necessity of defining them more closely. And there's the rub. "It is hard to encounter any pair of researchers in the field [of terrorism] using the same definition."[1]

The subject of political hostage-taking has been much written about from many and various standpoints – geographical, psychological, instrumental, ideological, motivational and so on. The most useful and memorable of these divisions, to my mind, is the threefold motivational one of F.G. Hacker in 1978[2] into "criminals, crazies and crusaders". In 1989, T.B. Kissane[3] added a fourth group, "the calculator", which included, among other groups, anarchists and racists. I shall replace this with a small subcategory of my own, "crazy crusaders", those whose motives are ostensibly political, usually Marxist, but whose obsession with them borders on the psychotic. "As a rule of thumb, we tend to call criminal or crazy or both the terrorist we disapprove of, but if we sympathize with the terrorist or his cause, we will be inclined to place him in the category of crusader."[4]

Miron and Goldstein[5] attempted to reduce these categories to two: "instrumental", that is those seeking purely material rewards, and "expressive", those wanting to be acknowledged and empowered and to control both the incident, the hostage and the third party. They concede that the first often transmutes into the second during the course of an incident but, in the case of political hostage-taking, the distinction is irrelevant, as the great majority contain these two elements from the outset.

Even among the straightforward crusaders the range and variation is too diverse to be encompassed comfortably within a single book. I shall deal only *en passant* with those politically motivated hostage-takers whose sole object was the extortion of money, ostensibly to further a political cause. In countries such as Colombia (where over 20,000 people died in political killings between 1986 and 1994, mostly at the hands of the security forces) or the Philippines, such seizures for ransom have almost become a way of life and run into many hundreds, if not thousands, every year. In the Philippines, for example, between 1993 and 1996, $11 million in ransom was paid for the release of more than 600 hostages, generally seized by one of two groups, the NPA (New Peoples' Army) and MNLF (Moro National Liberation Front).[6]

Nor, unless there are other important implications in their actions, shall I more than mention those hostage-takers whose sole aim was to seize control of an aircraft in order to divert it to a sanctuary of their choice – usually in Cuba or the Middle East. In a similarly marginal and slightly bizarre category are those like the Stansted Afghans or the voluntary human shield participants in Iraq in 1991 and 2003. I shall also only mention in passing the endemic and extensive hostage-taking by guerrillas and government police and militia alike in Asia, many parts of Africa and Latin America, and even in the Balkans* during the UN–NATO intervention, to secure information or the release of prisoners. These are more akin to the exchange of prisoners during more conventional war than to true hostage-taking. The role of state-instigated hostage-taking will be assessed, though in some cases the distinction between control, sponsorship and acquiescence is hard to determine. For example, did Gaddafi control or only sponsor Carlos the Jackal?

I shall have to ignore both criminal and crazy captors, as to consider them would render this book both unwieldy and beyond my competence. As I am not a psychologist nor a criminologist, I have found it more useful to consider each of some 200 post-Second World War hostage incidents in terms of its outcome. Was it a success for the captors, for the coerced or for neither? Was the outcome peaceful or bloody? Was it brought about by negotiation, force or chance? I shall not differentiate between sieges and kidnappings, hijackings and skyjackings, though whether they were accidental or planned will be an important factor in analysing the reasons for a particular type of outcome. Rather I shall consider them all broadly as seizures. A successful seizure from the captor's point of view is one in which he achieves all or most of his significant objectives in terms of propaganda, the release of prisoners or changes in government policy. Ransom and safe passage may sometimes be incidental benefits he secures along with his primary objectives, but they are not usually good indicators of success or failure. Since captors are often indifferent to their own fate, their success will not be considered as diminished if any or all of them are killed, captured or incarcerated while attempting to achieve their goals.

The seizure that fails is primarily one where the coerced authorities are able to deny the captors all but the most trivial of concessions and, secondarily, where they are able to secure the release of all the hostages unharmed. I regard the outcome as drawn if it falls anywhere between these two extremes and if both participants achieved some, but not all, of their objectives.

The two principal means of resolving hostage incidents – negotiation and rescue by force – are likewise divided into three parts. The negotiation that succeeds is one that results in the captors surrendering themselves without achieving any of their main goals or physically harming any of their captives. In one that fails, the captors either gain all of their ends and escape unscathed, or the coerced abandon negotiations in favour of force. A nearly successful negotiation – in industrial relations terms the mutually satisfactory resolution of a dispute – is one in which both parties secure some of their objectives, the

*Among the more prominent examples are Afghanistan, Bosnia, Congo, India, Kashmir, Nepal, Nicaragua, Niger, Sierra Leone and Uganda.

release of hostages unharmed, for example, in return for the release of prisoners held by the state or the publishing of a political manifesto.

Finally, a successful rescue is one in which all the captors' captives are freed unharmed and all the captors are either killed or caught. The murder of hostages by the captors prior to an assault – often the trigger to the decision to use force – or the death of police or military personnel, whose job implies voluntary acceptance of such risks, does not invalidate the success of the assault. Conversely, an unsuccessful rescue is one in which the captors escape or the captives are killed during the assault by them or by the attacking force. It is interesting to note that of the 1,001 hostage deaths and injuries during forcible rescues in one study, 781 were attributable to the attacking forces. In a similar FBI study, 12 per cent of hostages died.[7] It can be seen that by these terms I shall often assign exploits by special forces that are more generally considered to have been successful to the drawn (or not quite successful) category.

There have certainly been many very crazy individual hostage-takers whose demands have seemed reasonable to themselves, but only too impractically unhinged to the hostages. An elderly Dutchman held 18 people in the Rembrandt tower in Amsterdam in March 2002. He forced his captives to hold placards up to the windows abusing the electronics giant Philips, which had moved its offices long before. He was protesting against "the creative nonsense of widescreen television sets". After some hours he shot himself in the lavatory and all the hostages emerged puzzled but unscathed.

In the United States, a captor demanded to speak directly to God and only released his hostages after face-to-face dialogue with a negotiator who had dressed himself in white robes and whom the captor believed to be the Deity. In another US incident, in April 1997, the leader of a self-styled Independence for Texas movement took a couple of hostages for not having passports and declared war on the United States. Needless to say, he lost!

Such sad, if humorous, incidents are all too frequent and have been the subject of serious analysis by many specialists trying to understand the psychology of the crazy hostage-taker. I shall confine myself to a brief consideration, based on the work of others, of the mindset of gesture captors and crazy crusaders.

Crazy seizures should not be confused with the perfectly rational symbolic hostage-taking that also lies outside the scope of this study. In these there is no intention on the part of the captor to bargain for anything, let alone to harm or threaten their hostages. Their sole purpose is briefly to draw attention to a particular grievance. Typically, Afghan students seized their own embassies in Bonn, New Delhi and Tehran in June 1980 and took hostages for a few hours just to draw attention to the Soviet invasion of their country. Another capture of a home embassy occurred in Bonn and was carried out by Iraqi students in August 2002. It was ended without any serious casualties by a German police assault. In 1993 and 1995, members of the PKK – the Kurdish Workers' Party set up in 1978 by Abdullah Ocalan to campaign for an independent Kurdish state – simultaneously seized Turkish embassies in half a dozen western European capitals for a few hours in a carefully co-ordinated campaign. Since none of these European Union members could do anything more than draw the attention of the Turkish authorities to the claims of the Kurds, the seizures were intended to shame and enlist public sympathy rather than to coerce. PKK protesters with the same limited objective had seized the Copenhagen office of Lufthansa in August 1987, holding hostages and threatening to set fire to the building, and the Paris offices of Turkish airlines in November 1988. Again, in 1999, after the arrest of Ocalan on 15 January, embassies throughout the whole of Europe and North America were briefly seized. All these incidents ended without serious injury to any of those involved and cannot be described as anything but rational, if wildly optimistic, actions.

Even more rational are the hostage seizures carried out by criminals whose sole objective is financial gain. Whereas the crusader will openly proclaim his capture or his siege (since he cannot otherwise hope to gain his ends), the criminal kidnapper will go to great lengths to conceal the whereabouts of his captives in order to thwart the police and facilitate the private payment of ransom. Paul Wilkinson has pointed out that 90 per cent of all kidnappings in which a ransom is demanded are purely criminal affairs.[8] None of the above definitions should be taken to imply a moral judgement. A rescue in which all or most of the captors are deliberately and unnecessarily killed by the attackers on the orders, or implied orders, of the coerced may be repugnant and immoral, as in the cases of the Japanese embassy in Lima and the Iranian embassy in London, but I shall still treat them as successful, or at least nearly successful, rescue attempts. Those not directly involved in a hostage incident may look on it as consisting of a balance of conflicting moral imperatives. On the one side of the scales lies an act, or acts, of terror, on the other, the injustice, or injustices, being fought.

While it is usually an exaggeration to describe one man's terrorist as another man's freedom fighter, differences of viewpoint have made it extremely difficult to arrive at an agreed international definition of terrorism. The spate of terrorist attacks and hostage-taking incidents in the 1970s prompted the UN to try to formulate an international treaty governing the expected behaviour of states towards any act of terrorism either committed within their boundaries or abroad by one of their own citizens. The problem was that the recently independent countries and those fostering revolution objected to those people still struggling for independence being classified as terrorists. The contrary view was held by the colonial and former colonial powers and such prime target countries such as the United States and Israel. They argued that whatever the intent, the *mens rea*, of the perpetrator, it was the nature of the act itself that should define whether or not it was an act of terrorism. The means employed in skyjacking, hostage-taking etc were still fundamentally criminal means and their implementation should be treated as such. To this day the concept of *mens rea* is not considered in American law and no distinction is made between political and criminal kidnappings and sieges. They are both tried and punished in exactly the same way. Indeed, it is arguable, particularly since 9/11, that the political offences are punished the more severely. As we shall see later, there are foreigners who have been in American prisons for the best part of 30 years for committing offences similar to, but considerably less heinous than, those for which native perpetrators are released after ten or 12 years.

The UN's problem of defining terrorism was eventually resolved by skirting round it. Those areas such as hijacking, skyjacking and hostage-taking, in which there was some element of agreement, were tackled by lengthy and contentious sub-committees. Others, such as assassination and suicide bombing, were shelved. There is, indeed, "Confusion about whether terrorism is really a form a crime or a form of war, an instrument of protest or an instrument of control."[9]

This confusion has been confounded twice by President Bush's post-9/11 declaration of a "war on terrorism". Does this turn terrorists, particularly those associated with the "axis of evil", into legitimate combatants? If America has declared a war, then surely by international law it does and those interned in Guantanamo after the US anti-Taliban invasion of Aghanistan are held and treated illegally.

After a great deal of wrangling, the International Convention Against the Taking of Hostages was agreed and signed by the participating nations in New York on 18 December 1979. It did not come fully into effect as part of international law until 4 June 1983. Interestingly, the United States, which never fails to ignore international agreements it considers harmful to its interests, was not one of the ratifying states. Only the preamble and three of the Treaty's 20 articles need concern us in this study.

> Having in Mind the purposes and principles of the Charter of the United Nations concerning the maintenance of international peace and security and the promotion of friendly relations and co-operation among States,
> Recognizing in particular that everyone has the right to life, liberty and security of person, as set out in the Universal Declaration of Human Rights and the International Covenant on Civil and Political Rights,
> Reaffirming the principle of equal rights and self-determination of peoples as enshrined in the Charter of the United Nations and the Declaration on Principles of International Law concerning Friendly Relations and Co-operation among States in accordance with the Charter of the United Nations, as well as in other relevant resolutions of the General Assembly,

Considering that the taking of hostages is an offence of grave concern to the international community and that, in accordance with the provisions of this Convention, any person committing an act of hostage-taking shall either be prosecuted or extradited,

Being Convinced that it is urgently necessary to develop international co-operation between States in devising and adopting effective measures for the prevention, prosecution and punishment of all acts of taking of hostages as manifestations of international terrorism,

Have Agreed as Follows:

Article 1

Any person who seizes or detains and threatens to kill, to injure or to continue to detain another person (hereinafter referred to as the "hostage") in order to compel a third party, namely, a State, an international inter-governmental organization, a natural or juridical person, or a group of persons, to do or abstain from doing any act as an explicit or implicit condition for the release of the hostage commits the offence of taking of hostages ("hostage-taking") within the meaning of this Convention.

Any person who:

attempts to commit an act of hostage-taking, or participates as an accomplice of anyone who commits or attempts to commit an act of hostage-taking likewise commits an offence for the purposes of this Convention.

Article 4

States parties shall co-operate in the prevention of the offences set forth in article 1, particularly by:

taking all practicable measures to prevent preparations in their respective territories for the commission of those offences within or outside their territories, including measures to prohibit in their territories illegal activities of persons, groups and organizations that encourage, instigate, organize or engage in the perpetration of acts of taking of hostages; exchanging information and co-ordinating the taking of administrative and other measures as appropriate to prevent the commission of those offences.

Article 8

(i) The State party in the territory of which the alleged offender is found shall, if it does not extradite him, be obliged, without exception whatsoever and whether or not the offence was committed in its territory, to submit the case to its competent authorities for the purpose of prosecution, through proceedings in accordance with the laws of that State. Those authorities shall take their decision in the same manner as in the case of any ordinary offence of a grave nature under the law of that State.

(ii) Any person regarding whom proceedings are being carried out in connection with any of the offences set forth in Article 1 shall be guaranteed fair treatment at all stages

of the proceedings, including enjoyment of all the rights and guarantees provided by
the law of the State in the territory of which he is present.

Lawyers' language, with its proper anxiety to close any potential loopholes, can
be confusing and not every reader may be clear as to what constitutes hostage-
taking after reading Article 1. The French Ministry of the Interior is certainly
blunt and brief in its terms: "Hostage-taking is a criminal act which consists of
taking hold of one or several persons, in order to use them by threatening their
well-being (*intégrité corporelle*) to the end of exerting a constraint on a third
party."[10] This makes no distinction between hostage-taking incidents, so will
not do. In practice, it is not the approach generally favoured by the French who
tend to treat some fairly marginal cases as political ones and often look on
terrorists more as prisoners of war than as criminals.[11]

Personally, I prefer the rather simpler definition of hostages as used by the
Red Cross. It defines hostages as "persons who find themselves, willingly or
unwillingly, in the power of the enemy and who answer with their freedom or
their life for compliance with the orders of the latter (the enemy) and for
upholding the security of its armed forces".

But even this definition, with its obvious emphasis on the circumstances of
openly declared war, does not quite satisfy me, so I suppose I must attempt a
definition which will serve my purpose better.

"Political hostage-taking is that in which the well-being or lives of unwilling
captives are threatened by their captors in order to compel a government or
state authority to act in a way in which it would not otherwise necessarily have
acted."

Hostage-holding, however, is not simply a matter for states and policies. For
the individuals involved, negotiators, captives and captors alike, it can be either
a traumatic or an enriching experience. It has been in talking to officials,
former hostages and perpetrators, and in their written accounts over the
centuries, that I feel I have best been able to do the subject of hostage-taking
justice.

Chapter Three

Captors Win

hree-quarters of political hostage incidents end in success for the captors.[1] No wonder it has been such a popular tactic with dissidents, rebels and anarchists throughout the world. But are the essentials the same in all hostage-taking incidents in which the captors win, or do they differ widely according to circumstances? A closer look at five such incidents, and a glance at a couple of dozen more, may help to answer that question.

Long before the 1968 watershed, the prototype for large-scale political hostage-taking took place in Cuba.[2] Fulgencio Batista's second coup* in 1952 initiated an unparalleled growth of corruption. In return for bribes, which they could well afford out of their excessive profits, many major US corporations, with the blessing of their government, received massive contracts for public works, hotels and casinos. From all of these Batista, his family and his cronies, took a ten to 30 per cent cut, as they did from the tax revenues earmarked for health, education and other public services. Havana quickly became not only a gambling centre to match Las Vegas, but a safe haven for leaders of the "mob" and the ideal place for the "families" to meet to discuss the carve-up of their crime empire. The majority of US companies operating in Cuba were full of praise for Batista's suppression of gangsterism. They chose to turn a blind eye to the fact that the gangsters were now the government.

In 1953, Fidel Castro's first, under-resourced revolt against the Batista dictatorship was easily put down. He and his brother Raoul and those of his comrades who had not already been killed were thrown into jail. Then, on 15 May 1955, Batista made his fatal mistake. As a political gesture to appease

* The first had seen him ruling Cuba initially as the military commander and eminence grise behind a number of feeble presidents from 1933 to 1944.

discontent at the lack of democracy, he released Castro and his companions and expelled them from Cuba.

In December 1956, Castro, Raoul and the totemic Che Guevara slipped back into the country and recommenced their guerrilla insurgency. Batista was confident his ruthless and brutal police and military would comfortably contain the uprising by a combination of superior firepower and reprisal executions. Castro's rebels were penned into the largely agricultural Oriente province in the east of the island. Nevertheless, their strategy of dispersing in small groups among the sugar plantations and the almost unanimous support of the peasants and farmers of the region made it difficult for Batista to inflict any decisive defeat on the rebels. Nor could he deprive them of the ability to carry out a series of propaganda coups.

In February 1958 they kidnapped the motor-racing star Juan Fangio and by preventing him from taking part in a Grand Prix drew world-wide attention to their cause. In March, Raoul hijacked a bus among whose passengers were 27 US marines returning to their notorious base at Guantanamo from a day's furlough. On learning of this, a dozen US journalists, fed up with being restricted by the naval authorities to cover the rebellion from behind the barbed wire of the base, headed into the hills with the rebels. From here they not only filed copy complimentary to the rebels, but, more significantly, drew attention to the fact that the weapons supplied to Batista by their government were being used to kill civilians and crush democracy. They were, moreover, impressed by their good treatment and that of the hostages, by their freedom to go where they pleased under the protection of Castro's men, and by the first-class medical attention provided in Oriente for combatants and civilians alike.

Raoul, in particular, milked this situation for every drop of publicity. When a dozen American and Canadian engineers were seized, the Canadians were immediately released on the grounds that Canada was not supporting Batista as the Americans were. The marines were released in dribs and drabs as a ploy to keep the US consul, Park Wollam Junior, and a sympathetic CIA agent, Robert Wiecha, in a prolonged negotiation whose purpose was twofold.

Not only was world-wide awareness of Castro's cause and Batista's tyranny sustained, but the presence of the marines and journalists scattered throughout the province obliged Batista to suspend the use of the heavy weaponry that had hitherto given him the upper hand, through fear of killing an American citizen and losing the support of the US government. His abstention was in vain. President Eisenhower not only vetoed a proposal to release the marines by force, but withdrew the public government support which had done much to keep Batista in power.

The Americans love a fighter and in the eyes of the majority there could be only one winner between a cruel dictator and an idealistic rebel. That majority was, of course, unaware of Castro's Marxist beliefs and the US administration chose to keep it that way. That the rebel would himself become the longest-ruling dictator in the world and a political hate figure for the US government was an irony yet to be appreciated and one that most Cubans would choose to ignore as his rule was at least preferable to that of his utterly corrupt predecessor.

In a final snook cocked at the US, Raoul announced that the marines had been released to help out Eisenhower, who was desperate for men to send to Lebanon! By the end of 1959, Castro, though nominally only Prime Minister, was in complete control of the whole country. Batista, together with his family, close cronies and a great deal of loot had fled to the Dominican Republic in January of that year.

There is only one important difference between this successful seizure and the four that we shall treat next. The Cuban abductions were carried out by a guerrilla army already in the field, however tenuously, whereas the others were the work of small bands of politically motivated individuals without overt military backing. Most of the other elements in propaganda and power terms necessary for a successful political hostage-taking were already present in the Cuban incident. Our next case was a pure propaganda exercise.

On 10 September 1976, 86 passengers, mostly businessmen, were sitting in the departure lounge of John F. Kennedy airport in New York waiting patiently for their TWA flight No. 355 to Chicago. Those of them not reading would probably have been looking round at their fellow passengers with that idle look of low-level curiosity which helps to pass the time in these collective moments of boredom. That slightly tense-looking couple holding hands, the girl a pleasant looking blonde, the man, muscular, six foot tall and redolent of suppressed energy and both looking a little nervous, as if flying to meet the in-laws for the first time. The big fellow smiling amiably at his neighbour and the two in the corner chatting in low voices in some unintelligible foreign language. There appeared to be nothing out of the ordinary about any of them. Even if their fellow passengers could have looked inside their hand baggage they would have been puzzled rather than alarmed. Some cooking pots – funny present for one's mother-in-law – a couple of reels of black gaffer tape, some potter's clay with that same sweaty texture that watchers of too many B-movies have come to associate with plastic explosives. Two of the small cases for taking on the plane seem to be jam-packed with leaflets printed in letters almost too small to read. If the others had scrutinized the leaflets more closely, as they were later to get the chance to do, they would have been mildly intrigued, no more. They described the torture, imprisonment and even murders inflicted on the inhabitants of a region called Croatia by the brutal Yugoslav government on those demanding an independent Croatian state.

Croatia? Isn't that in Asia some place? Heck no, some crazy guys threw leaflets about an independent Croatia off the top of a skyscraper way back.

Belgrade, that's Yugoslavia, ain't it? Guess Croatia must be in Europe. Nothing out of the ordinary then.

However, had the passengers of TWA355 been able to look in a coin locker in Grand Central Station they would never have boarded their flight. It contained some of the same leaflets and a bomb together with instructions on how to disarm it safely.

Zvonko Busic,* the skyjackers leader, Petar Matanic, Frane Pesut and Slobodan Vlasic were all dedicated Croatian nationalists determined to draw the world's attention to the plight of their countrymen and Julie, Busic's American wife, passionately supported her husband's cause. Their plan was to hijack an aircraft, fly it to Croatia via several European capitals over which the leaflets would be scattered, release the passengers unharmed once four of America's most important newspapers had published their rather lengthy manifesto and then surrender peacefully. Maybe they would get five years' imprisonment for air piracy, but that would be well worthwhile if the world woke up to what was happening in the Croat part of Yugoslavia and backed the Croatian demand for independence. The bombs on the plane would not be real bombs – though no one but the five would know that. The bomb in the locker was real so as to convince everyone that the skyjackers could blow up the plane if they chose. It would never go off or hurt anyone. That was if everything went according to plan – but it didn't.

The skyjacking itself was a copybook exercise. Zvonko, Frane and Slobodan went simultaneously to the various aircraft toilets and turned their innocuous domestic items into very realistic looking bombs and explosives strapped to their bodies. Throughout the entire episode not a single person other than the captors doubted that these devices were real and could be detonated in an instant. Zvonko went into the pilot's cockpit. Frane and Slobodan seated themselves rather awkwardly at the rear of the plane. The passengers ate, drank and read, oblivious to what was about to happen while Julie and Petar pretended to do the same, ready to take up their role of control and reassurance. Within a few seconds the captain, Dick Carey, spoke to his passengers over the PA system, sounding calm and reassuring as captains of routine flights are always supposed to do.

"Well, folks, I have an announcement to make. This plane has been hijacked. The hijackers have some demands and will be explaining to you what is happening. Please try to remain calm so this thing can be concluded quickly and safely."

Most of the passengers look at each other in disbelief. He can't be serious! It's a joke, isn't it? That it isn't becomes apparent when Julie and Petar get up

* I am deeply grateful to both Julie and Zvonko for their help with this account which draws heavily on Julie's book, Lovers and Madmen, and their private papers and e-mails to me.

from their places and start to reassure the passengers that no harm will come to them. Still no one seems too perturbed and the prompt action of one of the stewardesses, Basia Reeves, in asking permission to serve food and drink underlines the normality of the flight. The passengers may eat, drink, move about the cabin and go to the toilet when they please. Aren't skyjackers supposed to give you a bad time and shout at you in Arabic? What's this all about then? Julie, with her familiar American accent, tries to explain. Then she has the smart idea of distributing one of the leaflets to each passenger. You can hear the silence of concentration as they read. Then a flood of questions. Several express apparent sympathy for the motives of the skyjackers now they have a better understanding of the reason for their action. A few even offer to help. Many of the passengers have their pictures taken with Petar and Julie as if this were some holiday excursion. Are they ingratiating themselves with their captors or are they genuine? One of the older passengers tells Julie calmly to her face. "I don't approve of hijacking, regardless of the cause, but that doesn't mean I can't sympathize with you and like you as a person." It seems that, despite the brevity of their contact, the Stockholm Syndrome – the development of empathy between captors and captives that we shall examine later – is affecting all but a couple of the passengers and the co-pilot. However, as Julie put it:

"We make the mistake of believing that, because the passengers are not spitting on us or calling us names, they agree with what we are doing and are actually our compatriots. It is hard to believe otherwise, so congenial is the atmosphere, so understanding the passengers."[3]

Captain Carey has already radioed, several times, Zvonko's careful instructions to the US authorities and to the police in New York on how the locker bomb can be safely handled and defused. Zvonko was not to know until it was too late that these instructions would be ignored. What is more, he has made a miscalculation in thinking that the aircraft he had targeted so carefully was capable of flying across the Atlantic and on to the capitals he had chosen without refuelling. Stops must be made in Newfoundland and again in Iceland where fuel, food and drink are taken on board, the toilets are emptied and some of the passengers with a good case to make are released after vetting by Julie. There is one condition. They must drop leaflets over Chicago and Montreal from the aircraft taking them home.

When TWA355 enters French airspace the atmosphere changes. At first the authorities refuse to let the plane land at a civilian airport, but when an angry Captain Carey points out that he has not the fuel to go anywhere else the plane is begrudgingly diverted to a nearby military airfield. Or was this the intention of the French security authorities all along? It is only seven months since the dramatically successful Djibouti armed rescue operation (see pages 107–8) by French special forces and they are feeling pretty confident. Maybe they can resolve this one the same way. Are they planning to do the one thing that is beyond the skyjackers' control? The Croatians are willing to die for their beliefs if necessary, but they are appalled at the thought that the passengers and crew, with most of whom they have established a partially sympathetic relationship in the past 24 hours, might be wounded or killed.

As the aircraft touches down it looks as if their worst fears may be realized. No sooner is the plane on the ground than French marksmen shoot out its tyres and surround it at a distance with squads of soldiers taking cover behind trucks and barriers. All of this without reference to the United States. What the skyjackers do not know is that the French have good reason to believe they are seriously dangerous people. Now both captors and captives alike are subjected to a dubiously effective softening-up process in which they are denied food, drink, fuel and the emptying of the overflowing toilets. The commanders in the control tower refuse to enter into any kind of dialogue, let alone serious negotiation, even when an almost hysterical Carey tells them that everyone will be blown to pieces if they do not comply. The principal effect of this tactic is to make the already anxious and frightened passengers angry with the French, not their captors, for endangering their lives. Their state of mind has not been helped by a Roman Catholic priest on board telling them that they are all about to die.

As far as the French are concerned TWA flight 355 is going nowhere. In any case, the Belgrade government has told them that the moment it enters Yugoslav airspace it will be shot down regardless of the death of so many captives. Some of the passengers cannot believe the Yugoslavs would shoot down a planeload of innocent people. Julie disabuses them: "Sure they would. They go around murdering them all the time on the ground. Besides, the [Yugoslav] government is scared of the effect the leaflets could have on the population."[4] The French show they can be as tough as any Slav. Surrender or face a firing squad they threaten. Zvonko, however, cannot surrender yet. He still does not know if the captors' demands have been met, so Julie must leave the plane with Lou, the co-pilot, and Knudsen, an influential passenger, to phone New York and see if the manifesto has been published. If it has, he will surrender. The French have no objection, after all it gets one captor and two captives off the plane even if the skyjackers' demands have not been met. If they have, then the skyjacking can be ended peacefully.

Julie's phone call does not help much. One contact says yes, the other does not know. Julie is not allowed to return to her comrades and not long afterwards an official hands her a copy of the *New York Times*. Yes! There's the manifesto!

But what's this on the other side of the front page? The locker bomb is discovered at 5.30 pm and taken to a firing range to be dismantled. Some time later that evening it explode and a policeman, Brian Murray, is killed and another badly injured. How can that happen after so much care has been taken to make sure it would be harmless? It transpires much later – too late to be of any use to the defence at the trial – that Murray's widow, Kathleen, has sued the NYPD for negligence because no standard safety precautions were taken and Zvonko's careful instructions had been ignored. Despite losing her suit, the evidence Mrs Murray produced and the lengths to which the police went to destroy or "lose" the crucial documents for the hearing seem largely to confirm Zvonko's claim that the locker bomb was never intended to hurt anyone.

However, at that stage Julie thinks it wiser only to pass on the good news and Captain Carey, in his customary calm tone, tells his passengers it is all over, but with a surprising rider:

> This is the captain speaking. We have all been through an incredible experience. But it is over for us. No one is hurt. However, it is not over for our hijackers. Their ordeal is just beginning. They have a cause. They are brave, committed people. Idealistic, dedicated people. Like the people who helped to shape our country. They are trying to do the same for theirs. I think we should all give them a hand.

One or two sceptics* apart, the passengers endorse his view. Not only do they applaud, but they surround their erstwhile captors when they leave the plane in case the French try to shoot them. Twenty-five of these same passengers write to the judge during the trial pleading for leniency. Three of them even visit Julie in prison. During the trial, letters of support, phone calls and even visitors come in from all over the world and not only from Croats. The five million dollars set for bail is quickly raised and is refused just as quickly on a technicality. Captain Carey, the chief prosecution witness, refuses to be trapped into condemning his captors and the prosecution psychologist whose evidence would support the defence is never called. After four days, the jury of eight women and four men find all five guilty of air piracy resulting in death, not, it should be emphasized, of murder. Judge Bartels, as a preamble to sentencing, declares that he does not consider the Croatians to be criminals or terrorists, but that their "noble cause" does not exempt them from the consequences of their criminal act. The three subordinates get 30 years apiece, but serve only 12.

However, life sentences for Zvonko and Julie are mandatory because of the policeman's death. The judge recommends that Julie be released on parole after eight years and Zvonko after ten. Julie is finally released after 13 years and Zvonko is still there at the time of writing – 27 years after the event. He is not even allowed to serve out his time in Croatia where his "Penelope" waits and campaigns tirelessly on his behalf. He remains dignified, philosophical and

* Dr Brockman is one of them and the captain's envoi quoted here is verbatim from his account in the Atlantic Monthly of December 1976.

resigned to his fate. He bitterly regrets the death of Brian Murray,* but he does not regret his fight for justice and independence for Croatians. Who knows, perhaps the skyjacking of TWA355 was the hole in the dyke that alerted people abroad to the tyrannies of the doomed Yugoslav regime. Croatia is now an independent state and Zvonko is one of its heroes. The episode exemplifies a successful seizure in that all the captors' demands were met. It also exemplifies the apparent preference of the American authorities for vengeance rather than justice.

Our next hostage incident, on 6 June 1985,[5] is one of the longest and most bizarre of skyjackings and appeared to be more like a Feydeau farce than a professional seizure with the captured aircraft ping-ponging to and fro between Beirut and Algiers five times. Yet behind the superficial madness there was considerable method, resulting in one of the most successful outcomes on record from the captors' point of view. The apparent confusion was itself a reflection of the confusion on the ground in strife-torn Lebanon, where the extreme Hizbollah, Party of God, faction was in conflict with the larger and more influential of the Amal groups led by Nabih Berri, though as we shall see in chapter four these were only two of the many contending factions in 1985.

On 14 June, shortly after take-off from Athens of TWA flight 847 for Rome, two Lebanese members of Hizbollah, armed with pistols and grenades, seized control of the aircraft. According to flight captain John Testrake – who should have been on holiday with his wife – the two men were in a highly excitable state, perhaps high or even mentally unbalanced, even if their declared motive was political. However, their apparently frenzied behaviour may have been exacerbated by the failure of a third man to catch the flight in Athens, leaving them shorthanded in their attempt to take control of an aircraft as large as a Boeing 747 with 155** passengers, five cabin staff and a flight crew of three. The captain carried out the airline's standing orders with reluctance but alacrity: "Do what the man with the gun says, fuel supplies permitting." The two captors were brutal and confused, but cunning, too. By taking over the passenger section of the aircraft and threatening to blow both themselves and the plane up, they obliged the co-pilot to unlock the cockpit door. When he had done so they broke off the lock and hinges so it could not be secured against them.

The brutality was evident, not only in the way in which they bound and beat unconscious US marine Robert Stethem and Major Kurt Carlson, and randomly struck flight engineer Christian Zimmerman, but in the manner in

---

* *With the Busics' help a wealthy Croatian set up a trust fund to which they contributed and Julie has given the family money from her related literary work.*

** *Different accounts give slightly different numbers, so I have stuck to Testrake's throughout.*

which they ran up and down the main aisle beating over the head with a torn-off aircraft panel, any passenger who failed to maintain a bent-forward posture. The confusion manifested itself in their ignorance of the range of the aircraft they had taken over and the distance, and consequently fuel required, to reach any of the possible destinations. This resulted in much dithering as to where they should go and revealed a lack of the meticulous planning demonstrated by the majority of hijackers. The confusion was compounded by the fact that they could only speak a few words of English and that the flight crew, with not a word of Arabic between them, seemed to think that by shouting in pidgin they could make themselves understood. Some kind of reasonable communication was eventually achieved through the German spoken by one of the captors and that of the chief stewardess, another level-headed professional, Uli Derickson. This resulted in the agreement that they would fly to Beirut to take on the fuel necessary to travel on to Tehran, Aden or Algiers. After having, rather oddly, asked Testrake to "land quietly" they refueled and the captors released 17 women and two children.

Destination number two was Algiers where, following much argument with the authorities and after releasing another 21 passengers and picking up the missing Hizbollah member, they flew back to Beirut. By now the airport, which was mostly under the control of Amal, was ready for them and had put up barriers on the runway to prevent another embarrassing landing. An angry Testrake, only too aware that his aircraft might be blown up at any minute, told the tower he was running low on fuel and intended to crash the barriers and land anyway. Since an accident, which might kill more than 100 people, would have been an even bigger embarrassment, the airport authorities quickly cleared the runway and permitted the landing.

But things were to get worse. Clearly unable to cope with what they had begun, the three captors on the plane demanded that Amal become involved. Amal refused and together with the airport's refusal to provide the hijackers with more fuel this was enough to snap the last strands of restraint. They would show these people that they meant business. Hoisting the unconscious Stethem to his feet like a sack of rubbish, they propped him in the open doorway, shot him in the head and tossed his body onto the tarmac 40 feet below. They got both their fuel and Nabih Berri, who was anxious in the light of the threatening noises emanating from the White House to avoid any further bloodshed, who agreed to add five of his men to the hijack team. Alarmed by rumours of an Israeli assault force offshore and by now aware that the American Delta force had been on their track for some time, albeit impotently, the hijackers freed a further 64 passengers and the cabin crew and set off once more for Algiers. There they received medical assistance, released a further three ailing captives and gave the crew their first opportunity to get a few hours' sleep.

The captives also learned for the first time what all this was about – the demand for the release of 756 Shia Lebanese prisoners held illegally by Israel after its withdrawal, with a sore head, from Lebanon. Even less realistically, they sought the end of Arab oil sales to the West and the withdrawal of Arab money from western banks. They also tacked on the almost obligatory call for the release of the 17 Shia men held in a Kuwaiti prison following a bomb attack. By now the captors had carefully pruned down their hostage-take until it consisted only of the 40 American passengers and three American crew who would give them the most leverage on Israel through its protector and patron – the United States. Yet again TWA847 set off for Beirut. Realizing this could go on indefinitely, Testrake and his engineer gambled on their captors' ignorance of the workings of a modern aircraft. By furtively disconnecting three of the four engines just as they landed in Beirut they made it seem as if they had suffered an irreparable breakdown that would prevent the Boeing taking off again.

The hijackers, however, could be just as cunning. With Delta Force panting along behind them, they scattered their hostages among members of Amal throughout Beirut, except four which were held by Hizbollah, leaving only the three-man crew on the plane to endure the ransacking of baggage, the accumulation of rubbish, the guards' endless fooling with the radio like demented disc-jockeys and their constant playing with their weapons and loosing off shots at random. Testrake was mightily relieved at the dispersal of his passengers. When asked what he thought about a rescue attempt, he told one of the interviewers at a press conference cleverly arranged by his captors: "I think we would all be dead men if they did, because we are continually surrounded by many, many guards."[6] No more was heard of Delta Force despite President Reagan's tactless huffing and puffing. Sensibly, neither Testrake nor his two colleagues took the opportunity to make a break for it when the rear doors were left open and the captors' weapons were left unattended. Whether this was prudence, cowardice or concern for fellow hostages is only a matter for conjecture, but it is a common response to such situations. Apart from two excursions to the airport firehouse for a shower and a night's sleep, Captain John Testrake and engineer Christian Zimmerman were cooped up for a total of 16 days in the confines of the cabin and cockpit. Co-pilot Phil Maresca had been bitten by a spider on his first night at the firehouse and was eventually ordered off the plane to hospital by a Lebanese doctor a few days before the end of the ordeal.

On day 16, all but four of the hostages, crew and passengers alike, were shepherded to a nearby school house and told they would be released into the care of the Syrians and sent to Damascus that day. After conferring among themselves about the absent four, the other hostages decided it must be all or none. Hizbollah, which held the four, had taken umbrage at yet more of Reagan's get-tough posturing and held their men another day. The fact was, however, that secretly, behind the rhetoric, the US had leaned on Israel, Syria, Amal and Hizbollah to engineer a deal. On day 17 of the longest recorded skyjacking all 42 of the remaining hostages were reunited and returned under Syrian escort to the American embassy in Damascus.

Testrake's account is remorselessly punctuated with a religious Christian evangelism that contrasts unfavourably with his captors' discreet observance of their religion and their absence of proselytizing. His narrative also betrays a not-uncommon American ignorance of other cultures and of conditions in other countries. However, this is redeemed by the mind-expanding effect of the shock of being taken hostage on a man used to soul searching. His 17 days in war-torn Beirut and his glimpse of the internecine conflict between its numerous factions brought him to a level of understanding and sympathy for his captors' motives and for their demand for peace and justice.

> Almost every one of them had a friend or a family member who had died in that shelling. I wondered if the *New Jersey*★ was what had convinced some of them to join the Hizbollah militia. I spent a lot of time thinking about it. Could we find a way to hit back at terrorism without hurting innocent people? Were we justified in firing indiscriminately into a city where many thousands of innocent people live – people who just happen to be caught in a war they don't want?[7] … We all had a chance to say that while we did not agree with their tactics, we had at least gained some understanding and sympathy for the Shi'ite point of view. Until the hijacking, none of us really understood what was going on in the Middle East. We didn't understand the reasons for the dissatisfaction and anger in Lebanon and had only vague ideas of what the fighting was all about. Our weeks of captivity had at least given us a better understanding of the situation.[8]

A skyjacking which to all appearance had been a frenetic shambles had been turned, nevertheless, into one of the most successful ever in as much as Israel, claiming a coincidence in which nobody believed, released all the illegally held Lebanese Shia prisoners in accordance with the hijackers' demands. In practice, the skyjacking had not been that badly managed. The captors, for all their vacillation as they flew between Beirut and Algiers, had succeeded in paring down their hostage group to the essential core of Americans who could provide the longest lever. They had thwarted the Delta Force rescue team and through their press conferences had obtained considerable publicity for their aims and cause. By my criteria, despite the tragic murder of Stethem and the

---

★ *On 14 December 1983 this US warship began a bombardment of Beirut and the Beka'a valley in retaliation for the suicide bombing of the US marine barracks in Beirut in which 241 marines had died on 23 October 1983. The bombardment lasted through January and February 1984 and up to 280 rounds were fired in a day, including what they chose to call "cookie cutters" – air bursting shrapnel shells. Some 3,000 civilian Lebanese were killed.*

hijackers' failure to realize their wilder claims, this incident was a resounding success for the captors. Our next example also established a long-standing record – this time for multiple skyjacking.

In 1970, one of the master strategists of the Palestinian Liberation Movement, Dr Waddid Haddad, planned a co-ordinated seizure of civilian aircraft belonging to different nations in a manner that would not be equalled until the horror of 9/11.

The aims of the PFLP in orchestrating the multiple skyjacking that came to be known as "Skyjack Sunday" were threefold – two overt and one implicit. The hijackers demanded the release of PFLP (Popular Front for the Liberation of Palestine) members imprisoned in Germany, Switzerland and Israel. Later they added Leila Khaled, their captured comrade, to the list. She had already brought them a great deal of the world-wide publicity that they now sought to augment. In August 1969 she had carried out a daring, well-researched and cleverly executed skyjacking of a TWA Boeing 707, flight 840 out of Rome where security was particularly lax. She and a companion forced their way into the cockpit and, armed with knives and grenades, made the captain divert to Tel Aviv. Khaled had previously calculated the 707's fuel consumption and had flight maps showing the route to Tel Aviv and from there on to Damascus. She also knew enough about the plane's cockpit procedures to ensure that her orders were carried out. At 12,000 feet above Tel Aviv she forced the captain to circle the city to carry out the second aim – to transmit propaganda messages via the airport control tower before flying on to safety in Damascus.[9]

The third, implicit, aim of Skyjack Sunday was to destabilize, or even topple, the regime of King Hussein of Jordan in order to create an independent Palestinian state in the northeast corner of the Hashemite kingdom adjacent to the borders of Israel and Syria. Ever since the founding of Israel and the expulsion of hundreds of thousands of Palestinians from their homeland, there had been a steady flow of refugees into the initially sympathetic Arab kingdom. By 1970, the Palestinians formed a substantial minority of the population of Jordan and exercised a considerable degree of lawless, armed autonomy in the cities and refugee camps. By late 1969, armed skirmishes between the Palestinans and the Jordanian authorities were running at a rate of several hundred a year. How to deal with their increasingly dangerous and much less welcome guests was something that sharply divided Hussein's cabinet – the doves wanted to negotiate and accommodate them, whereas the hawks wanted to suppress them by military means. It was against this unstable background that Dr Haddad masterminded one of his most ambitious plans.

On 6 September 1970, a SwissAir DC-8 and a TWA Boeing 707 were seized and flown to Dawson's Field, a former Royal Air Force military airbase in Jordan which the PFLP promptly took over and renamed Revolution Airport.

A third aircraft, a TWA 747, was seized and flown to Cairo to be blown up, empty, on the main runway. Unexpectedly, given that after her previous skyjack she had undergone facial plastic surgery to avoid recognition, the fourth attempt, under Khaled, failed. Her co-hijacker, a Nicaraguan, was shot and killed and Khaled was captured and packed off to a British prison where, in her own words in a letter to her mother, she was "treated more like a guest of state than a prisoner". No matter, six days later, another PFLP team took over a BOAC VC-10 carrying the requisite number of British passengers and flew it to join the others at Revolution Airport. Here the hijackers held 312 hostages, mostly British but with sufficient Swiss and Germans to exercise the desired leverage for their first purpose. To bring home their point as dramatically as possible, they took everyone off all three aircraft, released 256 of them, including all the women and children, and then blew up the planes in a carefully staged event for the world's television cameras. A core of 56 hostages was retained to keep up the pressure on the four governments holding Palestinians in jail.

The responsibility for resolving this crisis rested largely with Britain, which found itself confronted with a dilemma. On the one hand, it had always been Jordan's principal ally and patron, though Prime Minister Edward Heath was reported to have doubted whether there were "any advantages to be derived from prolonging, possibly only for a short time, the increasingly precarious regime of King Hussein".[10] Moreover, as each signatory of the 1963 Tokyo convention on hijacking was committed "never to negotiate with terrorists", Britain would not only cast doubt on its own resolution but also infuriate America if it broke ranks.* The cabinet[11] was well aware of all the potential consequences of yielding to the hijackers' demands. On the other hand, there were wider British Middle Eastern interests to consider, and the disastrous impact the murder of so many Britons would have on a parliamentary majority of only 31 and a troubled economy. With Britain no longer a significant power in the region, it would have been impossible to send a General Napier to rescue the hostages, or even the SAS, when the number of captives involved was so great. To have done so would have given the Palestinian leader, Yasser Arafat, just the opening he wanted to prove that the West was demonstrably anti-Palestinian. Heath took the only course of action open to him and an announcement on the BBC World Service's Arabic channel the day after the television spectacular told Arafat that Khaled and the six other Palestinian prisoners in Germany and Switzerland (but not, of course, Israel) would indeed be released "in a few days".

In the meantime, Hussein had dismissed his doves and let loose his hawks, particularly the contemptuous Bedouin, on the Palestinians. At first things went

---

* *As indeed it did, though Britain's riposte was that America's satellite, Israel, "wouldn't lift a bloody finger!"*

badly for the king. Some 5,000 of his soldiers deserted to the enemy, although his command structure remained intact and the bulk of his men stayed fiercely loyal. The Palestinians fought stubbornly and held their ground and Syria joined the fray by sending two armoured columns to support them, shortly expanding this to a full armoured division. Then the tide turned. Though Hussein's appeal, through Britain and America, to Israel, of all countries, to bomb the Syrian tanks was refused for fear of starting a war, Israeli jets did buzz the Syrians and Israeli diplomats made it clear to the newly incumbent Syrian President, Hafez al Assad, that the merest hint of air support would provoke a stern Israeli riposte. The Syrian tanks summarily withdrew. Arms were almost certainly supplied by Israel to Jordan. The Jordanian army steadily drove the militant Palestinians out of the cities and Egypt, Sudan, Kuwait and Tunisia sent their most senior politicians to negotiate a truce that amounted to a Palestinian surrender on 27 September. Securing the cease-fire was almost the last accomplishment of Egyptian President Nasser, who died a few hours later of a heart attack.

In due course the PFLP was driven back into the northeast corner of the country and Arafat, unable to bear the shame, slipped over the Syrian border and fled to Lebanon with a couple of thousand of his men to sow the seeds of yet further trouble – as we shall see. But Hussein's triumph had come too late to let Heath off the hook. By the time it was clear who had come out on top in the civil war, an embarrassed Britain had already sent Khaled home on 30 September together with the prisoners from Germany and Switzerland.

There is no doubt that the publicity and the release of the Palestinian prisoners was a tremendous morale booster for the PFLP, even if they had been unable to oust Hussein and had suffered a severe military reversal. The lesson they learned was that never again should they abandon guerrilla tactics for formal military confrontation. That the hijackers took heart from the obvious impotence of even powerful nations in the face of such tactics is indisputable. As Leila Khaled said many years later when she was a middle-aged housewife and a member of the Palestinian parliament:

> It was a good step for us that we saw governments could be negotiated with. We could impose our demands … The success in the tactics of the hijacking and imposing our demands and succeeding in having our demands implemented gave us the courage and the confidence to go ahead with our struggle[12] … You know, for us it was used to put a question in front of the whole world. Who are the Palestinians? And the answer was to be given by the revolution itself. Because you know the media was totally with the Israelis all over the world. We don't have our media. So this is one of the ways, and we did this as tactics just at the beginning of the revolution. Now our cause is known and the whole world is discussing it in one way or another.[13]

But perhaps the last word should be given to the unfortunate British Prime Minister of the day, Edward Heath.

> When you're negotiating with people like that, if you want to achieve your ends, it's very often the better way to do it without a blaze of publicity to begin with … We were always realistic. We were very practical about it all.[14]

After all, Mr Heath did not have to preside over probably the most embarrassing and successful seizure of them all.

"Excuse me, can you tell me if the OPEC conference is still in session?"

The journalists thus addressed hardly gave a second glance to the polite young man with the slightly foreign accent before confirming that it was. Even if they had looked more closely, it is doubtful if they would have recognized the notorious "Jackal", for Carlos had grown long hair, a goatee and sideburns since his most recent "hit" in Paris. His companions, four young men and a woman who carried their holdalls attracted even less notice than their spokesman – probably clerical staff or drivers waiting for their bosses, thought the journalists, if they thought about it at all. It was a quiet Sunday morning in Vienna on 21 December 1975.

Carlos the Jackal[15] had made a frightening name for himself since his first murder attempt, just two Christmases earlier, when he had shot and nearly killed Marcus Sieff, the Jewish chairman of Marks & Spencers, in his own doorway and escaped unscathed. A series of dangerous and savage exploits had turned him into another ideal, if slightly unbalanced, tool for Waddid Haddad. Now Haddad wanted him to put together a new team and carry out his most dramatic raid yet – to seize the entire Council of OPEC (the Organization of Petroleum Exporting Countries), kill Yamani and Amouzegar, the Saudi and Iranian Oil Ministers, and hold the remainder hostage until a manifesto had been repeatedly broadcast and a large ransom had been paid.

Carlos enjoyed the luxuries of life and commanded the operation from his suite in the Vienna Hilton. It was no use his team complaining. Wilfred Bose, the none-too-bright Hans-Joachim Klein, homicidal Gabrielle Krocher Tiedemann and three middle easterners who never went by anything but their code names – Khalid, Yussuf and Joseph – were there to obey, not to question. In any case, they had every confidence in their leader at the outset of this mission. Carlos had already secured details of the conference timetable and the location and layout of its meeting room and the access routes to it. On the eve of the raid, Carlos had gone to an unnamed embassy and collected machine pistols, machineguns, ammunition and explosives. Fifteen years later, it transpired that Libya had been behind all these careful preparations.

The group was not challenged by the two policeman standing by the door as it approached the ugly glass-and-concrete headquarters of OPEC squashed in between its taller neighbours. Nor were they questioned by the journalists, or anyone else, as they crossed the lobby and climbed the stairs to the landing outside the first-floor conference room and started shooting. Only two unarmed policemen stood between the Jackal's squad and the rather spartan oblong room where 11 of the world's most economically powerful men were gathered to fix the latest price of oil in an already sky-high and volatile world market. Bravely, the older policeman, Anton Tichler, tried to wrest Carlos' gun from his hand. As he was thrust away, Tiedemann came up behind him and shot him through the neck so that the bullet emerged through his throat. He was then dumped, bleeding heavily, into the lift and despatched to the ground floor. As Tiedemann finished her grisly task, an Iraqi plain-clothes security man grabbed her round the arms in a bear hug so she could not fire her weapon, but she managed to draw a second pistol and shot the Iraqi in the head.

Carlos, having locked the other policeman in an empty office, put a fatal burst of fire into the stomach of a Libyan official – presumably unaware of his country's involvement – who tried to stop him. What the Jackal did not know was that the sound of his shots had authenticated the other policeman's cryptic phone call to his headquarters.

"Inspector Janda. Department One. OPEC attacked. Shooting with machine pistols."

If Klein had done his job properly there would have been no working phones on which the Inspector could have called. Thanks to the prompt and courageous actions of the switchboard operator, Edith Heller, there were. It was Klein's task to take over the switchboard and stop all outgoing calls, but Edith had seen him coming and managed to alert the police to the attack. When Klein shot the mouthpiece out of her hand she grabbed another and in a fury the gunman emptied the rest of his magazine into the switchboard - not the most intelligent or effective way of disabling it. Edith was fortunate that she had been assigned to Klein, the one captor who had objected to indiscriminate killing as counterproductive. Any of the others would have killed her.

Firing a volley of shots into the brightly lit ceiling, Carlos walked into the OPEC conference room like some ham actor playing a gangster in a B-movie. But instead of killing Yamani as he had been ordered, he mocked him.

"Do you know me?" he demanded.

"Very well," replied Sheikh Yamani calmly, well aware that the Jackal had already tried to assassinate him.

The curious thing is why Carlos did not shoot the Saudi minister straight away as he had been ordered to do by Haddad. Instead, once he had divided his captives into "Liberals" (Algeria, Iraq, Kuwait and Libya), "Neutrals" (Ecuador, Gabon, Indonesia, Nigeria and Venezuela) and "Criminals" (Iran,

Qatar, Saudi Arabia and the UAE) and herded them into different parts of the conference room, he gave the captives the ritual reassurance that "no harm would come to them". The Liberals, who had been parked almost on top of the wired-up explosives, must have doubted his sincerity as much as the Criminals.

Did Carlos simply ignore Haddad's order? Or had it perhaps been a Thomas a Becket-type instruction rather than a direct order? Had it been countermanded since he had reached Vienna? Had Gaddafi, whose own economy was heavily dependent on oil sales, overruled the Palestinians for fear of destabilizing an already shaky market? It seems more likely to me, given the Jackal's temperament, that he merely enjoyed prolonging his captives' uncertainty and had every intention of killing the two condemned ministers in due course. That is, until the situation arose when his own safety might depend on keeping all the hostages alive now that armed police had surrounded the building. Already jumpy, the Austrian police would almost certainly have taken the murder of an important hostage as the signal to go in, regardless of the consequences. They had already been engaged in a fierce fire-fight with Klein, in which he had been seriously wounded and the assault leader had been ignominiously shot in the backside. At first Carlos ordered Klein to carry on with his duties, but when a medically qualified delegate pronounced him in urgent need of hospital treatment he was permitted to escort the wounded gunman out of the building. The hospital staff were amazed that anyone could carry on with such serious injuries and put him on a life-support machine. That Carlos was indifferent to the fate of his men, expediency apart, was made evident when he insisted on Klein being stretchered out to join the party when they flew out of Austria. "I don't care if he dies," he curtly told the Iraqi chargé affaires who had volunteered to mediate. "We came together and we'll leave together." Klein had his opportunity to gain a modicum of revenge at his murder trial in Germany in October 2000 when his evidence revealed the involvement of Libya and the probability that Carlos had embezzled the ransom money.

Rather oddly, it was a British secretary whom Carlos forced to type out, in French, the inevitable long-winded manifesto. However, the note of his demands, in English, was suitably curt.

To the Austrian authorities:

We are holding hostage the delegations to the OPEC conference.

We demand the lecture of our communiqué on the Austrian radio and television network every two hours, starting two hours from now.

A large bus with windows covered by curtains must be prepared to carry us to the airport of Vienna tomorrow at 7.00 am, where a full-tanked DC-9 with a crew of three must be ready to take us and our hostages to our destination.

Any delay, provocation or unauthorized approach under any guise will endanger the

life of our hostages.
The Arm of the Arab Revolution
Vienna 21/12/75

Whether daunted by the Jackal's reputation or simply stymied by the nature of the stand-off, the Austrian Chancellor, Bruno Kreisky, gave in to the demands. His chief concern seemed to be the safety of the (voting) Austrian employees rather than that of the other captives. At a little after 6 pm the same evening the manifesto, advocating the Palestinian cause and the need for Arab unification, was broadcast and again every two hours afterwards. Such was its length that it cannot have left much time for other programming!

Early the following morning, Carlos was filmed and photographed provocatively shaking hands with each of the OPEC employees as they were released. Having exploited that photo opportunity he then made much of embarking his remaining 42 hostages on the bright yellow post office bus that was to take them to the airport. The DC-9 with its crew, captors and captives took off for Algiers less than 24 hours after the initial attack was carried out.

Thereafter it must have gradually dawned on Carlos that his various sponsors were not entirely pleased with him. The first encounter was just what his ego needed. The Algerian Foreign Minister, Abdel Boutelflika, greeted him effusively. Klein was taken to hospital and most of the hostages were released, leaving only a dozen Arab representatives on the plane.

Next stop Tripoli and a warm embrace from Colonel Gaddafi, or so Carlos thought. He was entirely mistaken. Libya did not want to be identified in any way with what had happened and refused to supply a larger plane, demanded the release of their nationals and ignored the Jackal's threat to shoot the hostages. His bluff called, Carlos released the Libyans and five others leaving him with just his greatest prizes, Yamani and Amouzegar. Surely the Saudis would now supply him with the long-range aircraft he needed to get to Baghdad? They would not even speak to him while he held Sheikh Yamani prisoner. Grudgingly, the Libyans refuelled the DC-9 and Carlos set off for Algiers. He was to face the added humiliation of being refused a landing in Tunisia en route.

The Algerian Foreign Minister met Carlos once again at the airport, but this time there was a distinct frostiness in his greeting. Carlos returned to the plane and there ensued a long and heated argument within earshot of the captives about what should be done with them. The bloodthirsty Tiedemann and Khalid argued furiously in favour of shooting them, but the Jackal, realizing this particular game was over, released his hostages and vanished once more into anonymity somewhere in the Middle East. He had, after all, achieved most of his objectives – world-wide publicity, a massive ransom paid into a Yemeni bank★ and an escape route for Klein and himself.

It would be hard to classify such an extraordinarily high-profile coup, executed without the death or capture of a single captor, as anything but a success.

The five cases I have described were only the highlights of a plethora of successful seizures from the captors' point of view from the late 1960s to the 1990s.

★ *Figures vary between $20m and $50m, the source of funds between Saudia Arabia and Iran and their destination between the Revolutionary Cause and the Jackal's pocket.*

Other examples:

3 Sepember 1969, Brazil	US ambassador for 15 prisoners.
6 March 1970, Guatemala	US labour attaché for prisoners.
11 March 1970, Brazil	Japanese consul for prisoners.
24 March 1970, Dominica	US air attaché for 20 prisoners.
11 June 1970, Brazil	West German ambassador for prisoners.
22 July 1970, Greece	Skyjack VIP prisoner released who became MP in Jordan.
December 1970, Brazil	Swiss ambassador for prisoners.
10 February 1972, Sweden	Croats skyjack aircraft. Seven Croats released and flown to Madrid.
23 January 1973, Haiti	US ambassador for 16 prisoners and $70,000.
4 May 1973, Mexico	US consul for 30 prisoners and $80,000.
28 September 1973, Austria	Jewish emigrés seized. Transit camp closed. Captors flown to Libya.
6 February 1974, Singapore	Japanese embassy in Kuwait for 4 prisoners flown to Yemen.
24 April 1974, Chad	German and two Frenchmen held for 3 years for ransom and manifesto.

27 December 1974, Nicaragua	Fourteen prisoners including Daniel Ortega flown to Cuba.
5 January 1975, Germany	Peter Lorenz for five prisoners flown to Yemen.
4 August 1975, Malaysia	US and Swedish embassies seized for five prisoners flown to Libya.
22 October 1975, Palestine	US aid reps for two prisoners in Israel.
August 1978, Nicaragua	Sandinistas seize Congress, many prisoners flown to Cuba.
11 January 1980, El Salvador	Ambassadors of Panama and Costa Rica etc for publicity and seven prisoners.
5 February 1980, El Salvador	Spanish ambassador and 11 hostages for prisoners.
17 September 1980, El Salvador	Eleven hostages for investigation of murders by government.
1980, Honduras	One hundred and five hostages for 20 prisoners flown to Cuba.
5 May 1986, Chile	Hostages for press and radio attack on Pinochet and US.
10 September 1986, Norway	Hostages freed for anti-Iranian government statement.
14 September 1986, United States	Eleven hostages freed for radio appeal for peace in Lebanon.
September 1990, Netherlands	French ambassador for key prisoner and $1m.
25 April 1993, India	Indian Airlines plane and 155 hostages for three Kashmiri militants.

For fuller account of these episodes see Appendix One.

Chapter Four

Captors Lose

The impact made when four Palestinians under the direct command of the PLO seized the cruise liner *Achille Lauro**, an Italian ship travelling from Alexandria to Port Said, on 7 October 1985 completely overshadowed other much more significant hostage-taking incidents of that time – the TWA847 skyjacking of the previous June, the numerous abductions (many of them Americans) in the Lebanon and so on. It is puzzling that a failed act of piracy in which only one person died and where the hijackers were caught and tried should so have captured the public imagination. It was not even the first cruise liner to have been taken over in this way. A Portuguese cruise ship, the *Santa Maria*, was seized in January 1961 but, intercepted by US and Brazilian naval vessels, it landed its 600 passengers unharmed in Brazil after a few days. The *Achille Lauro* incident, however, provided the stimulus for books, films, television programmes and, in 1991, the second opera, *The Death of Klinghoffer*, of the American composer John Adams.

There is a moment in the opera when the captain, through whose reflections and reminiscences the storyline unfolds, listens, both fascinated and repelled, sympathetic and angry, to the explanation of one of the Palestinian hijackers as to why Klinghoffer has to die in an expiation for the suffering of the Palestinian people. The fact that Adams depicted the harrowing backgrounds of Jews and Palestinians with equal sympathy earned him much opprobrium in the United States.

It is no less puzzling that this act of piracy should have been possible in the first place. At the time of the take-over there was still a full crew and 95 passengers on board when their Palestinian fellow travellers took over the ship. The *Achille Lauro* was a 21,000-ton ship, 192 metres long and 25 metres in the

* *An elderly "Jonah" ship, its construction in 1938 was delayed by the Second World War meaning that it was not launched until 1947. By the time of this incident, it had already suffered three fires, in which three people had died, and a major collision. It was to catch fire again and finally sink on 2 December 1994.*

beam. To accommodate its full complement of 900 passengers and crew there was the usual wedding-cake construction of passenger decks with their warren of cabins and public areas. Below decks there was a labyrinth consisting of the engine room, a generator plant, bilges and stores with which only the crew were familiar. The usual elaborate structure of a big ship's bridge overlooked the whole. I recite these facts only to ask one question. How was it that four men, albeit heavily armed, were able to take control of so large and complex a space with so many people spread over so large an area for three days? (One woman remained undetected, locked in her cabin throughout the entire episode.)

Unlike the situation on an aircraft or on a bus where a hijacker can detonate a grenade or a small amount of explosive and kill everybody, there was no way the hijackers could even cripple, let alone sink, so large a vessel. What strange mental paralysis rendered all the passengers, with one notable exception, incapable of resistance? This is a general phenomenon among those taken hostage which I shall consider later.

Perhaps wheelchair-bound Leon Klinghoffer's experience of fighting physical adversity for many years had given him both the moral courage and the pure cussedness to urge his fellow passengers to fight back. Perhaps it was frustration with the inertia of his able-bodied fellow passengers that made him round on his captors to condemn their action. Perhaps it was simply because he was both an American and a Jew, and thus epitomized all the Palestinians had grown up to hate and to blame for their misfortunes, that provoked the ire of his captors and marked him as the first and only passenger to be murdered. Like nearly all those who are the most vociferous and convincing in arguing with their captors, he was chosen as the first victim when a hostage death was considered necessary to convince the coerced that they should comply with the hostage-takers' demands. There is no reason to suppose that he was singled out because he was unable to resist. It is more than likely that selecting the man in the wheelchair was done in a deliberate attempt to maximize the shock of the murder in the hijackers' desperate attempt to persuade the Syrian port authorities in Tatrus to let the ship dock. It was also a principal cause of the bitter arguments that are reported to have broken out among his murderers both before and after he was shot in the head and chest and trundled over the side of the ship by a terrified crewman.

Abou Abbas, the man behind the plan to seize the ship, has always insisted that this was a military plan that had gone wrong and that the intention was not to hurt anyone.

A decade later, when he had become a peace envoy for Yasser Arafat, he said: "The purpose of armed struggle is not simply to kill ... its purpose is to reach a political goal." He had already made an apology by that time for Klinghoffer's death, and also pointed out that his intervention had saved a great many lives. The Americans, not unreasonably, brushed his apologies and his excuses aside.

Hoffman was even more scathing, following NBC's success in tracking Abbas down when the US security services had so singularly failed to do so. "Presumably because it was to Abbas' advantage to let them. The glare of the camera lights ... transformed Abbas into the media star of the moment, rather than the kidnapper and murderer he really was."[1]

As is often the case, however, the mastermind plotting in the safety of his study does not take the psychotic tendencies of at least some of his front-line troops into account. Nor does he always anticipate the effect of a level of tension that can affect captors as much as captives and which can lead to a hair-trigger response whose consequences cannot be planned for.

The actual seizure of the cruise liner had been meticulously planned. The hijackers appear to have boarded the ship in Alexandria as genuine tourists having first waited for 80 per cent of the passengers to disembark for a tour of the pyramids from which they were to be taken by bus to Port Said. This left mostly the old, the feeble, the very young and the incapacitated and the indolent on board.

The original plan was that the four-man team should remain unobtrusively in their cabin until the *Achille Lauro* reached the Israeli port of Ashdod. There they would leave the ship, seize Israeli hostages and demand the release of 50 Palestinians held in Israeli jails and their own safe exit. Unable to resist the gunman's chronic temptation to handle his weapon they were spotted by a waiter cleaning their guns when he opened the door of their cabin. They grabbed the man and realized that they would have to act quickly before his absence was noticed. In several respects they were lucky. In the first place they were well out to sea and out of range of an easy counter-attack by a light, offshore craft.

Recognizing their inability to manage the ship without the co-operation of the captain and crew, the Palestinians, next move was to go to the bridge, threaten the captain's life and compel him to change the ship's course towards the Syrian port of Tartus. There they hoped to take refuge in a country sympathetic to the Palestinian cause. They also struck at a time, 1.15 pm, when many of the passengers were already gathered in one place for lunch. Even so, it is unlikely that only four men could have kept control for any length of time if there had been even the slightest degree of passive resistance and non-co-operation on the part of the crew. Their failure to thwart the hijackers smacks, if not of complicity, of at least some degree of sympathy for the Palestinian position. To assemble 90 passengers while simultaneously ensuring that every member of the crew is obeying your commands is not an easy thing to achieve. As has often been the case in other incidents, the shortage of manpower was a further cause of tension among the captors. Nevertheless, the hijackers successfully took control of the ship and, that evening, radioed their demands to the Egyptian authorities to pass on to Israel. They had shown themselves capable of adapting to the first unexpected change of plan. The second, however, proved more exasperating.

Unexpectedly, the Syrian port authorities refused to allow the *Achille Lauro* to dock in their harbour. In a frenzy of exasperation, the hijackers notified the Syrian authorities that they would kill a hostage every 15 minutes if they were not given docking facilities and, to confirm their intent, they shot the recalcitrant Klinghoffer. Fortunately for the rest of the passengers and the crew,* during the course of the following 15 minutes the hijackers received orders from their superiors to leave the passengers alone and carry on to Port Said where their return home in exchange for the release of the hostages would be negotiated. The Egyptians, initially unaware of Klinghoffer's murder, agreed to the deal. When the murder was discovered, the American ambassador in Cairo demanded the arrest of the perpetrators. The Egyptians mendaciously expressed regret that the four men had already left the country. They did not do so until several hours later.

It may not always have been the case, but in this instance American intelligence proved both swift and accurate. It was ascertained that the Palestinians would be flying to Tunisia in an EgyptAir Boeing 737 with the registration number 2843. The fugitives' exact route, planned altitude and take-off time, however, were not known. It is then that we get an early demonstration of the United States' post-Second World War willingness to flex its military muscle, regardless of international law. However, it is hard not to sympathize with the American determination to demonstrate that you cannot seize or kill any of its citizens, anywhere in the world, with impunity. As a former imperial power that had sent an army half way across the globe to rescue a few hostages in the 19th century, Britain was not unsympathetic. The fact remains that only the Italians, whose ship (i.e. territory) had been seized, or the Egyptians, in whose territorial waters the act of piracy had been committed, had any legal jurisdiction in the matter.

By chance, the USS *Saratoga*, a task-force carrier, was already in the Adriatic and the US National Security Council ordered its commanding officer, Rear Admiral David Jeremiah, to try to intercept the 737. By now it was dark and the F14-A Tomcat pilots criss-crossing the Mediterranean in a search pattern supported by an E2-C Hawkeye had close-shave encounters with two other passenger aircraft before spotting the crucial number 2843 on the tailplane of a third. Closing alongside and making their intent palpably clear, they ordered the pilot to land at the nearby NATO air base at Sigonella in Sicily. If the Palestinians had still been armed they would almost certainly have prevented the pilot from acquiescing, but they had surrendered their weapons to the Egyptians after securing their passage on the plane.

Once the plane had landed, the hijackers found themselves the subject of an

---

* *In the Adams opera the captain offers to be the next victim.*

absurd situation that while farcical had the potential for tragedy. Because the base was multi-national, the Italians and the Americans found themselves in armed contention for the prize. Sensibly, the US officer in charge, recognizing the risks of provoking a fight with the Italians on their own territory, called his men off and the hijackers were arrested and later tried by the Italians. No doubt piqued by the Americans' high-handed manner, the Italians turned down an American extradition request. To add insult to injury, two of the hijackers escaped while on parole, which the United States disapproved of their being given in the first place. Abou Abbas and the escapees were tried and convicted in absentia, but Abbas continued to operate unmolested in Palestine for many years.* Interestingly, because of the murder of Klinghoffer and the circumstances of the seizure, the Palestinians' defence lawyer was unable to plead the lesser charge of piracy and the conviction was for hijacking and murder on the high seas. It also prompted a great deal of soul searching among maritime nations about what to do about terrorism on the high seas. The laws relating to piracy now seemed inadequate and the International Maritime Organization thrashed out a convention on maritime terrorism sponsored, as it happened, by Italy and Egypt.

If the failure of the captors in our first case was due to a combination of circumstances, incompetence and American resolution, the unsuccessful outcome of our second was almost entirely due to the outstanding character of its principal captive, Sir Geoffrey Jackson, the British ambassador to Uruguay.

Why not? You think. You're 19 years old and studying for a degree that will almost certainly get you nowhere except into the ever-growing ranks of the unemployed. Your family chose the wrong side.

Once they were prosperous farmers, but since the collapse of the meat and wool trade after the war they have become progressively poorer. Uruguay, from being one of the wealthiest, most democratic and stable countries in Latin America, now hovers near the bottom of the chart. Of course, the family could have signed up with the big limo, big house, luxurious lifestyle of the small ruling class, but your father refused to be bribed and spoke out against the corruption that had gripped the country. He "disappeared" a long time ago and we all know what that means. Your brother rebelled as well. He is in the notorious prison in Montevideo along with hundreds of other political prisoners who have fallen foul of the regime of President Pacheco. All he did was take part in a student protest. Still, he's probably lucky to be alive and he wasn't tortured — much. One of these days the Tupos will get him out, you hope. That's why you joined, despite your mother's pleading. That and the frustration of living in a society ruled by people without ideals, without morals and without any prospect of being removed through the ballot box. If only

* *It gratified the Americans immensely when, during the second Gulf War, their commanders captured Abbas on 15 April 2003.*

there were some way to get Pacheco and his cronies out of office.

Then along comes your cell leader and summons you to a council of war. Twenty or 30 young men – and a couple of girls! That's against all the rules. You are supposed to know and meet only the four or five other members of your cell. Only the cell leader connects with Tupos beyond it. It is safer that way in case one of you is caught and interrogated – with a little help from the electrodes.

This man you don't know is hiding behind a large pair of dark glasses so he must be a bigwig. He's at least 28 or 30 years old. He's talking to you about Brazil where insurgents have kidnapped the US, German and Swiss ambassadors and swopped them for comrades in state prisons.

Then there's Guatemala, where the German ambassador, Count von Spretti, has been executed. Here in Uruguay that undercover cop, Dan Mitrione, was shot for helping to train Pacheco's new special security squads because the United States would not bargain for him.

Good old Movimento de Liberacion, Tupamaros, Tupac Amaru, the last Inca king who was murdered by the Spaniards in 1571 and yes, do we all know the joke about our name sounding like the bird that makes a horrid noise like a hyena, but we'll be the ones laughing in the end. What's he saying now? We should go for the British as well as the others. "After all, the British have drained our economy, obtaining benefits which amounted to thousands of times the invested capital and which never left the country with any tangible advantages. British ambassadors do good business for Britain."[2] He's got an idea for making them think twice about backing Pacheco? Well, why not?

Why not? You're 55 and you have been shunted into a graveyard posting where your liberal views can be kept out of harm's way. But make a real success of being ambassador to Uruguay and the next stop could be Paris or Bonn. Easier said than done when you have to deal with a regime whose methods you find repugnant, persuade it to let such wealth as there is trickle down much further, to let in the light of democracy, while you simultaneously sustain British commercial interests. Wishful thinking. You'll probably be kidnapped first as that seems to be becoming an even more popular fashion than the miniskirt.[3]

It looks as if the Tupamaros have their eye on the Brits. Lucky for Gordon Jones that he managed to roll out of the back of the pick-up they were driving him off in. Trouble is they're smart kids and now they're using closed vans. Well, you can only do your best to be an elusive target, and if they do get you they won't get much out of you. Family and officials alike for the high jump if there is so much as a hint of negotiation, let alone concession, were your orders. It's tough it out for me, do or die, literally perhaps, but I have my faith and a lot of forethought so ... why not?

The parallel monologues above are fictional, but the facts and many of the phrases are all drawn from personal accounts and, in particular, that of the British ambassador Sir Geoffrey Jackson, a model for every autobiography of hostage captivity that followed and one seldom equalled for its insights. Little could Jackson have known that he would have to "tough it out" for 244 days, a political hostage captivity record that would stand for more than a decade. Ironically, he had written not so long before to Jasper Cross, the British commissioner in Montreal, to congratulate him for surviving a week's captivity the previous October at the hands of French separatists who had murdered Quebec Labour Minister, Pierre Laporte, at the same time.

By 1971, the Tupamaros had created their own network of hospitals, ambulances, safe houses, ammunition dumps and schools. More relevantly for Jackson, underneath the teeming city of Montevideo, home to 80 per cent of Uruguay's population by this time, they had a network of "Peoples' Prisons" in which to hold their kidnap targets. Jackson found himself in one of these on 8 January 1971, locked into a small cage and under the constant scrutiny of the young Tupamaros guards who were hooded and who were changed and substituted frequently. This was not so much to prevent him recognizing them, but to ensure that their captive could not establish any kind of rapport with his jailers and turn himself from an object that could easily be disposed of into a human being deserving of compassion and sympathy and, therefore, harder to kill. That Jackson was able to establish just such a rapport with the majority of these young people is a tribute to both his character and his tactics. His first challenge was to preserve his personal dignity.

Caged, like an animal in a zoo, unable to do anything, however private, without being observed by your zookeepers "is without doubt a deep insult to human dignity and a serious blow to self-esteem".[4] The ambassador coped with this situation firstly by never being "the ambassador", never indulging himself in the fallacy of confusing status with self-worth. As Jackson wrote:

> I had, I said, already made it clear to my custodians that I was not holding out for protocol: "the ambassador" did not ask for the communal bucket as such, nor did I have any illusion of "excellency" when perched upon it. The substance of my mission was, however, another matter;[5]

A hostage who fails to recognize from the outset of his captivity that the office or position which has bolstered his ego and reinforced his authority previously is completely unrecognized by his captors will find that self-esteem hard to maintain.[6] The importance of that office to the Uruguayans, as much as to the British, was something Jackson tried to get across to his captors.

Through a combination of philosophizing and humour he came to terms with his encagement, recalling his Richard Lovelace that "stone walls do not a prison make nor iron bars a cage" and laughing at himself in a gently self-deprecating way. On one occasion, he recalled waking on the floor with his head wedged up against the bars and comparing himself to Wallace, the lion immortalized by Stanley Holloway who also lay "in a somnolent posture with the side of his head on the bars". How he must have wished at times to have been able to emulate Wallace as far as his guards were concerned.* In fact he made every effort to engage with them while making it clear that he did not condone their conduct, even if he did have some sympathy for their motives.

He kept himself in some kind of shape physically by doing the Canadian Air Force exercises that had become popular at that time and by endlessly pacing to and fro in the confines of his cage. But although he was so closely confined, the conditions in which he was kept were not too onerous by the standards of most kidnap hostages. He had a plentiful supply of good books, he was allowed to draw, to embroider and to play cards. This latter he used as one of the many means to enter into humanizing dialogue with his guards, who enjoyed the games he taught them and taught him other games in return. The fact that his captivity did not deprive him of mental stimuli, from reading to writing a children's book in his head, enabled him to endure better the cramped conditions of his cell.[7]

He used another aspect of his self-discipline as a means of engaging the guards' sympathy. Food was supplied in a very irregular manner, feast followed by famine. When there was a surplus he put some by, not just to avoid getting fat or for his own future use, but because he felt genuinely sorry for the improvident youngsters who bolted every mouthful put before them and whom he supplied in times of dearth. Nevertheless, when they offered him a glass of wine he courteously, but firmly, declined, for to have accepted such a symbolic offering would have been to imply a friendship and approval which he did not feel. He could never allow himself to forget that "behind all the ideological protestations of the New Revolution lies the ultimate and unchanging sanction of raw force".[8]

Jackson also established a connection with his guards by sketching caricatures of them with the materials provided. But while they laughed at these he "remained under no excessive illusion; more than once, in between drawings, the alarm, the silence, the darkness and the click and feel of the cocked weapon reminded me that these were but concessionary glimpses of our common humanity, to be superseded at any moment by the larger, overriding, omnipresent and deadly empiricism."[9] All these interactions gave Jackson something akin to power over his captors rather than the other way round. But that it was so was due to his astonishing sense of self-discipline, his recognition that to control his captors' behaviour to any degree he first had to control his own. This he did by the thoughtful analysis of the twin basic requirements of the captive's day:

---

* *"Lion's eat Albert…"*

Whether it is an original discovery or not I cannot say, but I have concluded that the captive requires two classes of routine, corresponding to two distinct human needs – the need to break up his day and the need to fill up his day. I had already developed many such routines and, with company, was to develop more. In retrospect, I can rationalize what at the time I suspect I did intuitively to survive, which was to confront the loss of the dimension of time – and the effective extinction of any future tense – by the creation of landmarks in my small eternity.[10]

The company to which he referred was the arrival of a fellow prisoner, who was treated in a far worse manner than he, who became an object both for pity and conspiracy to maintain the psychological upper hand.

The mantra, which Jackson recited at least twice a day and with which he preserved his sense of self- and mental control is somewhat long-winded and must have filled ten minutes of his time whenever he turned to it. It is, however, worth quoting in full, both for an understanding of Jackson's situation and of the psychology of the survivor captive:

1. I am in a totally passive situation – a prisoner, guarded and immobilized. It is up to me to turn this into an active situation, by seeking survival through the preservation of my health and, when it comes to the point, my life.

2. I am in a totally negative position – no freedom, no family, no friends, no news, no time, no light, no faces, no green growth, no world. It is my obligation to turn all these negatives into a positive by identifying in them a purpose, pursuing it and attaining it.

3. There is no reason to hate these people (my "hosts"). Nor, however, may I be sentimental about them. I must, therefore, make no concession to them, and give them no satisfaction.

4. These people, however objective I force myself to be, have done my family, my government and my country an immense injury. I have no right to add to it by anything I may do, and conversely the absolute obligation to seek by any means I can, to transform that injury into a good, for my family, my government and my country.[11]

Whether this mantra would have sustained him throughout the length of captivity that was endured by the captives in our next example we cannot know, but it is a safe bet that it would. Fortunately, quite fortuitously, he did not have to put it to that test. On 6 September, the Tupamaros burrowed under Montevideo's main prison and freed 106 of their comrades. They left a placard in the tunnel that showed them not without a touch of student humour. "Movement for National Liberation Transit Authority. Please keep to your left."[12]

Since the release of these prisoners was the principal reason for kidnapping Jackson, there was no longer any point in keeping him and, on 9 September, he was released to wander the streets of Montevideo until he could find a taxi to take him home. For his captors his detention had proved fruitless. The strict no-negotiation order he had imposed had been obeyed and no concessions were made. For Jackson the time was by no means wasted for he had revealed himself to be a man of remarkable character and a philosopher of no little insight. That his government never fully made use of his exceptional talents afterwards was its loss and the typical fate of those who have embarrassed their masters by being kidnapped.

It is hard to know where to begin on the sad tale of Lebanon and the digression, in historical terms, that is the story of its 59 foreign hostages.

Was it on 2 November 1917 when Lord Balfour committed Britain, the protecting power, to creating a state for the Jews in Palestine? Or on 14 May 1948 when the State of Israel came bloodily into being and tens of thousands of uprooted Palestinians were scattered throughout the Levant? Or on 27 September 1970 when an exasperated King Hussein finally drove the more militant majority of Palestinians out of Jordan and Yasser Arafat took 2,000 of his diehard core of fighters with him to Lebanon? Was it in April 1975 when civil war between the ruling Christians and the frustrated Muslims broke out in Lebanon itself? Or was it in June 1982 when Israel lost patience with Lebanon for allowing Palestinians to raid and kill across their common border and invaded, thus adding the Lebanese Shia to its enemies? The US did not endear itself by vetoing a UN resolution condemning Israel's incursion. Or was it, as Amnesty International claimed in July 1997, because:

> Lebanese nationals, mostly those suspected of armed opposition to the Israeli occupation of Lebanon, had been held for years in detention in Israel or by Israeli-controlled forces, cut off from the outside world, often without charge or trial … or held beyond the expiry of their sentences as hostages to be used as a bargaining counter with Islamist militia groups?

Rather, I think, it was the cumulation and combination of all of these events and the ineptitude of Western interference in its affairs that reduced Lebanon, once the most beautiful and prosperous country in the Middle East, to a nightmare of anarchy, hatred and fear.★

Against this background in the 1980s a minor epidemic of kidnapping of westerners grew, burgeoned and faded. I say "minor" because the taking of

★ *Those seeking to disentangle the complex history of Lebanon in the second half of the 20th century can do no better than read Robert Fisk's heart-rending account – Pity the Nation.*

Western hostages was only the newsworthy tip of a massive iceberg of lies, myths, propaganda and terror of which the Lebanese themselves, of every faith and sect, were the principal victims. Tens of thousands of Muslims were kidnapped by Christians, Christians by Muslims and the Lebanese resented the fact that the West only took interest in its own hostages. As Walid Jumblat, leader of the Druze,★ said at the time. "There are hostages in Lebanon so why make a fuss about a few foreigners?" And another angle was put on the same question by Robert Fisk: "Why was it that Western hostages were called 'hostages' – which they were – while Lebanese Shia Muslim prisoners held in an Israeli-controlled jail in southern Lebanon were referred to by journalists simply as 'prisoners'? These Lebanese were also held illegally, without trial…"13

Jumblat's view was shared by Mrs Thatcher, who certainly did not wish to give the captors the pleasure of seeing her make a fuss. Indeed, she quashed a Foreign Office initiative to trade the hostage Alec Collet for a supply of kidney machines which his captors were willing to entertain. Collet was later killed. As Thatcher's spokesman, Charles Powell, said: "We were well aware of what might happen to the British hostages in Lebanon, but this was not a consideration that we could allow to shackle our policy." Thatcher made it clear in the House of Commons that she would not negotiate with terrorists. It is puzzling to know why the kidnappers did not just kill their British captives once they had no trade-in value. Perhaps they just could not believe or understand Thatcher's attitude.

The European Union and the United States, however, while equally adamant in public in their refusal to do deals with hostage-takers to secure the release of their nationals, did so behind the scenes. France and Germany traded successfully by supplying hundreds of millions of dollars worth of medical supplies and other equipment, but never arms or money. Not surprisingly they resented being lectured by the Americans on not having dealings with terrorists. The United States did try to have such dealings secretly, but unsuccessfully, which was not surprising in the light of Kissinger's famous remark that it was "the responsibility of hostages to get themselves out". Not only was the US supplying anti-tank missiles to Iran, but its only attempt to buy the release of a hostage ended in fiasco with $200,000 dollars paid and not a hostage to be seen. During the Reagan administration, the man on the Lebanon desk at the State Department had never even been to the Middle East. As one American caustically commented of his fellow American politicians: "There are two kinds; those with passports and those without."

It is possible to detect a pattern in the 59 (by my count, see Appendix Two) kidnappings of Europeans in Beirut between 1982 and 1989. Three quarters of

★ *The Druze religion is a monotheistic combination of Christianity, Islam and Judaism. Its adherents in Lebanon live mainly in the mountains.*

them occurred from the first quarter of 1985 to the first quarter of 1987. In each of these three years, the majority took place in the first quarter of the year – nine, nine and eight respectively – in the wake of some action by the West that had provoked the indignation of the Palestinians and the Lebanese. In 1985, the CIA engineered an attempt to blow up Sheikh Fadlallah, an important Shia cleric and a leading figure in Hizbollah. Although it left Fadlallah unscathed, it killed 80 civilian passers-by. In 1986, it was the *Achille Lauro* affair and the US's assassination attempt on Gaddafi by bombing his palace in Tripoli. Gaddafi's three-year-old daughter and some 90 civilians were killed. The raid was launched from British bases, and that was something that was not forgotten by her enemies. In 1987, the duplicity revealed by the gradual breaking of the story of the Iran Contra affair had a similar effect.

For all the violence in other aspects of the Palestinian campaign against Israel and America, during the hostage period in Lebanon only eight of the captives were killed and one, possibly two, of these died of exacerbated natural causes and were then dressed up for propaganda purposes to look like executions. The first British prisoner escaped, the only hostage to do so, and a Frenchman died of cancer while in captivity. The next two Britons to be seized were released almost immediately.

Of those deliberately killed, four were British, three of whom were murdered on 16 April 1986 immediately following the Tripoli bombing. A video of the hanging corpse of Alec Collet was sent to the British authorities, though it has been argued that he died of natural causes and was already dead when hanged. One Briton, with a reputation for pestering female students, and an Italian may have been killed for non-political reasons, though the Italians had sent a small contingent of troops to Lebanon in 1983. Two Americans died because of their connections with US security services. William Buckley, the CIA station head, was tortured and gave a most cleverly obscurantist "confession" before being murdered, though it is possible that he, too, died naturally and was dressed up for the camera. Videos of him being tortured were sent to the US embassy. Marine Colonel William Higgins was killed in retaliation for the kidnapping of Sheikh Obeid in July 1989.

Of the European hostages, the Americans and the French were the early targets. The first foreign captive – if you discount the Jordanian chargé d'affaires in 1981 – was David Dodge, Rector of the American University in Beirut, who was kidnapped on 18 July 1982. This was something of an irony as AUB was the main route to higher education for many Lebanese. He was taken out to Iran, the only Western hostage ever held outside Lebanon, and released a year later. Nine of the 15 Americans and five of the 13 Frenchmen had been taken by mid-summer, 1985. American military support had ensured Israeli victory over the Palestinians in 1967 and 1973; the French had been closely involved in Lebanon since the beginning of the century. Britons were the next to be taken captive. Brian Keenan, an Irishman, was treated by his captors as if he were British, much to his annoyance and despite his protestations. Thus the three nations who had been most actively involved in Palestinian and Lebanese affairs, mostly in support of the exclusively Christian government, accounted for almost two-thirds of the captives. The only other nationals taken in significant numbers were Swiss – one suspects some may have been mistaken for French, Germans with five each and Russians with four.

The Russian case is an interesting one because all four were taken at the same time. One, Arkady Katkov, was killed, but the other three were rapidly released when the Russians, via the Druze, captured the brother of one of the captors and reputedly posted first one finger then another to those holding their men with dire threats of what would happen to its owner if they were harmed. As a Beirut-based Russian journalist, Konstantin Kapitanov, observed: "Nobody is going to kidnap Russian citizens in Lebanon."[14] The remainder of the hostages, an Indian, a South Korean, a Norwegian, a Dutchman and a Belgian, may simply have been in the wrong place at the wrong time.

A number of other interesting patterns emerge. Three quarters of the hostages were either killed or released within a few weeks, in some cases a few days (19) or were detained for several years (24). Only a quarter were held for intermediate lengths of time. The earlier in the hostage-taking years that you were taken the better your chances were of being released quickly. No women or children were ever held as hostages. The three European women seized were sent home, in one case immediately and in the other two after a few days. To have held them would not only have been deeply offensive to the principles of Islam, but highly impractical in what was an exclusively male captor force.

It is, in fact, completely against the tenets of Islam, as interpreted by contemporary Moslem divines* at least, to hold anyone hostage, a fact both acknowledged and ignored by most of the jailers with whom it was raised.

Nor did it make any difference to your vulnerability to have played a positive role in the life of Lebanon. Most of the captors were ignorant of such contributions and ignored them if they were not. It was sufficient to be foreign. Priests such as Weir and Jenco, teachers such as Regier, Ciccipio and Dodge, and pro-Palestinian journalists such as Anderson and Levin, were all taken. However, Fisk and three other Western journalists, two of them women, survived, though in constant fear of kidnap. Fisk tells an amusing story against himself:

> In my own car I drove around Beirut like a lunatic Nikki Lauda, foot touching the gas pedal at traffic lights in case gunmen approached. At a junction on Corniche Mazraa, I saw a man in the mirror. He was walking to my car door and I crashed the traffic lane, swerving round trucks, a policeman screaming at me. Only when the mirror's panorama

---

* e.g. Maulana Wahiduddin Khan: "This is a great sin and cowardice and is entirely forbidden in Islam."

increased did I see that the man was a street tout trying to sell me a ticket to the national lottery."[15]

Perhaps in the latter stages of the kidnapping period those in charge realized the value of having honest and objective reporters in Beirut who, while they condemned the captors, were even more severe on the conduct of Israel and America.

Relying as they did on western support, the Christian militias, who controlled east Beirut, left kidnapping westerners to the Muslim groups who controlled the western half of the city. But, as Antokol observes:

> Groups have come and gone with bewildering speed and complexity. Several groups might claim responsibility for one kidnapping, while no group might assert its claim for another. Some organizations are heard of only once. The location of a hostage, even the country in which he is being held, can be almost impossible to determine. Fixing responsibility for a kidnapping with any degree of certainty is sometimes out of the question … so unless a specific and incontrovertible claim is made by a specific group, such as Amal or Hizbullah, we shall use the [umbrella] term Islamic Jihad.[16]

The British ambassador, John Grey, refined the argument: "The first few days of any kidnapping are crucial. If you can find out who has them right at the start it is sometimes possible to get them released quickly. But once a few weeks have passed, the earth almost seems to close over them and then it becomes a far more difficult task."[17] The picture is further confused by the fact that professional criminal gangs would sometimes carry out a kidnap and then sell their captive on to the highest bidder. The "odd" nationals may well have been victims of this practice.

Of the main Muslim captor groups, Amal were the more pragmatic, though they were split into two factions that sometimes fought each other. Nabih Berri led the larger and more moderate faction which had more direct control over its kidnappers than the others. He secured the release of the two Frenchmen, Regier and Joubert, within two months of their capture and also took charge of all but four of the hostages from the TWA skyjack in June 1985 (see pages 36–40). Both Amal factions came under the direct influence of a sometimes-embarrassed Syria, and Damascus was often used as the face-saving way station for hostages en route to freedom. Correspondingly, the more theocratic Hizbollah came under the influence of the equally theocratic regime in Iran, though its kidnappers frequently acted independently of their sponsors. Almost immediately after Ayatollah Khomeini came into power, the number of kidnappings increased and, as the most fanatical and disciplined of the hostage-takers, Hizbollah came to dominate that trade.

Methods of abduction were almost identical among all groups of captors.* The routine of a target would be observed and he would then usually be seized in transit rather than from the safety of his own home or office. His car would be forced into the side of the road and its escape route blocked off. Unwanted passengers would be threatened with a gun, while the captive was dragged out of his vehicle and bundled into a getaway car. In it he would be forced to crouch down on the floor covered with a cloth or by one of the captors in order to avoid detection at the various militia roadblocks of rival organizations. He would be taken to a safe house with, in most cases, an underground block of several cells, though ordinary apartments were sometimes used. There he would usually be chained by his feet or his wrists (or sometimes both) to the wall and subjected to random beatings and mock executions. He was not starved, but was only allowed to urinate, defecate and wash at the whim of his guards. If there was any suggestion that the prisoner might have been detected, the captive would be moved to another location. Transit between prisons was one of the captive's more unpleasant experiences. He was usually swathed in parcel tape from head to foot with barely an aperture to breathe. The parcel would then be stowed in the boot of a car or under the tailboard of a truck in the midst of the fumes and dust and driven at a fearful speed to the next destination. That destination was often the remote Beka'a valley, a location in which it was harder to mount a rescue mission and which prevented penetration from rivals. There the captive languished in an agony of uncertainty as to his fate, deprived of knowledge of the outside world, and any information as to what was being done on his behalf could only be obtained via scraps of overheard news broadcasts in Arabic, which very few of them spoke. Occasionally, he would be tantalized by being allowed to see an English language newspaper or magazine or to have a radio or a television for a short spell, only to have it taken away again if he vexed his guards.

During the whole nine years of the Lebanon hostage affair "confusion twice confounded" prevailed on both sides, captors and captives alike. Paradoxically, despite the abnormality of their surroundings and treatment, it is the captives who seem to have been least confused. Indeed, the majority emerge enlightened by the experience, each having evolved his own means of survival, a subject we shall look at in greater detail later. That so many survived this ordeal is something best recorded in their own words.

> For three years I didn't see daylight. Blindfolded and chained to a chair in a basement somewhere in west Beirut, with Syrian artillery pounding the very building I was trapped in, I was confronted with the fact that evil has no "why". With terrifying lucidity, my captors, who regularly subjected me to mock executions, simply said that question no longer existed ... The interest of a journey is not only in its destination, ...

* *This description of a kidnapping is based on the more common factors of the 59 abductions listed.*

Blackened by fire, hidden for years, a painting, like the self, can still be restored. In the end, there is always a future."[18]
Jean-Paul Kauffman

The guards threw away uneaten food. Our unclean hands had touched it and thus it was forbidden to the zealots that held us. Each time I saw this I was angry. To be considered an untouchable was a humiliation I could not stand ... Freud described insanity as "a flight from a traumatic reality to another world of madness". I saw it, I travelled it, I left men trapped in it, not wanting to return.
Brian Keenan

With so little to occupy my mind, the smallest events took on the greatest significance. I was able to control the generator myself and later the switching on or off of the light. That small amount of control over my own environment meant a great deal to one as deprived of free will as I now was ... I suppose establishing the direction I was facing, using the sun to tell the time, going back into the past to discover ways to survive the present, was my way of coping.
Jackie Mann

Jackie, an ex-Battle of Britain fighter pilot well past his allotted three score years and ten, was in solitary for two years and beaten almost daily, yet he made more attempts to escape than all the other hostages put together.

I wanted to believe that the beating had been a mistake ... but now I couldn't escape the realization, long held but never so forcefully presented, that the guards could do anything they liked. There was no higher power, no avenue of appeal. They were free to abuse us at the slightest whim.
John McCarthy

No matter how much I recount the negative in cell horrors or tales of chains, or travelling taped up under the bed of a truck, or dark holes, or a terrible beating or three suicide attempts, the positive of the experience comes through in the end.
Thomas Sutherland

And what of Terry Waite, the only captive to put his head in the lion's mouth voluntarily only to have it bitten off? Suffering from asthma and kept bookless in solitary for almost four years – longer than all but one of the other hostages – he has no regrets. He has been castigated by some for muddying the waters, but the fact remains he was the only person ever to come face to face with the hostage-takers to negotiate. Pride and vanity played their part in his decision to go back after the Iran Contra scandal had just become public knowledge, but so did genuine compassion for the situation of the hostages and great courage.

I really did have a battle with myself whether to go back or whether to stay away. To me it seemed like this: if I had been working from a political base, then it would have been political suicide to go back, and personal suicide probably, as I had been clearly warned to stay away. But I was not working from a political base. My base was a church base, it was a humanitarian base, and to the best of my ability a spiritual base. It seemed to me that it would be entirely wrong, when these hostages were being deserted left, right and centre by every vestige of hope, that I, as a representative of the church, should also desert them. I felt there was a slim, slim chance of picking up the threads again. I felt as scared as hell and I felt terribly vulnerable and I thought, damn it, my pride was hurt. I mean, we all think of our reputations, but it was the reputation of the church as well.[19]

Terry Waite

I'm determined not to let these bastards beat us.[20]

Ben Weir

The demands of all the hostage-taking groups were not dissimilar: the release of 17 members of Dawa* imprisoned in Kuwait for bomb attacks in December 1983, the release of those held in Israeli (and sometimes European) prisons and the removal of outside influences, particularly those of Israel and America, so they could get on with fighting their civil war to a bloody conclusion. I have classified the nine years of hostage-taking in Lebanon as a failure because virtually no part of these demands were yielded to the captors. Yes, the Iranians did secure weapons from the US with which to fight the US-backed Iraqis, but this was not due to any pressure brought about by the hostage-takers, but simply a consequence of Reagan's obsession with toppling left-wing regimes in Latin America and allowing Oliver North to get involved with the Iran Contra affair in order to finance that obsession clandestinely. The Americans did get one hostage back for their trouble and even then they asked at first for one who was already dead. Yes, the Kuwait 17 were released from prison, but this was due solely to Saddam's 1991 invasion of Kuwait and their subsequent escape in the confusion that followed.

The ending of the Iran-Iraq war in the summer of 1988, the eventual UN declaration that Iraq was the aggressor, the involvement of the UN in hostage negotiations, the re-involvement of Britain and other western countries in the reconstruction of Iran and the renewal of diplomatic links, the death of Khomeini on 3 June 1989, the election of Rafsanjani as President of Iran in July, the collapse of the Soviet Union, the replacement of the bumbling Reagan and North by the far more professional and competent Bush and Scowcroft, the decision of Israel to release substantial numbers of captives – these were all

---

* A pro-Iranian Iraqi opposition party trying to topple Saddam.

far more instrumental than any political pressure in securing the eventual release of all the western captives by the end of 1991,* bar two Germans, who were held until June 1992. As one captor put it to Anderson on his release: "Hostage-taking is a waste of time. We didn't get what we thought out of this. We are not going to take any more hostages."

With more than a sigh of relief the President of Lebanon was able to declare: "The Nightmare of Lebanon is over."[21]

Other Failures:

31 July 1970, Uruguay	US (aid) official Dan Mitrione kidnapped by Tupamaros. Demand release of all political prisoners in Uruguay. Government refuses. Mitrione killed 10 August.
7 August 1970, Uruguay	Tupamaros kidnap US agricultural adviser, Claude Fly. Demand manifesto publication. He falls sick and is released without concessions.
31 August 1970, Holland	Thirty-two armed Amboinese youths kill a guard and seize Indonesian ambassador at home. Demand independence for South Molucca. Family held, but captors surrender next day.
18 April 1974, Italy	Red Brigades kidnap Mario Sossi, public prosecutor. Tricked into releasing him before the release of the prisoners they demanded.
24 April 1975, Sweden	Baader-Meinhof seize West German embassy and 11 hostages. Demand release of comrades. Germans refuse. B-M explodes bomb. Escape fails. One B-M commits suicide. Rest captured.
16 March 1978, Italy	Red Brigades kidnap Aldo Moro, leader of the Christian Democrats. Demand release of prisoners. Government refuses to negotiate. Moro shot, no prisoners released.

* *For a detailed, but lucid, account of these complex negotiations see Giandomenico Picco's book,* Man Without a Gun. *Picco was the UN representative, trading considerably on his standing as the man who had negotiated the end of the Iran-Iraq war.*

8 March 1993, Costa Rica	Nicaraguan Contra gunmen seize Nicaraguan embassy and 24 hostages. Demand $6 million and Nicaraguan government shake-up. $250,000 paid. No political shake-up.
April 1993, Costa Rica	Five members of Command of Death seize Costa Rican Supreme Court and 19 justices. Demand $20 million. Tricked into disarming before boarding plane and captured.

Chapter Five

Seizures Drawn

I n examining over 200 political hostage-takings, I have only been able to find two that could be described as a draw between the captors and the coerced, and even then a certain elasticity of definition is required. All the others have either been ended by force or negotiation or resolved by unilateral decisions in which the captors either win decisively or lose equally heavily.

The Baader-Meinhof gang, founded in June 1970 as the Red Army Faction, carried out its first kidnapping following a series of sabotage attacks throughout continental Europe. Peter Lorenz, a right-wing candidate for the impending elections in West Germany was kidnapped on 27 January 1975. Unsuspectingly, he admitted to his heavily secured home a young family friend, who also happened to be a member of Baader-Meinhof, and was then seized by her companions. The captors demanded the release of five of their comrades who were being held in West German prisons. Chancellor Schmidt gave in and the kidnappers appeared to have won the battle. However, it could also be said that they lost that particular war. Their secondary objective had been to make a protest against right-wing candidates, but an indignant electorate responded by handing the Right substantial gains. A 1–1 draw. I shall look more closely at Baader-Meinhof when studying crazy crusaders.

The second example could also be construed as a case of successful negotiation, but as the real negotiators were the hostages themselves rather than free representatives of the two coerced parties, the US and the Colombian governments, I have chosen to think of it as a 0–0 draw.

Dominican national day falls on 27 February, and in 1980, as was often the custom with the embassies in Bogota, a party was being thrown for the diplomatic community in the Dominican embassy. One of the many guerrilla groups of Colombia, M-19 (named after the day of the rigged election of 1970) had been studying the calendar and looking for the embassy with the worst security and the best prospect of capturing a good collection of diplomats. The occasion presented by the party at the Dominican embassy fitted their picture perfectly. Waiting till the Soviet diplomats had left the festivities early – tip-off or coincidence? – 16 well-armed* members of M-19 had no difficulty whatsoever in taking over the embassy and holding 54 of its guests hostage. They soon realized that they had a record haul in their net – 15 ambassadors and sundry consuls and chargés d'affaires as well as the small fry of caterers, waiters and embassy staff. The prize catch was the US ambassador, Diego Asencio.[1]

The captors soon threw back the small fry and whittled their catch down to a more controllable number, 20. The problem was, as is often the case, that having planned and executed the take-over most efficiently, the captors appeared to be at a loss as to what to do next. Their demands were clear enough – the release of 311 prisoners from Bogota's La Picota penitentiary, a $50 million ransom, a flight out to Cuba and the publication of an indictment of the misdeeds of the Colombian government. This last demand, at least, Asencio could have some sympathy with, since he had no illusions about the nature of the regime to which he was accredited: there is no doubt that the Colombian authorities perpetrated many breaches of human rights – torture, forced imprisonment and death squads. This was all too commonplace in a country whose 27 civil wars had accounted for between 100,000–300,000 dead.

However, the US ambassador was well aware of the dangers he was now exposed to, despite the courteous and respectful treatment both he and his fellow envoys received at the hands of their captors.

> As diplomats we were expendable, and we knew we could be sacrificed if it became necessary to safeguard policy, that is to protect our colleagues in the future. It was a painful realization, and at times it was difficult to deal with when the cruel reality of the issue confronted me.[2]

In fact, his most difficult interlocutor was his own government, which did not think he should still be acting as ambassador while also negotiating on the captors' behalf. Ascencio strongly disagreed, feeling that the special circumstances made it essential for him to retain both roles. The strength of his opinion did not prevent the State Department once this incident was over from bringing in regulations that deprived any diplomat of all the powers of his office the minute he is kidnapped.

---

* *The previous year, M-19 had tunnelled under the national armoury and stolen several thousand weapons of all descriptions.*

Asencio was perhaps lucky to get a posting to Brazil three years later. He felt himself even luckier to be alive and is convinced that he would probably not be had not he and some of his fellow ambassadors intervened in the negotiating process at the invitation of Number One, Rosamberg Pabon, the leader of the guerrillas. All the captors addressed each other by number as a means of avoiding identification by the various military eavesdropping devices. Asencio was far more worried about the possibility that a combination of the gung-ho approach of the military and the provocative rhetoric of the captors would lead to a bloody assault in which as many captives as captors would be killed. Asencio and his three fellow ambassadors on the steering committee were surreptitiously able to tone down the revolutionary rhetoric of Number One's notes to the authorities. They advised the M-19 negotiators what stance to take in the closed van parked between the two forces in which negotiations took place and initially even had one of the steering committee accompany the M-19 representative. Asencio and his colleagues also gradually persuaded Number One and his companions to tone down their demands, so that after 61 days the M-19 "special column" accepted just one million dollars and a flight to Cuba. They were wise enough, in the light of others' experience of trickery, not to release the last of their hostages until all the captors were safely out of harm's way.

While there are numerous examples of crusader hostage-takers and even more examples of crazy ones, crazy crusaders are as rare as the number of drawn outcomes of hostage-taking. As we shall see in chapter 11, however, most hostage-taking groups have at least one psychotic personality among them. The crazy crusader groups consist almost entirely of mentally and emotionally disturbed individuals.

They are drawn together by an almost hypnotized addiction to Marxist or Maoist beliefs (which they endlessly recite but seldom live up to) and an attraction to a charismatic leader to whom they surrender the last vestige of individual conscience. They also, incidentally, have a higher proportion of women members than most other groups. The political obsession allows them to justify to themselves their real motivating forces – a fascination with violence, a deep sense of personal persecution and a sense of inadequacy and hatred for most of their fellow men.

The two groups that exemplify this dangerous mixture are the Symbionese Liberation Army and the Red Army Faction, better known as the Baader-Meinhof gang. Two other organizations were inextricably involved with the Baader-Meinhof group, the 2nd of June movement, and RZ.* The Red Army Faction was named after the left-wing terrorist organization the Japanese Red

* *Revolutionary Cells, whose best-known exploit was the OPEC [see pages 43–7] seizure in 1975 .*

Army and first appeared in June 1970. The faction suffix was added to convey the entirely false impression that the group was part of a world-wide Marxist movement. The Baader-Meinhof gang began its more spectacular activities with the armed rescue of its leader, then no more than a petty criminal, from a library to which he had been allowed out of prison to visit for "research". The rabid nature of its public utterances became apparent even then.

> Did the pigs really believe that we would let Comrade Baader sit in jail for two or three years? Did any pig really believe we would talk about the development of class struggle, the reorganization of the proletariat, without arming ourselves at the same time? Did the pigs who shot first believe that we would allow ourselves without violence to be shot off like slaughter-cattle? Whoever does not defend himself will die. Start the armed resistance! Build up the Red Army![3]

Over the next two years there followed an unprecedented spate of shootings and bombings in which symbols of the capitalist state – judges, policemen and businessmen – were shot at randomly and indiscriminately. The gang also blew up the offices of media mogul Axel Springer in Berlin and set off a series of other explosions in cities such as Augsberg and Munich. Infuriated by American involvement in Vietnam, the gang also exploded pipe bombs outside US forces' barracks and clubs that killed and wounded several service men. After the Springer bombing, its press release showed no let-up in the hysteria of the language.

"Springer would rather risk seeing his workers and clerical staff injured by bombs than risk losing a few hours' working time, which means profit, over a false alarm. To capitalists, profit is everything and the people who create it are dirt."[4] This message was signed 2nd of June Commando.

However, by the end of 1972, all the main leaders – Andreas Baader, Ulrike Meinhof, Jan Carl Raspe and the real power behind the throne, Baader's mistress Gudrun Ensslin – together with many of their chief lieutenants had been arrested and charged with four murders, conspiracy and 54 attempted murders. They were finally convicted in 1977 of 30 of these and the murders, as well as the conspiracy. It seems as if, with the aid of compliant lawyers, the leadership was still able to direct the gang's activities. On 5 September, Hanns Schleyer was kidnapped and held as a bargaining counter for the release of the leadership.

Stiffened by vociferous public opinion on the matter, on this occasion Chancellor Schmidt refused to deal with them. On 18 October, the four imprisoned leaders attempted suicide. Three of them succeeded. Raspe and Baader with smuggled guns and Ensslin by hanging. The fourth, Irmgard Moller, stabbed herself several times in the chest, but lived. It would have been easy enough for their sympathetic lawyers to get the instruments of their suicides to them. Later, Moller claimed that her comrades had been murdered by the authorities and conspiracy theorists liked to think that the Baader-Meinhof leaders had been conveniently disposed of by the state. It seems unlikely, for there was little to gain from such a solution since the four had been arrested so long ago and had already been convicted. Moreover, the almost-simultaneous murder of Schleyer – "After 43 days, we have ended Hans-Martin Schleyer's miserable and corrupt existence" – suggests a co-ordinated gesture of defiance or perhaps despair.

The psychopathic nature of so many members of Baader-Meinhof is not only evident in their statements and the indiscriminate nature of their shooting, but in their subsequent wholesale self-destruction. Even before "the night of death", this obsession with suicide had begun with the hunger-strike suicide of Holger Meins in 1974 and Ulrike Meinhof's suicide by hanging in 1976 in prison. Nor was this an organization that permitted the self-doubt of defection. When Ingeborg Barz intimated her reluctance to take part in a bank raid in 1972 she disappeared, almost certainly killed by the gang. Added evidence of the mental disturbance of Baader-Meinhof leaders was published in 2002 in a neurological study of Meinhof's brain that revealed damage from a 1960s' brain tumour operation that could have lead to psychotic behaviour.

Not only did the activities of Baader-Meinhof damage the electoral chances of the left in Germany for many years, but as one commentator observed, it "paved a road to nowhere with their rigid and unrealistic idealism, then littered it with dead bodies and broken hearts".[5]

The roots of the psychoses of the Symbionese Liberation Army (SLA) lay in the growth of the black consciousness movement within the harsh penal system of the United States, where Donald DeFreeze, alias Cinque, its charismatic leader, was nurtured. Paradoxically, the troops of this "army" devoted to righting the wrongs of black people were all white. Schreiber expands this paradox:

> The political focus of its campaign was always fuzzy and at times the rhetoric and violence exceeded any obvious political or social rationale. Given the composition of the SLA, however, this political naivety is not at all surprising. It stemmed from student radicalism grafted onto the poisonous strength of black hostility, which had been cultivated over years of frustration with the polite racism of white society. The black prisoners were angry but had no program save violence. The white students were angry as well but had no program either, only rhetoric.[6]

Patti Hearst, the SLA's most celebrated member, ascribed to it a rather more grandiose and unrealistic objective: "They wanted to overthrow the government of the US. They called themselves an army. They planned on forming cells and going on until they started a full-scale war in this country."[7]

Despite the incessant physical training, mental indoctrination and self-criticism, almost the only significant action of the SLA was the kidnapping of Patti Hearst on 4 February 1974. The granddaughter of the media tycoon and billionaire William Randolph Hearst, Patti was snatched naked from her shower, bundled into a dark cupboard and bombarded with an incessant stream of SLA rhetoric and radical propaganda for many days. Whether this process was indoctrination or simply the initiation procedure for someone already sympathetic to the SLA's aims is a matter for speculation, however. Hearst had already left home and shacked up with her boyfriend in a small apartment near the Berkeley University campus where he taught. Berkeley, at that time, had a reputation for radical politics and Hearst's boyfriend was deeply involved in them. One wonders if that was part of his attraction for the disaffected daughter of the most *haute* of *haute* bourgeoisie.

Whatever the explanation, the fact remains that within two months of her abduction Hearst had identified with the SLA and later took part in a raid on the Hibernian Bank in San Francisco. The picture of her doing so became a significant symbol for revolutionaries everywhere, for it showed that someone from even the most privileged of backgrounds could be won over to a left-wing cause. Her body language in the security video of the raid does not suggest reluctance. The language and tone of the later tapes to her parents, in which she berates them for the ineffectiveness and tardiness of the free food for the poor programme that was the price of her release appears genuine enough. Though chaotic and prone to racketeering, the food distribution did take place, but Patti did not come home. She told her distressed and uncomprehending parents:

> I have been given the choice of, one, being released in a safe area or, two, joining the forces of the Symbionese Liberation Army and fighting for my freedom and the freedom of all oppressed people. I have chosen to stay and fight.[8]

She would claim later that she made this choice through fear of retribution if she left the SLA – a not entirely unreasonable fear in view of the paranoid tendency of crazy crusaders to kill those who desert the cause. Nevertheless, one has to ask certain questions. Why, when eventually arrested and asked her occupation, did she reply "Urban Guerrilla"? Why, when the SLA had been reduced to a rump of herself and two others, plus a few hangers-on, did she not avail herself of the numerous opportunities to leave the by-then emasculated organization? Why, when the other two were caught shoplifting and a gunfight ensued, did she fire her companion's machine gun (not her own) to cover their retreat? Patti Hearst should perhaps be allowed to speak in her own defence:

> Changes had come over me subtly since I had been brought into this strange world of

> the SLA. In time, although I was hardly aware of it, they turned me around completely, or almost completely. As a prisoner of war, kept blindfolded in that closet for two long months, I had been bombarded incessantly with the SLA's interpretation of life, politics, economics, social conditions and current events. Upon my release from the closet, I had thought I was humouring them by parroting their clichés and buzzwords without personally believing in them. Then, following the nightmare of the bank robbery and being branded along with them as a "common criminal", a sort of numbed shock set in. To maintain my own sanity and equilibrium while living and functioning day by day in this new environment, I had learned to act by rote, like a good soldier, doing as I was told and suspending disbelief. [9]

At her trial, during which, at the instigation of her highly paid lawyers, she invoked the Fifth Amendment 42 times,[10] she pleaded in mitigation that she had been brainwashed. The court was unconvinced and she was sentenced to seven years in prison. The fact that while awaiting trial she was allowed to stay at her parents' home under house arrest with four private bodyguards, and that she received a presidential pardon from Jimmy Carter after only 22 months in prison speaks volumes for the influence of wealth in plutocratic America rather than the unsoundness of the court's judgement. It is fair to say that she has often expressed regret for her actions and has lived unobtrusively with the bodyguard she married and her two daughters ever since her release from prison. For the purpose of an examination of the mental make-up of crazy crusaders, it is irrelevant whether she was coerced into a life of crime through fear for her life or out of conviction.

Her autobiographical account of these events provides a fascinating insight into the obsessive world of these particular crazy crusaders. Though the army never amounted to more than seven or eight foot soldiers, the SLA leaders, first DeFreeze and then after his death Bill Harris, both dubbed themselves Field Marshall and spoke grandiloquently of liberating and converting the masses. There was an almost phallic attachment to their weapons and a fanatical pursuit of physical fitness in preparation for deeds that were never actually done, a couple of small-time bank robberies apart.

The all-night sessions of political and self-analysis suggest an unhealthy concentration on insecure egos. They displayed an irrational fear of discovery that forced them to move to new accommodation almost every time a street patrol policeman passed by. Most striking was the demise of the leadership of the SLA with the same self-destructive determination as that of Baader-Meinhof. When the police finally caught up with Cinque and the core of his followers in a house in a poor black neighbourhood, they surrounded it and called on him to surrender. Whether by accident or caused deliberately, a fire broke out and rather than give themselves up the SLA members immolated themselves in the flames.

These two gangs of crazy crusaders were both primarily terrorists and criminals rather than political hostage-takers, but hostages they took. Baader–Meinhof made one highly successful kidnap, of Peter Lorenz, and one that failed, of Hanns–Martin Schleyer. The SLA's only kidnap was that of Patti Hearst, but in terms of both propaganda and conversion (by whatever means), it can only be described as a success.

Chapter Six

Bungled Rescues

The great majority of rescue attempts in political hostage incidents fail. This is a true even if a more lax definition than mine [see page 28] is applied. As shown in chapter two, three-quarters of hostages killed in rescue attempts die from the "friendly fire" of the police, military or special services trying to rescue them, or in many cases trying simply to bring the incident to a sudden conclusion.[1] Even in what are usually quoted as copybook rescues,* one or two hostages have been killed in the crossfire during the assault on their captors. However, because they were otherwise so effective and may well have prevented the deaths of many other hostages, I shall treat them in a subcategory of proxime accessit rather than as out-and-out failures.

The most notorious of completely bungled rescues is undoubtedly operation Eagle Claw, the United States' attempt to recover 52 captive diplomats from its embassy in Tehran, but seven other notable failures will also be examined for their lessons: the Munich Olympics in 1972; the 1974 Ma'alot school rescue in Israel; the 1979 seizure of the Grand Mosque in Mecca; the 1978 and 1985 Egyptian attempts to end skyjacking of their aircraft in Cyprus and Malta; the 1998 case of the hostages held in the Yemen; and, more recently, the Russian endeavour to free the hostages held by Chechens in a Moscow theatre in October 2002.

The root cause of the Eagle Claw disaster lay in British and American policy towards Iran in the early 1950s. The neo-Marxist Prime Minister, Mossadegh, was partly dependent on the Iranian Tudeh party, the manifestation of Communism in Iran. Blinkered by their obsession with the Cold War, Britain

---

* The Iranian embassy in London [see pages 117–21]; the Dutch train and school siege [see pages 114–17]; Entebbe [see pages 108–14]; or Djibouti [see pages 107–08], for example.

and America failed to see that in so religious a country as Shia Iran, the prospect of a communist take-over was zero. Britain was afraid of losing its considerable oil interests and America, besides wanting a piece of the black gold action, was afraid of losing its Tacksman listening posts along the Soviet-Iranian border that were a crucial part of its Cold War eavesdropping strategy. Between them they engineered the coup in 1953 that removed Mossadegh and brought Mohammed Reza Pahlevi back to power as Shah.★

The United States, now exercising global power, was looking for client states through which to control critical regions of the world, not least the Middle East, whose oil supplies were so essential to the gas-guzzling US economy. Military advisers and weapons poured in, along with American commercial interests. By June 1978, there were some 54,000 Americans in Iran.[2] Much of the weaponry was far too sophisticated for the then largely peasant conscript army, but it was just one part of the Shah's theme of modernization to which most Iranians, hoping to improve their miserable economic lot, were not averse.

When I first travelled throughout much of Iran in 1957, this expectancy still existed, though already the growing gap between a poor populace and an increasingly wealthy elite with the Shah at its head was beginning to be resented. When I returned to many of the same places ten years later, the picture was very different. The military, smarter and more efficient now, were everywhere. The Shah's secret police, SAVAK, had cowed almost all the secular opposition into silence by means of abduction, brutal imprisonment, torture and murder, and free speech was a thing of the past. But it was beyond the power even of the Shah to still completely the tongues of the mullahs, the imams and the ayatollahs. The mosque, particularly in the regions centring on the holy cities of Meshed and Isfahan, had become the one place where dissent could still be openly expressed and discussed.

The American government's crucial diplomatic mistake was to construct a relationship with one man, the Shah, rather than with a nation, a people or a government. The obtrusive American presence and the substantial support by the United States for an oppressive regime because of irrelevant Cold War considerations was deeply resented by most Iranians.

As Moses put it in his masterly and lucid analysis of the Iran hostage background: "They insisted on living in Iran as they lived in America, and literally tonnes of American food and other goods were delivered to Iran weekly and ostentatiously consumed in plain view of economically deprived Iranians."[3]

My own experience confirms this. The Americans I met in my travels in the region were as generous and hospitable as they always are, but shut behind the

---

★ *Mark Gasiorowski argued in the* Journal of Middle Eastern Studies *No. 19, 1987, that but for the coup the 1978 revolution would probably never have happened.*

walls and fences of their compounds and construction camps, flying in everything they needed rather than buying locally, ignoring local customs and sensibilities, particularly dress codes for women, they very rarely had even a word of Farsi or any knowledge of the culture and history of the country in which they worked. This created the impression, wrongly in many cases, that they despised their Iranian hosts. Not surprisingly, they were despised in turn.

Two straws broke the camel's back. The Shah was deposed in January 1979 and fled the country, which was then governed by a religious faction under Ayatollah Khomeini. The Shah, suffering from a serious cancer which he had kept secret from all but a few, had been wandering rather pathetically around Europe looking for both treatment and a refuge. In September 1979, America admitted its former protégé into the country. It could hardly do otherwise. This was seen as a spit in the eye of Iran. Then, on 1 November, US national security adviser Brzezinski met Bargazan, the relatively moderate Iranian Prime Minister, and his Foreign Secretary, Yazdi, in Algiers. This meeting, at US insistence, only served to discredit the two Iranians in the eyes of their people, particularly the students. The ability of the two politicians to hold back these young radicals was destroyed, as, fairly shortly, were their political careers.

On 4 November, some 3,000 students, several hundred of them women, cut the chain securing the main gate of the US embassy and poured into the compound. Within a couple of hours they had taken over the whole complex and 66 hostages. More or less immediately, all bar one of the black hostages – seen as the fellow oppressed – were released, leaving 53, one of whom was later sent home for medical treatment. Senior embassy officials believed that after two or three hours' inconvenience, Iranian security forces would clear the students out as they had done in February when a similar incursion had taken place. The United States' ignorance of the tensions of Iran's internal politics meant that they did not realize that neither the moderate nor the radical tendencies in Iranian religious politics could afford to disown the students. Indeed, within a couple of weeks, Ayatollah Khomeini had seen the advantage of adopting them and did so. On 17 November he issued a decree that the US embassy would not be handed back until the Shah and all his property were returned to Iran. Later, following the US reference of the dispute to the International Court of Justice, further conditions were added that America should apologize and make unspecified reparations. After the Shah's death in July 1980, these rather unspecific terms were consolidated into four quite specific ones: (1) a promise from America not to interfere in Iranian affairs; (2) the return of the Shah's assets; (3) the unfreezing of Iranian assets in US banks; and (4) the dropping of all legal and financial claims against Iran. Although Iran did not enter a plea to the Court, it is hard not to have some sympathy for the sentiments of a letter written to it at the time.

... this question only represents a marginal and secondary aspect of the overall problem, one such that it cannot be studied separately and which involves, inter alia, more than 25 years of continual interference by the United States in the internal affairs of Iran, the shameless exploitation of our country and numerous crimes perpetrated against the Iranian people, contrary to and in conflict with all humanitarian norms...[4]

The Court ruled 13–2 in America's favour.

The US had displayed breathtaking diplomatic ineptitude both before and after the flight of the Shah in January 1979 and the declaration of an Islamic republic by Ayatollah Khomeini in April. Despite the presence of so many CIA people, there was no clear intelligence about the likely outcome of the power plays taking place in the three-cornered struggle between the secularists, the moderate clerics and the theocratic Khomeini and his followers. There were no Iran specialists in either the embassy in Tehran or in the National Security Council at home. Ambassador Sullivan had continued to send reassuring messages until, in November 1978, he, too, began to predict the fall of the Shah. The shooting of some 10,000 demonstrating Iranians by SAVAK and the military during the previous 12 months may have gone some way towards convincing him. One of hostage Daugherty's guards told him that they were deeply insulted that even the CIA men "could not speak their language and knew nothing of their culture, customs and history".[5]

America's immediate response to the seizing of the embassy was its usual one – go for your six-gun and blast someone. Options were discussed from a full-scale military response to mining the Gulf to prevent Iranian oil being exported. There were voices expressing caution even then and drawing attention to the illegality of such actions in international law. The United States' first practical response was to freeze some $12 billion worth of assets, mostly in US banks, on 12 November. Because of the implications for the American economy, indeed for the world economy, these banks almost immediately began to look for channels of communication to resolve the financial impasse. These channels were to play an important part in eventually resolving the hostage crisis by meeting one of its central conditions, which could be summed up as "our hostages for your money".*[6]

The wisdom of the more restrained approach was endorsed on 17 December, when the Soviet Union's advance guard invaded Afghanistan.[7] For the US to have been militarily involved in Iran at the same time could well have led to a force-to-force confrontation between the two superpowers. The American administration was also baffled by the apparent complete indifference of the Iranian government to enter into any dialogue, let alone

* For detailed accounts of the financial negotiations see the chapters by Robert Carswell and Richard J. Davis and by John E. Hoffman in American Hostages in Iran, Yale, 1985.

negotiation, about the hostages. Only one civil servant, Gary Sick, had pointed out that the problem was unlikely to be resolved until the internal power struggle had been resolved. No one seemed to appreciate that Khomeini, with his simplistic view of world politics and the role of the "Great Satan" in them, held the key.[8]

Nevertheless, there was great pressure on the indecisive Jimmy Carter to "do something". The American public was smarting at the humiliation and its country's apparent inability to respond effectively. Unfortunately, like most indecisive men, Carter finally reacted precipitately and unwisely. On 16 April 1980, the President summoned a meeting of his foreign policy staff to consider a particular course of action. Colonel Charles Beckwith, commanding officer of Delta Force, America's equivalent of the SAS, since its formation in 1977, appeared before the committee to outline the plan for rescuing the hostages which he had formulated and rehearsed in the seclusion of the Arizona desert. Great care had gone into the tactical detail, even down to monitoring Iranian television broadcasts to see which gates were locked and how the Iranians were armed. Killing these guards and probably members of the Iranian civilian population, and the deaths of as many as 30 commandos and hostages were all part of the plan. However, it was not the tactics but the whole strategy of Eagle Claw that was a nonsense. As one commentator put it: "The plan was much too elaborate and complicated and based on poor intelligence. It also presumed a total disregard for the loss of Iranian civilian life."[9]

Secretary of State Cyrus Vance and his deputy Warren Christopher* were stunned at the folly of the whole idea and expressed the strongest opposition. Vance had already warned Carter, who saw the Shah as "an island of stability in one of the more troubled areas of the world", that he was "operating with too limited an understanding of Iranian political realities".[10]

> He believed that Khomeini was using the hostages to consolidate control of the revolution. To kill them would end their usefulness. He opposed military force because it risked the hostages and would damage US interests in the Gulf. He also believed that a military strike would unite the Muslim world against the United States and its allies. He maintained that the Tehran hostages would be released once Khomeini realized that they had become a political liability rather than an asset.[11]

Vance later resigned over the Eagle Claw decision, but not until the raid was over through fear of jeopardizing its already negligible chance of success. Yet, despite the fact that even its begetter gave his team only a 30 to 40 per cent chance of success, Carter gave it the go ahead. So, on 21 April, the 132-man commando team gathered in Egypt before flying on to the island of Masirah off the coast of Oman, presumably with both Omani and British connivance.

* *For his most enlightening account of events in Washington during the crisis see* American Hostages in Iran.

It would be hard to imagine a more complicated plan than the one conjured up by Colonel Beckwith and so uncritically endorsed by Carter and his foreign affairs advisers. It read more like a *Rambo* film script than a serious incursion and rescue plan. Agents were to be infiltrated into Tehran where they would set up a number of safe houses. A recce of the projected landing site, code-named Desert One, in the Dasht (desert) E Kavir, 200 kilometres southwest of Tehran would be undertaken to confirm its suitablity, put out landing beacons and check the level of radar surveillance.

On night one of the operation itself, three MC-130 transport aircraft would land the combat controllers, interpreters and truck drivers. Next, three EC-130s would arrive equipped to refuel the eight RH-53 helicopters that would be flown in from the carrier *Nimitz* in the Arabian Gulf. Once refuelled they would fly the task force itself, consisting of 107 men, to the suburbs of Tehran where they would be met by the infiltrated agents and guided to the safe houses to lie up for the night. The helicopters would leave for another desert hiding place to await the summons of Delta Force on day two. I hope you are with me so far!

On the second day of the operation, the MC-130s and EC-130s would return to Iran, this time to land 100 Rangers (elite troops) at Manzariyeh to secure the airfield 100 kilometres southeast of Tehran. The C14 transport aircraft would then land and stand by to fly everyone out of the country, while the EC-130s prevented the Iranian air force at the fairly distant base at Mehrabad from counter-attacking. The task force itself would be dropped by the re-summoned helicopters near the US embassy. It would assault the buildings, free the hostages and rendezvous with the helicopters again at an adjacent football stadium. From there, everyone would fly to Manzariyeh, board the C14 and fly home to live happily ever after, leaving only the fragmented wreckage of the scuttled helicopters for the Iranians to chew over. Phew!

Needless to say the script was not followed. The preliminaries were the only element of the operation that went according to plan. The agents were infiltrated and a month before the strike a Twin Otter flew to Desert One and landed an air force combat controller, Captain Wade Ishimoto, who roared round the area on a trials bike, laying out the beacons to help the larger aircraft land. He also established that there was no radar coverage below 3,000 feet. So far so good, but what followed was a disaster.

The helicopter pilots, a mix of army, navy and air force men with little experience of operations such as Eagle Claw, were ordered to fly at 200 feet "to avoid radar". This meant that they had to contend with the *haboob*, a whirling dervish of tiny particles in a dust storm that reduced visibility almost to zero. By the time they had struggled their way through these conditions to rendezvous with the refuelling aircraft, they were already running over an hour behind schedule and mechanical failures had cut the number of helicopters to six. When the hydraulic system of a third RH–53 packed up, meaning that it could no longer carry a full load, there was no longer sufficient capacity to carry out the mission. Even if the commandos could have been delivered to the target by shedding fuel, the five remaining helicopters would have had neither the range nor the load capacity to get both assault troops and hostages out.* The mission was aborted before it had properly begun, but its tribulations were far from over. Already the roadblock section had been unexpectedly forced to take over a bus and its 44 passengers. Shortly afterwards, it managed to blow up a fuel tanker. The flames not only lit up the night sky for miles around, but the driver of the fuel tanker escaped in a following truck. Beckwith's naive hope that the tanker might have been on a smuggling run and so would not report the invasion was typical of the wing-and-a-prayer approach to the whole affair.

Now, tragically, one of the surviving helicopters, blinded by the swirling dust sucked up by its rotor, collided with a parked C-130. Both aircraft immediately burst into flames. Eight men died and many more were injured. In the ensuing chaos, a decision was made to evacuate the entire force in the remaining fixed-wing aircraft and the order to abandon and blow up the remaining helicopters was ignored. The Iranians were able to recover, not only the sophisticated technology, whose details they were able to pass on to their new Soviet sponsor, but also confidential documents containing details of the whole operation which nearly cost the infiltrated agents their lives.

The immediate consequence of this fiasco was to destroy the painstaking process by which the new premier of Iran, Beni Sadr, had started to bring Khomeini round to the idea that the hostages were no longer of any value. It also resulted in the hostages being dispersed throughout Tehran so that no future rescue attempt would be worthwhile and led to a marked deterioration in their conditions. Unbelievably, another rescue plan was concocted and code-named Honey Bear. Eagle Claw had ended with its talons stuck up its own backside. Honey Bear would almost certainly have come to an equally sticky end. Fortunately, it was not put to the test, as the hostages were released by other means.

Four factors – three quite unrelated to either US pressures or US mistakes – eventually ended the 52 hostages' 444 days in captivity: (1) Khomeini's grasp on power had become so firm that he no longer needed the hostages as a tactical weapon, (2) The invasion of Iran by Iraq on 12 September 1980 meant that Iran needed the goodwill of the country that, despite recent Soviet military assistance, had still provided the bulk of Iran's military equipment and was, therefore, the only source for munitions and spares, (3) The assets frozen in US

---

* *Total to be airlifted 160; helicopter capacity 30; 5 x 30 = 150; 160 into 150 won't go. However, if Beckwith's casualty estimate was right and the wounded were left behind it might just have been possible.*

banks were needed to help finance the war and (4) The skilful and selfless mediation of the Algerians, abetted by the tact and nous of Warren Christopher, meant that both sides could back off without losing face.

On 20 January, under Carter's last Executive Order (No. 12283), $7.5bn were placed in an escrow account for Iran in London and, just two minutes after Reagan's election victory and Carter's defeat, the hostages were sent on their way home.

Afterwards, some disappointed Democrats argued that Reagan had done a secret, and in effect treasonable, deal with the Iranians not to release the hostages until after the election, thus depriving his opponent of an electoral ace. This became known as the "October Surprise". While some of his campaign managers may have encouraged a delay, there is no reason to doubt the Democrat-controlled congressional committee's finding that there was no case to answer. It was simply a matter of the final arrangements being sorted out in a rather muddled rush. The financial transfer was even done on the basis of word given and a back-of-an-envelope signature. Nor did the Iranians have any reason to delay things as one of their negotiators, Behzad Nabavi, later explained: "Even the Iranian government was insisting that the Americans should be set free before Carter's term ended … (it) was of the view that if the dispute was not settled under the Carter administration everything had to be repeated under the tenure of the next President (if Reagan were elected)."[12]

I have gone into this failed rescue attempt at some length because it perfectly exemplifies what happens if, firstly, careful political analysis is not made before a rescue is launched and, secondly, the basic rules of any rescue operation are ignored. There are, in my view, 12 rules for successful rescue attempts:

1. Know your enemy and do not fight if you can negotiate.
2. Operate in friendly, rather than hostile, countries.
3. Keep it simple.
4. Get in and get out as fast you can and make sure of your escape route.
5. Do not play away from home unless you know the stadium really well.
6. Make sure you have adequate back-up resources if things go wrong or break down.
7. Use specialized forces that have been knitted into a team long before the attempt.
8. Plan and rehearse tactics and weapons carefully.
9. Distract or bemuse the captors and take them by surprise.
10. Cause no hostage deaths directly or indirectly.
11. Ensure proper medical and psychological care for rescued hostages.
12. Have a clear and unique chain of command with one person in absolute control.

You can break one, two, or even sometimes three of these rules and still get away with it. But you cannot break all of them as happened in Eagle Claw. The Americans are not alone in their embarrassment. Even the vaunted Israelis had to learn the hard way – through a bungled rescue.

In 1947, the UN partitioning of the British protectorate had put the Arab village of Tarchiha, 20 kilometres to the east of the coastal town of Nahariyya, into what was to have been Palestine. Israeli militia had other ideas, seized the village and drove out its inhabitants. In 1950, Tarchiha was flattened and the new town of Ma'alot was built where it had once stood. It thus had symbolic significance for both sides and as always in Israeli-Palestinian disputes there are two versions of the story of what happened on 15 May 1974, the day of Israeli Independence celebrations that year. The versions that follow are an amalgam of various accounts.

The Israelis claimed that a party of schoolchildren on a field trip to Golan had bedded down for the night on the floor of a school in Ma'alot. During the night, three terrorists, dressed as Israel Defence Force soldiers, burst in and seized both the school and some 90 children. A few of the children escaped by jumping out of a second-floor window. The DFLP★ guerrillas wired the school with explosives and demanded the release of Arab prisoners held in Israeli jails. They set a deadline of 6.00 pm the same day for this to be done or they would start to kill the hostages. At 3.00 pm, an emergency session of the Knesset, the Israeli parliment, decided to do as they had been asked, contrary to the principle of no negotiation with terrorists, since children were involved. An Israeli army special combat unit had already been called to the scene. The Palestinians refused to extend the deadline to allow negotiations to take place, so at 5.45 pm the rescue operation began. As a preliminary, a sniper shot, but failed to kill, one of the three terrorists and shots and explosions were then heard from within the school. The combat unit responded by launching the assault and killed all three terrorists, but not before the terrorists had killed 21 children and wounded most of the others.

The Palestinians tell another story. At 6.00 am, three Palestinian *fedayeen* seized the school in Ma'alot and some 90 17-year-olds who belonged to the quasi-military youth organization Nahal, who had been training in the area. Fifteen escaped through an open door and two were allowed to leave because they were ill. They then sent out two of the youths with a list of the 26 prisoners they wanted released by Israel and flown to Damascus and a request that the French and Romanian ambassadors mediate. When the prisoners arrived in Damascus, a code word was to be passed to the ambassadors and the hostages would then be released. If this were not done by 6.00 pm the *fedayeen* "would not be responsible for the consequences" – a euphemism meaning that

----

★ *Democratic Front for the Liberation of Palestine, a splinter group of the Popular FLP.*

they would start killing hostages. The Israelis agreed to negotiate, but deliberately prevented the French ambassador from reaching the scene in time to do so. The Palestinians would have been perfectly willing to extend the deadline by two hours if asked. In their opinion, this proves that the Israelis never seriously intended to negotiate and only offered to do so as a front for getting their assault force into position.

Forty minutes before the expiry of the original deadline, the special combat unit stormed the building and, in the ensuing battle, all the *fedayeen* were killed and some of the youngsters were killed by their exploding grenades and others by the wild firing of the Israeli soldiers. The Israelis refused to conduct post mortems to establish the truth of the matter. Within hours, the Israeli air force had bombed villages and refugee camps in Lebanon, killing 52 civilians.

The French and Romanian ambassadors were inclined to favour the Palestinian, rather than the Israeli, version of events, although they said so in the usual restrained diplomatic language and the formidable Israeli propaganda machine made sure that it was their country's version that reached the public through the world's media.

It is not for me to take sides here, but the Palestinian version does seem the more plausible in the light of what generally happens in military rescue attempts, though the truth probably lies hidden somewhere between the two.[13] Reports in the Israeli press from surviving youngsters indicate that the Palestinans did not mistreat their hostages in any way, so they might well have been unlikely to shoot them in cold blood. That the Israelis miscalculated their ability to free the hostages by force rather than "negotiate with terrorists" seems much more in keeping with tough woman premier Golda Meir's style and seems to be confirmed by the steps taken straight afterwards to create Israeli special forces for just such tasks. The Yechida Meyuchedet Le'Milchama was formed with its members selected from the military after the same kind of rigorous screening employed by the SAS. Who knows? Such diametrically opposed accounts can only indicate just how hard following President Bush's proposed "Road Map" for Middle East peace will be.

The Egyptians were not quite so quick to learn from their mistakes, indeed they compounded them. In the Nicosia Hilton on 19 February 1978, two Palestinian gunmen assasinated Youssef Sebai, editor of a newspaper that had supported the Israel–Egypt peace agreement and who was a personal friend of Egyptian President Anwar Sadat. Because the gunmen now also held a number of hostages, the Cypriot authorities agreed to allow them to leave Cyprus with 11 of them, including several Egyptians, in an aircraft provided by the Cypriots. The hostage-takers could find no country willing to accept their flight and, running low on fuel, were forced to return to the small airport at Larnaca. There the Cypriot authorities, under the watchful eye of President

Kyprianou, began to negotiate for the release of the hostages and the four-man crew.

An outraged President Sadat of Egypt had already despatched a commando force in a C-130 Hercules to Larnaca where it was permitted to land, but expressly forbidden to interfere in the hostage incident unless invited to do so. The Egyptians, probably conscious of the direct personal interest of their President, ignored the prohibition and prepared to launch an attack. Even as they took up their firing positions, a courageous, if somewhat foolhardy, Cypriot officer approached them and ordered them to desist. By now the negotiations with the hostage-takers were on the brink of success, so when the order to retreat was flouted, the Cypriots felt they had no option but to fire on the Egyptians. The Egyptians enthusiastically returned the fire. Thus a fierce gun battle broke out between the two forces of "good guys" to what must have been the utter bewilderment of the "bad guys". Kyprianou and his entourage beat a hasty retreat as the bullets began to fly. By the time the Egyptians were overpowered, 15 of them were dead, as many wounded, along with some Cypriots, and the Hercules had been destroyed. During the course of this exchange, the puzzled hijackers had been persuaded by the crew of their aircraft to give up both their weapons and themselves and to release their hostages. The wounded on both sides, rather like opposing teams after a bruising rugby match, went off together to Larnaca hospital.

Seven years later, on 23 November 1985, Egypt Air flight 648 from Athens to Cairo was skyjacked by one of Abu Nidal's freelance hijack teams under the patronage of Libya. Three smartly dressed young men produced handguns and grenades, took over the aircraft and began collecting the passengers' passports with the obvious intention of identifying and separating out the Israeli and American citizens. One of three plain-clothed sky marshals on board, instead of pulling his passport from his pocket, pulled out his gun and shot and killed one of the hijackers before he and two flight attendants were shot and wounded. The other two marshals had their guns in the luggage lockers!

The shots fired punctured the fuselage of the plane which plunged from 35,000 feet to 15,000 feet before the pilot was able to regain control of it. The remaining two hijackers demanded to be flown to Libya or Tunisia. The pilot managed to persuade them that if that was where they wanted to go, they would first have to land in Malta and refuel, which they accepted. The Maltese airport initially refused them permission to land and turned out the landing lights. As in other skyjackings, faced with the choice of running out of fuel and crashing in some unpredictable spot and a blind landing where crash facilities were on hand, the pilot chose the latter. The Maltese authorities refused to provide fuel and the island's premier, possibly lacking the appropriate skills and experience, began to negotiate with the hijackers. He did manage to secure the release of 11 women hostages and the two wounded flight attendants.

As soon as the skyjacking became known, both America, whose citizens were at prime risk, and Egypt, whose aircraft it was, initiated rescue operations. America despatched its Delta Force, but its men never even reached Malta as all three of its aircraft broke down (on purpose?). The Egyptians landed a commando team at Malta's Luqa airport and stood by.

The negotiations dragged on for 22 hours, but these skyjackers were better organized and more ruthless than their predecessors had been. When refuelling was persistently refused they began shooting hostages and pitching the bodies onto the tarmac at roughly ten-minute intervals. First two Israelis, then two Americans and finally, after a gap of three hours, a third American, Jackie Pflug. She later wrote a book about her experience for, astonishingly, though all of them were shot in the head, she and two of the others lived. She attributes this to the Palestinians using home-made ammunition. This seems unlikely unless they had being trying to reduce the explosive charge to make the rounds safe to use on an aircraft.

At 8.30 pm, urged on by their US advisers, but without the consent of the Maltese government, the Egyptians launched their attack. Even though they had rehearsed on a similar aircraft shortly before, again it seems as if they were inadequately prepared. They used no distracting tactics and even tipped off the Palestinians as to their intent by turning off the airport lights. They then used smoke rather than stun grenades, which caused secondary fires when thrown into the passenger cabin. However, that was probably of little consequence, as the massively excessive charge in the cargo hold had not only given the commandos access to the plane, but had also set light to the plastic parts of its structure. The toxic fumes given off accounted for many of the subsequent deaths. When two commandos finally managed to get into the aircraft, passengers report that they fired indiscriminately. This may have been an observation bred of panic and inexperience, or it may be that the commandos were heeding the tacit suggestion of the Maltese authorities that any surviving captors would be an embarrassment, whatever the cost in hostage lives. They were disappointed. Although one of the two remaining hostage-takers was among the 58 people who died, their leader and executioner, Omar Rezaq, was not.

Rezaq was sentenced to 25 years in prison by the Maltese, but was released after seven. He went to Ghana and from there to Nigeria where, to his astonishment, the FBI was waiting for him. Dubious as the legality of such an extra-territorial kidnap was, he was flown back to the States and sentenced to ten years for air piracy. It was thought politic not to sentence him to death.

Kidnapping tourists in the Yemen* was once something of a cultural pastime with its own rules and rituals. Tourists in the deserts and mountains were held up en route and abducted by local tribesmen. They would be taken to the tribal camp and treated as honoured guests. Once some minor concession had been obtained from the government, they would find themselves showered with gifts and be sent on their way, unharmed and usually thrilled rather than alarmed by their experience.

At 11.00 am on 28 December 1998, a very different cultural tradition took over. Seventeen British, American and Australian tourists were travelling in a five-vehicle convoy between Habban and Aden, about 250 kilometres southeast of the capital, Sana'a, when a large truck surged onto the road between the first and second vehicles. Armed men, firing warning shots into the air, surrounded the convoy and took 16 of the tourists and their four Yemeni drivers captive. One tourist and his driver managed to escape and eventually raised the alarm. The hostages were taken up into the nearby mountains to a hideout from which Abu al-Hassan, the leader of the captors, was soon on his satellite phone to Abu Hamza, a notorious Muslim cleric in London, who is suspected of being behind the kidnapping. Abu al-Hassan reported that "the ordered goods, 1,600 cartons marked British and American", had been collected. Abu Hamza urged him not to maltreat any of the 12 British hostages and to use them as a negotiating lever for the release of nine prisoners held in Sana'a jail. Al-Hassan confirmed that was his intention and then called up the authorities for the Abyan district in which the hostages were held and, more importantly, the President's half-brother, Sheikh Salih Haidara al-Atawi, who had considerable influence in security and judicial decisions. In addition to his basic demand for the release of the nine prisoners, al-Hassan threw in a last-minute loss-leader by seeking the suspension of UN sanctions on Iraq, something that the Yemeni government could not even influence let alone grant. To his dismay, and later to the dismay of the British government which had been urging negotiation, he was turned down flat.

By this time, the captives realized they had been taken by an offshoot of Islamic Jihad, the Islamic Army of Aden-Abyan. In practical terms, however, they felt they had little to fear. They were being treated well in the traditional way and both captives and captors ate their evening meal together round the campfire in a quite companionable manner. Early the following morning, the elderly Sheikh Haythmi Ashal, with the concurrence of the Yemeni security forces which needed time to position themselves, tried to negotiate with the hostage-takers. Thinking he would soon be getting a response to his demands from much higher up the security ladder, al-Hassan refused to discuss the matter, though the Sheikh was offered and accepted the traditional protective

---

* What is now the Democratic Republic of Yemen was, from 1838 to independence in 1967, the colony of Aden with a British protectorate exercised over an extensive hinterland.

hospitality of tea and food. Shortly after Ashal left the hideout, Yemeni troops took up positions ready for an attack.

What happened next is not clear. The Yemenis claimed that al-Hassan's men threatened to shoot the hostages, thus prompting the troops to attack immediately. The Yemeni Prime Minister later informed his British counterpart, Tony Blair, that "if it was not for the speedy intervention, none of the hostages would have remained alive, and this is because the terrorist gang gave no chance for dialogue". It is clear from evidence provided at the subsequent trial of al-Hassan that the first two or three shots were fired by the captors. Neither is it disputed that some of the hostages were used as shields during the subsequent two-hour gun battle. The defence argued that the first shots were fired simply as a warning and that the army then opened fire indiscriminately. The hostages confirmed this, except for one Australian woman captive who endorsed the Yemeni version. Again, it is not disputed that two of the hostages were deliberately shot by their captors during their unsuccessful attempt to escape. Whose bullets killed the other two was never established. One suspects that the refusal of the Yemenis to allow the British and American police investigators to look into this suggests that the army was responsible. Two or three of the kidnappers were killed in the battle and the rest were captured. One of the latter was an Egyptian member of Islamic Jihad.

That the Yemenis did not share the view of the British government led to a sharp deterioration in relations between the two countries. The Yemenis accused half a dozen British passport holders of being terrorists and the British tried to block the accession of Yemen to the Commonwealth. Fortunately this spat did not last long, but the different assessments of the significance of the incident illustrate the difficulty of evaluating the success or failure of rescue attempts when they are being judged by people with very different cultural and social values. From the British point of view (and in terms of the definitions used in this book) the failure to negotiate and the death of three Britons and an Australian during the rescue marked it as a failure. The Yemeni government offered its formal condolences, but seemed to imply that it could not see why such a fuss was being made about a few deaths when most of the hostages had been freed and their captors had been either killed or captured.

Rather more than a few deaths were involved in my next example.

The first day of the Islamic year 1400 Islamic (20 November 1979 AD) saw the carefully planned and neatly executed seizure of the Qaaba, the heart of the Grand Mosque in Mecca – the most sacred place in the Sunni Muslim world. There were 50,000 pilgrims there at the time. This was clearly intended as a crucial first step in toppling the Saudi monarchical regime itself. Following the seizure, there were simultaneous riots and bombings throughout Saudi Arabia.

Accounts as to the number involved in the initial take-over of the mosque vary from 500 to 3,500. The core of the attacking force contained a substantial number of men recruited and trained in other parts of the Arab world from Yemen to Egypt, from Iraq to Sudan, but the majority were Saudi. Similarly, the number of hostages is given as anything from 300 to 6,000. Allowing for the confusion of such a large-scale coup, the conversion of large numbers of the hostages to their captors' cause and an inherent regional tendency to exaggerate, something nearer the lower numbers is more probable.

The attack on the Grand Mosque had been well prepared. With the assistance of a colonel in the National Guard, which was responsible for security in Mecca, a large quantity of arms and ammunition, probably originating from South Yemen, had been smuggled into the mosque in advance. Ample supplies of food and water, not just for the attackers but also for the hostages, were stocked up as well. It is hard to see how this could have been done without the connivance of at least some of the clerics responsible for the running and governance of the mosque. The seizure was led by Juhayman al-Utaibi, a former corporal in the National Guard, who proclaimed student Mohammad al-Quraishi to be a Mahdi, a leader of faithful Muslims who will appear at the last days of the world.

Quraishi led a series of sermons and discussions focussed not only on the need to restore the purity of Islam, but on the undoubted corruption, waste and brutal repression of the Saudi regime. He soon persuaded all but a small minority of his listeners not only to subscribe to his views, but also to take up arms in his cause. Many of them were issued with weapons.

A demoralized National Guard – the Saudi rulers were already much concerned by widespread disaffection in its ranks – made a feeble and abortive attempt to retake the mosque, which was easily repulsed. The Saudis then asked France for help and Captain Barill and three NCOs of the GIGN, the French counter-terrorist force, arrived on 23 November to help. The captain and his team had just ten days to train the inexperienced Saudis in this type of close-quarters fighting and to organize the material needed for the assault. To enable the Frenchmen to enter the sacred precincts they were made honorary Muslims. When the second assault began on 4 December, the captors retreated along with many of their captives to the extensive catacombs beneath the mosque complex. To render the cave-to-cave combat a little less lethal to the rescue force, two tonnes of what was coyly described by the French as "combat gas", probably a narcotic of some kind, were flown in from France and used to flood the underground passage. Behind a barrage of stun grenades, the rescue force then fought its way, corner by corner, through the labyrinth. As the first panic-stricken pilgrims and hostages fled from the mosque they were mistaken for terrorists and many were shot down by their rescuers. This happened twice. Figures from different sources of those killed vary from 300 to 10,000. Although the lower figure is almost certainly the more accurate, the comment of hardened anti-terrorist fighter Captain Barill that there was a "horrible slaughter" and that he is unable to talk about it suggests the toll was high. On 9 January 1980, 63 of the remaining ringleaders were beheaded.

Yossef Bodansky[14] has suggested that these events may even have influenced Osama bin Laden in his growing belief that only a theocracy, if necessary imposed by terror, could successfully combat the corrupting influence of westernization in the Arab world.

One of the few other rescue attempts to employ chemical weapons, other than tear gas, took place in a Moscow theatre 23 years later on 27 October 2002. Following a series of Chechen bomb attacks in Moscow, it seems strange that several jeep-loads of heavily armed Chechens could drive up to the culture club on Dubrovka Street in a rather run-down suburb without arousing any suspicions. Nonetheless, at 9.05 pm on 23 October 2002, 41 Chechens (23 men and 18 women, who claimed to be the widows or mothers of men killed by the Russians), occupied the club just after the start of the second act of *Nord Ost* (North East), a popular Russian musical* and strode on to the stage firing shots in the air. For a split second the audience of over 700 in the almost-full theatre must have thought this an ingenious twist in the plot, before being stunned into a passive acceptance of the fact that they had all been taken hostage. This particular musical had been chosen as the target because the theatre was always full and as the first indigenous musical and one based on Russian heroism it had a symbolic significance.

The captors, under the leadership of Movsar Barayev, a well-known Chechen resistance fighter or rebel, according to your point of view, were making a demand that they must have known could never be granted. They could not have imagined that the threat of killing several hundred Russians and visiting foreigners would compel President Putin to withdraw all Russian troops from Chechnya and grant it independence. It was as if they wished their demand to be publicly rejected so that, after extracting every possible moment of publicity from the take-over by protracting it for as long as possible, they could commit a spectacular and suicidal atrocity to underline their determination to be free of Russian rule. The pronouncements of these *smertniki*, suicide squad members, during a live television interview, substantiate this impression. Barayev himself said: "Our dream is to become *shakhidi*, martyrs for Allah." One of the women had joined because "the Russian occupiers have flooded our land with our children's blood". And a male captor told the interviewer: "I swear by God we are more keen on dying than you are keen on

---

* *Based on a nationaly famous novel,* Dva Kapitana, *or* Two Captains, *by Soviet-era writer Veniamin Kaverin, the musical tells the tale of Sanya, a young boy who discovers the diary of an explorer who went missing on the way to the North Pole. The boy then grows up to become a pilot who goes looking for his hero.*

living. Each one of us is willing to sacrifice himself for the sake of God and the independence of Chechnya."[15] Such an attitude made the offer the head of the FSB (Federal Security Bureau), Nikolai Petruschev, to guarantee the lives of the Chechens if they released their hostages completely irrelevant. The Chechens, however, did want to talk to a negotiator of their own choosing, the *Novaya Gazyeta* journalist, Anna Politkovskaya, whose forthright articles and reporting on Chechnya had won their respect. She was in Los Angeles receiving an award for women who have shown courage in journalism when the call came. She flew back to Moscow at once and at 2.00 pm on 25 October she was walking apprehensively into the theatre with Dr Leonid Roshal to negotiate while he attended to sick hostages along with the three doctors who were in the audience. During the three hours in which she was talking to Bakar Abubakr, one of the commanders of the captors, it became apparent that this was one of the breakaway groups of Chechen fighters that act independently of the moribund official leadership. Moreover, Abubakr simply wanted to state the Chechen case rather than to negotiate. Inexperienced as she was, Politkovskaya, a woman of great courage, did persuade the Chechens to let her and Dr Roshal bring in bottled water and fruit juice, which they did later.

Once the Chechens had assumed complete control of the theatre, they released 105 hostages straight away, mostly women and children, Muslims and non-Russians, such as Georgians. Amid the rather casual toing and froing of television crews, doctors and journalists in and out of the theatre, a further 40 hostages were released or escaped during the 58 hours of the siege. Again, it is surprising that television, radio and press, along with many anxious relatives and spectators, had gathered in the freezing cold outside the theatre before there was any sign of the FSB and its Alpha anti-terrorist unit. Several hostages gave media interviews before they were debriefed by security specialists and the captors were able to watch what was happening round the theatre on the various television channels showing in the foyer.

Another very contemporary aspect of this siege was the extensive use of mobile phones by both captors and captives. The Chechens were able to keep in touch both with the authorities whom they could threaten and with their supporters and informants as far afield as Georgia and Turkey. The unanticipated disadvantage from their point of view was that the FSB was able to trace the calls and make several arrests of co-conspirators as a result.

By about 11.00 pm, armoured vehicles and 250 Alpha unit troops, including rooftop snipers, had surrounded the theatre and the long stand-off began. At this stage the Chechens did not kill hostages deliberately unless they were trying to escape. They claimed that one woman killed in this way was an FSB agent and that another man shot in the eye was hit accidentally when they fired on a hysterical boy whose nerve broke and who bolted for the exit. Indeed, it seemed to be Barayev's intention to prolong the siege with its massive international media coverage for as long as possible before he brought it to its planned, dramatic conclusion. That it was his intention to blow the theatre and all within it sky-high is clear from the evidence produced by many of the hostages. The children's cardiac physician, Maria Shkolnikova, told Reuters on her mobile that "a huge amount of explosives have been laid throughout the place". She also reported that all the female captors were laden with explosives and, mistakenly, detonator wires that only had to be touched together to set off a chain of explosions.

This message was but one example of Berayev's psychological subtlety in allowing the hostages to use their mobile phones. He knew that they would plead with the authorities through their loved ones firstly not to attack the theatre and secondly to end the war in Chechnya. There were, in fact, small demonstrations outside the theatre during the siege appealing for just that. To emphasize the point, he had Shkolnikova read a declaration about the Chechen war on the steps of the theatre. Equally calculating was his way of making the conditions of the hostages increasingly uncomfortable so as to increase the urgency of their pleas to the outside world. He refused an offer of hot food, so the captives had to survive for most of the siege on the water and chocolate that were available from the theatre's own supplies. Nor would he allow them to use the theatre toilets, but made every one of them defecate and urinate in the orchestra pit in full view of each other and under the supervision of their captors. Other than these very occasional toilet trips, captives were not allowed to move out of their seats.

In the circumstances it is hard not to sympathize, as Tony Blair did in the House of Commons, with President Putin for the dilemma in which he found himself. Clearly Putin could not even discuss the demand for a withdrawal from Chechnya and he made this quite clear. He also had to recognize that as time passed it was increasingly probable that the Chechens would either start executing batches of hostages, as they had threatened to do, or would blow up the whole building and 500–600 people with it. The decision to make an assault in that situation was almost inevitable and the military aspect of it was very effectively carried out. A conventional assault could only have ended in disaster, so the FSB's first step was to incapacitate the captors as much as possible before attacking. There was clearly no way of doing this without incapacitating the captives as well.

The chemical agent chosen was a derivative of fentanyl, a powerful, opium-based narcotic, a similar derivative of which is used in surgical anaesthesia. It has a slight, but not readily identifiable odour and is invisible. Its principal effects are to induce drowsiness and insensitivity to pain. Prolonged untreated exposure, particularly on any subject, such as the hostages, weakened by exhaustion, immobility, dehydration, starvation and stress, can cause serious respiratory problems and sometimes death. There is an effective antidote, naltrexone, that can be given by tablet or injection and is effective if used soon after exposure. The gas was introduced to the auditorium mid-morning on the third day through the ventilation system and would have begun to take effect in seconds. The initial feeling of drowsiness passes quickly to unconsciousness. This was the most risky moment of the whole operation, for if the Chechens had realized what was happening, they would certainly have detonated their explosives. The probable reason they did not is that, although it was mainly the women who were the human bombs, evidence from other Chechen bomb attacks suggest that it would have been one or two of the men who had the radio-controlled detonators. The woman would also have had physically to close the electrical circuits – a kind of safety precaution – before the explosives could be detonated. As the producer of *Nord Ost*, Georgi Vasilyev, commented afterwards: "in an operation of this kind everyone could have been killed."

To coincide with the gas attack, and to distract the attention of the Chechens from what was happening inside the auditorium, the Alpha squad made a full-frontal assault on the entrance to the theatre and foyer, killing all the captors who were located there. The assault force then made its way into the basement below the auditorium, so that when it emerged from this unexpected direction, it took the hostage-takers who were not yet unconscious by surprise. Within a few seconds they had all been shot dead, some of them obviously executed while already unconscious. Cynical critics have said this was to save the risk of publicity and further terrorist attacks that would have been associated with a trial. The practical and far more likely explanation is that the Alpha squad could not risk leaving a single Chechen, either only wounded or semi-conscious, who could then have detonated the explosives with a last-gasp effort. The Alpha squad has also been criticized for using this particular gas and accusations were made of a breach of the Chemical Weapons Convention, which Russia vigorously denied. The fact is that any other readily available chemical would not have done the job as surely or as safely. As a former Alpha unit commander explained: "The use of the gas gave us a fraction of a second to be the first to shoot and prevent hostage-takers from pressing the detonation button or connecting the wires – this is why the gas attack was carried out."

As far as President Putin and the state-controlled media were concerned, "We managed to do the near impossible: save the lives of hundreds, hundreds of people. We proved it is impossible to bring Russia to its knees." – a view that was generally endorsed by western leaders. Had that been the whole story then this rescue would have been, at worst a case, of proxime accessit. But it wasn't the whole story. If the follow-up been as efficient as the assault, criticism of the methods used would have been hard to justify, but it was a shambles. There were not even stretchers available to carry the unconscious hostages from the theatre, so they had to be dragged out bodily before being dumped on the steps or in the street in postures that exacerbated the respiratory risks, to await a tardy ambulance service. Nor was bundling the half-conscious victims into buses to take them to hospital much wiser. Worst of all, the paranoid secrecy at every level about the identity of the gas employed was, as *The Times* commented, "disgraceful and reminiscent of the worst days of the Soviet era". This secrecy meant that, when victims did reach hospital or received medical attention at the site of the siege, doctors had no basis on which to know how best to treat these emergency patients. It would have been relatively simple to have had specialized medical teams provided with naltrexone, the proven antidote, standing by ready to follow the troops into the auditorium as soon as the shooting was over. Since the whole operation, from the time the gas was first released into the auditorium to the time the last hostage-taker was killed lasted no more than five to ten minutes, many lives could have been saved by such simple foresight. As it is, at the time of writing, 129 hostages, about a sixth of the total number of those taken hostage, have since died, all but half a dozen or so directly from the effects of the gas. The Health Minister was right to point out that its effect was exacerbated by the debilitated state of the captives, but that, too, should have been anticipated.

Another serious error in the aftermath was the crass attempt by someone in the FSB to discredit the Chechens by releasing video footage showing them to be degenerates with bottles of whisky, cigarettes and syringes lying about their corpses. This implication, in the context of a willing Islamic martyrdom, was utterly absurd – especially as whoever arranged it even forgot to break the seals on the whisky bottles.

By my definitions, the unnecessary death toll and the unconvincing propaganda turned what could at least have been classified as a near miss into another bungled rescue.

The Old Testament belief in an eye for an eye has been the driving force behind both Israeli political and military strategy since long before the creation of the State of Israel. "Neither Jewish ethics nor Jewish tradition can disqualify terrorism as a means of combat," wrote Yitzhak Shamir of the Stern Gang, and later Prime Minister of Israel, in 1943.[15] In the wake of the massacre of members of its team at the Munich Olympics in 1972, it adhered strictly to that philosophy.

Early on the morning of 25 September, passers-by saw five men in track suits climbing the six-foot-high fence surrounding the Olympic Village. They thought it was just another bunch of curfew-breaking young athletes "climbing in" after a night out. They were, in fact, five members of the relatively new Palestinian strike force, Black September, joining three of their comrades who had already inveigled their way into the compound by means of forged passes.

The well-armed team then calmly proceeded to the Israeli building and knocked on the door.

When wrestling coach Moshe Weinberg answered the door, he realized what was about to happen and shouted to his companions to escape. Weight-lifter Joseph Romano rushed to the door and tried to force it shut. The Palestinians shot him dead. Weinberg snatched a knife from the kitchen and stabbed one of the attackers. They shot him dead. Some sixteen members of the Israeli team did escape, but nine were taken hostage.

In response to Black September's demand for the release of 200 Arab prisoners held in Israel's jails, many without trial, the German Interior Minister, Hans-Dietrich Genscher, tried, unsuccessfully, to persuade the Palestinians to surrender their hostages in exchange for money and a safe passage out of the country. Several other prominent politicians offered themselves as substitute hostages with equally little success, but the persistent attempts to negotiate did postpone several times the original noon deadline for hostage killing to begin.

For Germany, trying through these very Olympics to assuage the guilt of the Holocaust, Jewish athletes being taken hostage was a public relations disaster. The decision was taken to carry on with the Games to demonstrate that no act of terror could shut down the world's most significant sports gathering of nations competing in friendship and goodwill.

Some journalists were critical of the decision, one even described it as like "dancing at Dachau". Nevertheless, the decision was probably the right one, but the methods used to resolve the crisis were completely wrong.

Conspiracy theorists saw neo-Nazis behind the catalogue of errors that followed and claimed that the failure was deliberate. Cock-up rather than conspiracy is the more likely explanation and cock-up it certainly was. The Bonn government decided to give in to Black September's demands to the extent of agreeing to arrange a safe exit from Germany for the Palestinians and their captives, but pointed out that their wider demand could only be granted by Israel.

At 10.30 pm that same night, a large, dark green bus drew up in the basement of the Israeli building and the captors, brandishing their weapons nervously, herded their captives onto it for the next short stage of the journey. In the Olympic Village plaza they transferred to two waiting helicopters. These were to fly them to Furstenfeldbruck airport for transfer to a Lufthansa jet to take captors and captives out of the country to a destination of their choosing. It was at this last stage in the transfer process that the German police decided they had the best chance of staging a rescue, though they seemed to have little idea how to go about it. In mitigation, it should be said that this was at a fairly early stage in the hostage-taking epidemic of the 1970s and very few countries had done any advance thinking, let alone planning, about how to deal with such situations.

The proposal to use sharpshooters to kill the hostage-takers individually as they moved their captives to the plane was a perfectly reasonable one in the circumstances and the one most likely to minimize hostage casualties, provided it was put into practice accurately and all the snipers fired simultaneously. But whatever the excuses, the operation failed miserably through lack of adequate planning. Why were only five snipers provided to kill eight captors? Why did they have the wrong rifles? Why were most of these without telescopic sights and none with infrared? Why were the riflemen chosen not top marksmen? Why were there no walkie-talkies for the snipers to talk to each other and their commander? The Bavarian police's excuse, that they could not get hold of any walkie-talkies, was pretty feeble in view of the hundreds at the Olympic camp being used by security men and stewards and dozens more in the hands of the journalists covering the story which could have been borrowed. One sniper was even positioned in the line of fire of others and was later wounded.

Another part of the rescue plan was to place armed police in ambush inside the Lufthansa aircraft, but the policemen chickened out at the last minute and voted to leave the scene, taking the aircraft crew with them. Their chief later explained: "We were trained for everyday offences, to be close to the people, unarmed — but not for an action against paramilitary-trained terrorists." As a result, the Black September men who went to check out the plane found it crewless and realized at once that something was up. As they ran back to the helicopters the marksmen opened fire. The Palestinians hurled themselves under the helicopters where they presented a hard target and returned fire in a gun battle that lasted for several minutes.

Enraged at being tricked, the captors shot the hostages in one helicopter and tossed a grenade into the other. All nine Israelis were killed, as was one German policeman in the crossfire. Five of the Palestinians were shot dead and the remaining three captured and taken into custody. However, they never came to trial because, on 29 October, other members of Black September skyjacked a flight from Syria to Germany and demanded their release. This they obtained, having given, some say, an undertaking to carry out no more Black September terrorist acts in Germany.

In some ways the sequel to the Munich Olympics incident is as interesting as the incident itself. Infuriated at the release of the three Palestinians, Golda Meir, Israel's Prime Minister at the time, ordered the creation of a special secret assassination squad as an extension of Mossad's clandestine activities. This squad, codenamed "Wrath of God", tracked down and murdered, without any judicial process, two of the three men directly involved, and eight of those Israel considered to have been involved in other ways.[16]

They failed to kill Jamal al Gashey who, after years in hiding, emerged to tell a BBC Sport interviewer in September 2000 that he had no regrets as the attack had focussed the world's attention on Israel's injustice towards Palestinians. Nor did the hit squad ever catch up with Abou Daoud, the man who planned the raid.[17]

Other Bungled Rescue Attempts:

12 May 1975	Kampucheans seize US merchant ship *Mayaguez*. Marines attack island where the hostages are not being held, 41 of them killed. Kampucheans were returning hostages at the time.
13 November 1985, Colombia	M-19 seizes Bogota Palace of Justice. Army attacks and 100 people are killed, including the President of the Court and ten other justices.
12 September 1986 Karachi, Pakistan	Twenty-two people died in a blaze of gunfire when Pakistani security forces stormed a PanAm Boeing 747 after four Palestinians had held the plane for 16 hours.
14 January 2001, Philippines	Gun battle between Abu Sayyaf kidnappers and government forces in which three out of four hostages die in rescue attempt.
5 June 2002, Philippines	US hostage Martin Burnham and Philippine nurse Ediborah Yap killed in rescue attempt by Philippine army, one hostage saved.

Chapter Seven

Successful Rescues

Completely successful rescues, in which all of the hostages are freed alive and without subsequently fatal injuries, are relatively few and far between in light of the vast number of hostage casees. Moreover, only one of those, the rescue of the Lufthansa passengers in Mogadishu on 17 October 1977, was played out away from home ground.

On 13 October, two apparently innocuous couples travelling on Dutch and Iranian passports walked through the virtually non-existent security screening at Palma de Mallorca airport. They were members of the PFLP and, having cleared customs with their weapons undetected, joined the other 82 passengers and the five-man crew on a Lufthansa flight for Frankfurt. It never got there. Shortly after take-off, as the passengers were finishing lunch, the plane was skyjacked. For the next three days there followed a highly bizarre game of musical runways. The aircraft either touched down and refuelled or was turned away at Rome's Fiumicino airport, Larnaca in Cyprus – where the local PLO representative tried to negotiate with the skyjackers – Beirut, Bahrain and Dubai where, suspecting intervention, the skyjackers forced the plane to take off again, and then Aden. There the captain, Jurgen Schumann, who had been sending out radio messages about the hijackers in a pre-arranged code, pretended that there had been damage to the landing gear that he had to inspect. Knowing that his covert communication had been blown by an indiscreet journalist who had published the coded messages in the press, Schumann made a run for it. The skyjackers caught him, took him back into the plane and shot him in the head in front of all the passengers. His body was left in the aisle as a warning. The co-pilot was then made to fly towards Kuwait, but diverted to Mogadishu in Somalia.

Communiqués of a different kind established that, from the start, this was an unusual skyjacking. This was because it was closely linked with a previous terrestrial kidnapping that was not yielding the expected results. A couple of hours after the aircraft was taken over, imprisoned Baader-Meinhof leader Gudrun Ensslin read a communiqué to the German police demanding the release of the same 11 comrades as the Red Army Faction had already demanded in exchange for the life of German businessman Hanns-Martin Schleyer. An hour later, "Captain Mohammed Walter" made a virtually identical demand from aboard the skyjacked plane, which was still standing on the runway in Rome. In addition to the release of the prisoners and a payment of DM100,000 to each of them, he added a ransom of $15m, the release of two PFLP members held in Turkey and safe passage to Vietnam, Yemen or Somalia, where it transpired they were to get a very different reception from the one they expected. The communiqué concluded with a threat to the lives of the passengers and to Schleyer, kidnapped 39 days earlier by the Red Army Faction.*

One of the prerequisites for a successful rescue is early authorization from a sufficiently high authority to ensure no obstacles are put in its way. In this case, the crisis committee of the German cabinet was already meeting daily about the Schleyer case, so the go-ahead was given to Grenzschutzgruppe 9 (GSG 9**) and within two hours of the Lufthansa flight taking off from Rome, GSG 9 was en route to Cyprus. The Lufthansa jet eventually arrived in Mogadishu in the early hours of 16 October with GSG 9, unbeknownst to the skyjackers, close on its tailplane. Also unknown to the PFLP team was the fact that the Somali government had not only agreed to allow the Germans to attempt a rescue, but agreed to co-operate fully with them. Thus, while the actual rescue team consisted of only 18 men and their commander it was backed up by Somali troops. Without this support it is unlikely that GSG 9 would have been able to muster sufficient force on the spot to carry out the rescue successfully. In particular, the Germans could not have been certain that the active PLO unit known to be in Somalia would not have backed up its colleagues militarily.

Negotiators won sufficient time for the rescue squad and support troops to take up their positions by bluffing the skyjackers into believing that their demand for prisoner release had been met and that their comrades were even now en route for Mogadishu.

At just after 2.00 am local time on 17 October, when the vigilance of the weary captors would have been at its lowest ebb, the Somalis lit a fire 100 metres away from the nose of the aircraft. As anticipated, all four PFLP members rushed forward into the cockpit to see what was happening. The GSG 9 team blew open all the doors to the aircraft simultaneously, tossed in

---

At about this time Schleyer's son agreed to pay the ransom demanded for his father, but the handover turned into such a media circus that the Red Army Faction broke off the deal.

** *Literally Frontier Protection Squad*

stun grenades and followed up by rapid entry and small arms fire directed at the conveniently concentrated skyjackers. The whole operation, from the lighting of the fire to the killing of three captors and the wounding and capture of the fourth, took only seven minutes. A stewardess and one member of the GSG 9 team were wounded. None of the passengers or other crew was hurt. This was a copybook rescue, but, together with the suicide of the three Baader-Meinhof leaders [see pages 71–2] later that morning, prompted those holding Hanns-Martin Schleyer to murder him two days later.

If the Mogadishu rescue was both technically perfect and morally satisfying, the rescue of the hostages from the Japanese embassy in Lima in 1997 lacked moral satisfaction entirely. Nevertheless, by my own criteria it must be accounted as successful.

Plus ça change! Twenty five years after their Uruguayan counterparts had kidnapped Sir Geoffrey Jackson and broken into Montevideo prison to release their comrades, the Movimiento Revolucionario Tupac Amaru (the MRTA), the Tupamaros of Peru, seized the Japanese embassy in Lima. They made almost identical demands: the release of their comrades from prison and the reform of the brutish prison conditions; economic reforms that would enable some of the great wealth accumulated by the few to trickle down to the multitudinous poor; the restoration of civil liberties; and an end to the torture, murder and false imprisonment of any one who opposed the government of "President" Fujimori. The inverted commas were often used at this time because Fujimori, a Peruvian citizen of Japanese origin, had carried out a coup against himself, as it were, in order to stay in office.

On 17 December 1996, 20 young Tupamaros took hostage nearly 600 distinguished guests at a party in the Japanese embassy to celebrate the Emperor of Japan's birthday.

Peru's President, Fujimori, was supposed to have attended but did not. Had he been there, the outcome of the ensuing siege might well have been very different. As soon as they had seized control of the buildings and grounds of the embassy complex, the guerrillas released all the women and children. During the course of the following week, they released the elderly, the sick – and those pretending to be sick – and many others until the core of captives had been reduced to some 72. Among this number were Peruvian government ministers and senior military officers, judges and foreign ambassadors. Although the majority of hostages were released by the Tupamaros on humanitarian grounds, cutting the numbers to a manageable size was also a sound tactical decision.

During the 128 days of their captivity, the hostages were treated impeccably, apart from the deprivation of their freedom. They were well fed and cared for and were allowed to mix freely and to pursue a wide range of social activities – from playing chess and cards to singing and cooking – often together with their captors. As one hostage later described it: "It was like a cocktail party without the liquor."[1]

Fujimori categorically refused to negotiate. As far as he was concerned the prisoners whose release was demanded were in "prison tombs [where] they will rot and will only get out dead".[2] The Japanese Foreign Minister flew to Lima to beg him to negotiate for fear of a bloody outcome if force were to be employed. He was rebuffed. Later Fujimori did make a pretence of negotiating to enable his counter-terrorist forces to prepare their assault. Ostensibly he was offering the MRTA captors safe passage to Cuba in exchange for the release of the hostages. The Tupamaros declined his kind offer, not only because it gave them none of the things they were risking their lives for, but also because they knew that they would never reach the airport alive.

The rescue plan itself was ingenious if complex and long-winded. It may have owed something to the Unites States and British counter-terrorist specialists who were advising and assisting their Peruvian counterparts. It entailed forcing miners from Peru's silver mines to dig five tunnels under those embassy buildings where the hostages were being held. The miners then mysteriously died or "disappeared" lest word of their work and the nature of the impending attack were to get back to the Tupamaros, which it probably would have done. Some sounds of the tunnelling did reach those in the embassy, but the hostage-takers failed to recognize their import.

On 20 April, a company (approximately 100) of counter-terrorist commandos was deployed in the tunnels while the sappers prepared their petards. On 22 April, the charges were detonated and the commandos poured into the embassy to engage the surprised and half-stunned Tupamaros. There followed one of the more shameful episodes in the history of counter-terrorism. As one soldier later revealed,[3] Fujimori's instructions had been quite explicit. "The order was to leave no one alive. For us, the instruction was to leave no prisoners."

Only one captor survived the attack, and he was tortured and murdered soon afterwards. Those Tupamaros who were not killed in the gun battle were summarily shot with a bullet in the head, including their leader, Nesta Cerpa. Two teenage girls were clearly heard surrendering by an officer monitoring the attack. The next thing he heard was the sound of the shots that killed them. In the room where the judges were held, two more who surrendered were put up against the wall and machine-gunned. Before being killed themselves, the Tupamaros could quite easily have been as ruthless and carried out their threat to kill their hostages if they were attacked, but they did not. Not a single one of them was hurt. The Peruvian Minister of Agriculture, Rudolfo Munante, recalled how one young man had entered the room where Munante and some of his fellow captives were held with the obvious intention of shooting them. However, he could not bring himself to do it, such was the bond that had developed between the captives and the captors during the four-month siege. He turned away and walked out of the door to be shot down outside a moment later.

President Clinton congratulated Fujimori on the successful outcome of his operation, an operation in which United States training and equipment had played no small part. Two of the attacking troops were killed and one hostage died, but of a heart attack, not from gunfire or wounds. Whatever may be thought of the morality of the extra-judicial murder of captors who surrendered and who had shown themselves as both humane and merciful to their hostages, however just their cause, however brutal Fujimori's response, from a purely military point of view, this rescue operation was a success.

Having a senior American NATO general kidnapped under their noses on 17 December 1981 by the Red Brigades provoked the Italian police into a frenzy of activity. Unusually, Brigadier General James Dozier was abducted from his home in Verona, where he had taken a rather dismissive view about the precautions being advised by American security officers in the light of a considerable recent increase in the Red Brigades' activity. His wife was tied up and he was taken from his apartment in a large trunk by four men who had gained admission by posing as plumbers. Also unusually, his captors made no specific demand of what they wanted in return for his release. The police feared that this indicated that the kidnapping was for propaganda and punishment purposes only, as several other Red Brigades actions had been.

After ten days the captors issued a communiqué stating that Dozier's "trial" had begun. The communiqué was accompanied by an authenticating photograph of the general and the inevitable rambling statement of political aims and complaints. This one was entitled "The Strategic Resolution" and ran to 188 pages.

General Dozier was held captive for 42 days in conditions that were calculated to maximize both his discomfort and disorientation. Yet in all that time he was never interrogated for any of the sensitive military information which his captors must have known that, as a Deputy Chief of Staff for Allied Land Forces South Europe, he would possess. The general dismissed his captors as "rather amateurish", a somewhat insouciant reaction to his stressful captivity.

Meanwhile, the Italian police were rounding up and "vigorously interrogating" anyone suspected of being a member of the Red Brigades or of being even tenuously connected with them. There were even allegations of the use of torture, although these were never substantiated but, whatever the methods used, they proved highly effective. After just over a month of intensive detective work, the police persuaded an informer to take them to an apartment where he said Dozier was being held. This was a considerable improvement on the American efforts to find their man, which had entailed bringing a psychic over from the United States and instigating a raid on an innocent Italian family on his advice.

For three days the Leatherjackets – as Italy's Nucleo Operativo Centrale di Sicurezza (NOCS) are known on account of their leather caps – studied plans and watched the apartment closely until they were satisfied that Dozier was indeed being held there. The NOCS also needed time to work out the best way to effect a rescue. Then, on 28 January 1982, the Leatherjackets started up a number of adjacent bulldozers to cover the sound of their approach and burst into the apartment. One captor who was holding a gun to Dozier's head was knocked down before he could pull the trigger and the other four surrendered without a fight. The whole rescue took just 90 seconds. It also yielded a substantial collection of arms and explosives.

The Dozier rescue was the first time Italian police had managed to catch up with a Red Brigades commando. Prior to this action the Brigades had carried out a series of kidnappings, bombings and killings in Italy with apparent impunity. However, from now on, more and more arrested members revealed evidence to the state and betrayed their comrades so that the authorities were finally able to stem the tide of violence.

Other Successful Rescues:

26 October 1974, Netherlands	Skyjacker and three criminals attend prison church service. Take congregation and pastor hostage. Nine convicts, one woman and children released. Authorities pretended to negotiate. After 106 hours, captors get hysterical. Dutch anti-terrorist BBE penetrates church door with thermic lance. Shots fired but no one killed or wounded. Captors recaptured and hostages released.
5 March 1975, Israel	Eight Palestinians come by sea, seize Savoy Hotel, Tel Aviv and take guests and staff hostage. Barricade in top-floor room. Demand release of prisoners in Israeli jails. Eight hostages murdered, 11 wounded before IDF rescue mission same afternoon. Palestinians blow themselves up – seven killed, one captured.
13 March 1978,	Three South Moluccans seize town hall and take

Netherlands	72 civil servants hostage. Release of previously arrested Moluccan train hijackers demanded. Psychological profiling of captors convinces authorities that armed rescue is the only option. BBE storms building. Short fire-fight. No casualties.
19 June 1980, Iraq	Three gunmen take over British embassy in Baghdad. British ambassador invites Iraqi security forces to intervene. An hour later, all three gunmen shot dead. No other casualties.
2 May 1981, Bolivia	Bolivian Socialist Falange (right-wing organization) led by former presidential candidate, Carlos Barbery, seizes oil refinery and 52 hostages demanding resignation of President. Refinery stormed. No hostages hurt.
12 December 1982, United States	An anti-nuclear protestor holds eight tourists hostage in the Washington Monument, in Washington, DC, before he is shot dead by a police sniper.
5 September 1986, Pakistan	PanAm plane and 400 passengers seized in Karachi. Crew escape. Captors start to shoot hostages, 17 die. Security forces storm plane. All hijackers killed or captured.
26 March 1991, Singapore	Four Pakistanis seize a Singapore Air A310 Airbus on a 45-minute flight to Singapore from Kuala Lumpur to demand the release of the husband of Benazir Bhutto, Asif Ali Zardari. Singaporean commandos shot hijackers dead.
17 January 1992, Philippines	Michael Barnes seized by New Peoples' Army to collect ransom to help overthrow the government. Police locate the apartment where Barnes was held. The Philippine Light Reaction Force storms the apartment and frees Barnes. Fourteen hostage-takers killed. No other casualties.

25 April 1993, India	Indian Airlines plane hijacked by a lone hostage-taker who manages to conceal his weapons in a leg cast. Indian Special Counter-Terrorist Unit force the emergency doors, surprise and kill the hijacker. No other casualties.
24 December 1994, Algiers	Four Islamic fundamentalists posing as baggage handlers board an Air France flight and take 227 passengers and 12 crew hostage. Demand release of spiritual leader from Algerian jail. Women and children released; three hostages killed.

Chapter Eight

Proxime Accessit

he template for hostage rescues overseas was cut not, as is generally supposed, at Entebbe, but at Djibouti on 3 February 1976. As a group of young French children travelled early that morning from the military base where their fathers were stationed to their school near Djibouti docks, their bus was hijacked by four members of the Somali Coast Liberation Front. The hijackers then forced the driver to take the bus to within a couple of hundred metres of the border with Somalia. Two more FLCS members joined the bus there and issued their demand – the immediate independence of the French-controlled coastal territories of Afars and Issas. If the demand was not met, they would cut the 30 children's throats. The local French military commander was quickly on the spot and tried to negotiate. Not only was the hijackers demand one that was impossible to grant, but it quickly became clear to him that they were in a highly excitable state and might indeed carry out their threat. Moreover, he realized that as the sun rose higher, temperatures in the bus would become intolerable and in any prolonged siege the children would be as much at risk from heatstroke and dehydration as from the hijackers. An urgent message was sent to Paris describing the dilemma. There was only one solution. The government despatched the Groupement d'Intervention de la Gendarmerie Nationale (the GIGN) to his aid.

The GIGN had been formed in 1974 following the debacles at the Munich Olympics (in 1972) and the seizure of the Saudi embassy in Paris the following year. This rigorously selected, highly trained and experienced anti-terrorist force had already enjoyed a number of relatively small-scale domestic successes, but this was their first challenge on foreign soil. There is always one unit of GIGN on stand-by every hour of every day of the year and a nine-man team, each equipped with his own specialist FR-F1 sniper rifle and Manurhin 73 revolver, arrived in Djibouti eight hours later and immediately took up position in the nearest cover to the bus a little under 200 metres away. Each sniper was linked to the commander of the unit, Lieutenant Proteau, by a throat microphone.

The hijackers were also well organized and four of them were always on the bus at any one time. But the GIGN is trained to be patient as well as tough. Critical to their plan was the ability to shoot dead all four hijackers on the bus simultaneously to prevent any reprisals being taken against the children. So they waited in the scorching heat. Their back-up cover of Legionnaires had been in position since shortly after the incident began.

Ingeniously, Lieutenant Prouteau had persuaded the hijackers to allow sandwiches to be sent in for the children. They were doctored with a mild sedative which the lieutenant guessed would not be detected by the Somalis who would feel obliged to eat only their own food. Soon all the children were lying down asleep and safely out of the line of GIGN fire. The hijackers, meanwhile, continued to patrol inside the bus four at a time.

At 3.47 pm all four were in suitable target positions and Proteau gave the order the snipers had been waiting for. The marksmen of the GIGN are considered some of the finest in the world and are often called on to train other specialist forces. They do not miss. They didn't. The four men on the bus were all killed instantly, but the two not on board opened fire on the GIGN positions, as did the Somali border guards. While the Legionnaires engaged the latter, the GIGN team covered the intervening ground to the bus. One of the surviving hijackers re-boarded the bus from the Somali side as did the GIGN. He was shot dead, but sadly not before he had killed one child and fatally wounded another. Two adults and three children were also wounded. The sixth hijacker was captured. The whole operation had taken only ten hours. The lessons of Munich had been well learned and, but for those two hostage fatalities, the Djibouti incident would have been the perfect hostage rescue under conditions of great difficulty.

The next rescue attempt was made under even more taxing circumstances.

Entebbe[1] is a name that is universally recognized on account of the singular event that took place there on 4 July 1976. The hostage-taking that preceded it, as usual in the 1970s, was made possible by lax security. There was no one manning the metal detector at Athens airport and the fluoroscope was getting only the most cursory inspection. No one looked closely enough at the passports that pronounced their bearers to be the citizens of Bahrain, Peru, Ecuador and Kuwait to suspect that they might be forged. As Captain Becos, the pilot behind the unlocked cockpit door of Air France flight 139 to Paris, discovered at 12.28 pm on 27 June shortly after take-off from Athens, those passports belonged to three men and a woman who had just taken over his aircraft by force. Two of them were members of the

PFLP, whose leader Waddid Haddad had almost certainly planned the operation, and the other two belonged to the closely associated German RZ (see page 70).

As soon as news of the skyjacking became known and that there were 77 Jewish passengers on board, the Israeli authorities assumed that the plane's probable destination would be Ben Gurion airport in Israel and preparations were made to deal with that contingency. However, after refuelling at Benghazi, flight 139 flew south and with only a few minutes' fuel remaining landed at what had obviously always been its intended destination – Entebbe, the main airport of Uganda. As owners of the aircraft, and therefore primarily responsible for its safety and that of its 233 passengers and crew, the French explored all possible diplomatic channels to try to end the hijacking throughout the eight days of the incident. To no avail. Israel, once it knew how large a proportion of the passengers were Jewish and that the plane had been seized by Palestinian hijackers, doubted if any diplomatic solution was possible. Mad sergeant Amin, the megalomaniac dictator of Uganda, had expelled every Israeli from the country over which he ruled in March 1972, after Israel had refused to supply him with Phantom jet fighters.

Not until they were safely on Ugandan soil did the skyjackers voice their demand for the release of 53 convicted comrades imprisoned in France, Germany, Israel, Kenya and Switzerland. A deadline for agreement was set for 2.00 pm Israeli time on 1 July, otherwise the plane and its passengers would be blown up. These demands were made all the more forceful once it was known that, shortly after their arrival at Entebbe, the Jewish passengers had been segregated from the rest. The 148 non-Jewish passengers were flown back to Paris in two batches on 30 June and 1 July. Captain Becos and his crew refused to leave any of their charges behind, so stayed with the remaining hostages. Only a few hours after the hugs and tears of an official welcome in Paris and being reunited with their families, the released hostages were discreetly debriefed by Israeli intelligence agents. What they learned, together with what the French and other European agencies had pieced together from their sources, made it fairly clear that Amin was not just conniving at the hostage-taking, but actively assisting in it. Moreover, a number of other PFLP members had joined the original hijackers and Ugandan troops were assisting them to guard the prisoners and to secure the airport. Thus, for the first time in the history of air piracy, a state went beyond finance, training and encouragement to participate actively in an operation.

While the politicians back in Israel debated and debated the respective merits of surrender, negotiation and force, a small group of senior officers from the Israel Defence Force and the Israeli air force were applying their minds to the possibility of having to implement the latter course of action. How could a rescue operation be carried out 3,200 kilometres away from home? Could enough be learned about Entebbe airport and its defences and layout? Could a plan be formulated and a rescue team be recruited and rehearsed in the time available? The answer would have been no had the hijackers not inexplicably postponed their deadline to 4 July. Why did they do that? Was it the persuasiveness of retired Colonel Burka Bar-Lev, an old acquaintance of Amin's whom Israel's Defence Minister, Simon Peres, had instructed to get in touch with the dictator and find out what he could? Was it that Amin did not want to be embarrassed at the Heads of State meeting of the Organization for African Unity due to take place that weekend? Was it that the hijackers wanted Amin himself with them to back their play when the second deadline expired. We are unlikely ever to know, but extended it was and with it the whole prospect of Israel's military planners staging an effective rescue.

Ninety minutes before the expiry of the original deadline, Prime Minister Yitzhak Rabin asked the Chief of Staff of the IDF whether he could carry out a military rescue. "Not yet," he replied. With the unanimous consent of his cabinet, Rabin agreed to negotiate and asked the French to pass that acceptance on to the hijackers. It was noted that Simon Peres and Minister of Police, Shlomo Hillel, agreed only on condition that negotiation was to be a delaying tactic pending the launch of a military rescue. At this point, the Israelis were still unaware that the deadline had been extended, although by then Amin had informed the hostages. I believe, therefore, contrary to most interpretations, that at the moment it was made, the unpalatable agreement to negotiate with hostages was genuine. Of course, as soon as it was realized that there were three additional days in which to come up with an alternative, the negotiations became no more than a smokescreen to hide the preparations for one of the most famous of all military raids.

The plan itself was relatively simple. The rescue party would be flown to Entebbe in four Hercules transports and two Boeing 707s would be converted to provide a mobile hospital and a flying communications and command post. The rescuers, a mixture of paratroopers and experienced anti-terrorist infantry men from the Golan brigade, were under the leadership of Lieutenant Colonel Jonathan Netanyahu, son of a future Prime Minister. They would disembark, seize the old terminal where the hostages were held, killing as many of the hostage-takers as necessary, secure the fuel depot that might be needed for refueling the transports, prevent the Ugandan troops from counter-attacking and destroy the Ugandan air force MiG fighters that might otherwise pursue and shoot down the rescue aircraft on their return journey. The plan was relatively straightforward. Execution of it, however, would be a different matter.

The Israeli air force had flown Hercules long-range transports regularly into Entebbe during the days when an Israeli mission in Kampala had to be supplied. The distance was no obstacle and the layout of an international airport is available in various flight manuals to anyone who wants to fly to it. The problem was, what might have been done to change or block runways since the hostages arrived? Would there be anti-aircraft defences? Would the runway lights be on when they landed?

Ingeniously, the latter problem was tackled by studying the timetables of commercial airlines flying into Entebbe and squeezing the assault in between two that were only a few minutes apart in the hope that the airport controller would simply not bother to turn the lights off between landings. In case he did, the specially chosen pilots practised landing a Hercules in the dark with no assistance but their own lights until they were touchdown perfect. The other problems would have to be left to solve themselves on the premise that, since nothing even remotely like this rescue had ever been attempted before, no one would be expecting it to be attempted this time.

Two other crucial problems remained. How was Colonel Netanyahu to get his 200 men across the 200 metres between where the Hercules would have to come to a halt and the old terminal without rousing the suspicion of either the hijackers or the Ugandan airport security guards? And once he got them there, how would they find their way round a building they did not know quickly enough to kill any defending hijackers before the hostages could be harmed? Again the answer to the second problem resolved itself by a stroke of luck before the first was overcome by a stroke of genius. The old terminal had been built by an Israeli contractor who still just happened to have the plans. General Kuti Adam, in charge of planning what was now known as Operation Thunderball, immediately ordered the construction, film set-style, of a full-scale model and the rescue squad rehearsed disembarking from an old Hercules and taking over the building in the minimum time over and over again. What they did not find out until it was too late was that one of the doors on the plan had since been blocked up, but other than that snag, rehearsal and performance turned out to be identical.

The problem of covering 200 metres of open ground without arousing suspicion and being gunned down was solved by one of those flashes of inspiration that can turn a dubious proposition into a resounding success. Second in command on the ground, Major Muki,* who had been responsible for much of the preliminary planning, remembered that Amin liked to drive round in a large black Mercedes with a substantial escort. Suppose instead of disembarking the troops on foot to face a 200-metre sprint in full battle kit they were to drive right up to the door of the old terminal? And that is exactly what happened. On 4 July, an hour before midnight, a black Mercedes – hastily transformed from its original white and flying a Ugandan flag – drove imperiously down the ramp of the Hercules onto the runway. It was followed by two Land Rovers packed with the men of the advance units wearing the

---

* *A number of officers, presumably for continuing security reasons, are referred to in reports only by initials or code-names.*

olive-green battle dress uniform common to armies the world over. Not until they were about to turn aside to cover the last few metres to the door of their target were they taken for anything other than a typically unexpected visit from Amin or one of his senior officials. Then two alert Ugandan sentries felt something was amiss and challenged the convoy. The gloves were now off. The two Ugandans were shot down and Muki led his men at a run to the door of the old terminal, while behind him other paratroopers were setting beacons on the runway in case the landing lights needed for the withdrawal take-off were turned out.

The first assault section, led by the major, burst into the part of the old terminal where the hostages were being held. Orders were loudly shouted in Hebrew and English for the captives to stay lying on the floor where they were. Unfortunately, one of the hostages, possibly mistaking the men carrying guns who had just charged through the door for his executioners, hurled himself at them and was mistaken for a captor and shot. After a brief and one-sided gunfight with the captors on guard the hostages were free, but another of their number had perished and they still had to remain where they were until the rest of the rescue plan had been carried out.

The second section of troops took care of those off-duty captors who were sleeping in another room, whilst the third raced to the top floor to neutralize the Ugandan soldiers whose guardroom it was. This part of the operation, from the vehicles leaving the Hercules to its successful conclusion, took only three minutes. Six hostage-takers, two Ugandans and two hostages were killed. The only casualty suffered by the rescuers was their own commander. Netanyahu had stayed outside the building in order to direct all three of his forward sections, but he was exposed to Ugandan fire from the control tower and was fatally wounded in the neck. His epitaph is best written in his own words when exhorting his men before the attack:

> The basic assumption in our work is to prepare in the best possible fashion, so that we may stand quietly on the day of judgment, when it comes, in the knowledge that we did everything we could in the time that we had.

So carefully had the operation been planned and rehearsed that even with its original commander out of action it ran on smoothly under the overall second-in-command, Lieutenant Colonel S. Five minutes after the old terminal had been taken, the remaining three Hercules had rolled to a halt on the runway; the main force of Armoured Personnel Carriers and infantry emerged from the first two. This back-up force engaged and silenced the Ugandan troops in the new terminal building and in the control tower, where it suffered its only other serious casualty. A sergeant, just 12 hours short of his demobilization date, was so seriously wounded that he was paralysed for the rest of his life. The remaining sections of the back-up force secured all the approach roads to the airport to prevent the possibility of Ugandan reinforcements arriving from Kampala.

While the fighting was taking place, Israeli air force technicians began unloading the high-powered fuel pumps whose presence was just another example of the foresight with which the rescue had been planned. They were soon pumping fuel from Entebbe's own bunkers into the four transport aircraft. This could have been the most dangerous phase of the whole rescue, for refuelling in this way was likely to take nearly an hour and so expose the Israelis to the risk of a serious counter-attack. When news was radioed through from the hospital Boeing at Nairobi airport that refuelling of all the Israeli aircraft would be permitted there on a "blind eye turned" basis, it seemed a heaven-sent opportunity to shorten the duration of the rescue. Lieutenant Colonel S. gave the order to evacuate the hostages at once. The fourth, empty, Hercules taxied as near as it could to the doors of the old terminal and the soldiers shepherded their relieved, but bewildered, fellow countrymen and their loyal French aircrew onto the getaway plane in just seven minutes. Fifty-two minutes after the wheels of the first Hercules had touched the runway, the hostages and the seven dead and wounded were on their way home.

The support troops stayed on just long enough to destroy the seven Ugandan MiGs stationed at Entebbe and to re-embark their equipment before taking off in the wake of their comrades. Ninety-nine minutes after the rescue began on the ground there was neither hide nor hair to be seen of a hostage or an Israeli soldier at Entebbe. Despite having to fly through a bad electrical storm over Lake Victoria en route, the leading Hercules had landed within seconds of the time planned and the entire operation had been completed ahead of schedule.

All told, six hostage-takers, 39 Ugandan soldiers and three★ hostages died.

The whole Entebbe operation was by any interpretation of international law an act of war, but the Israeli ambassador to the UN, Chaim Herzog, saw it differently.

> The Israeli action at Entebbe came to remind us that the law we find in statute books is not the only law of mankind. There is also a moral law, and by all that is moral on this earth, Israel had the right to do what it did. Indeed it had also the basic duty to do so.

The governments of the West agreed with him on the whole. Many of the members of the Organization for African Unity condemned Israel's action, thus

---

★ *An elderly lady, a Mrs Bloch, had been taken to Kampala hospital with a heart problem and died there. It was rumoured that she had been murdered by a vengeful Amin.*

flagging the disagreements that would bedevil future UN discussions aimed at drafting an International Convention on terrorism. However, what Entebbe did show was that the battle against terrorism need by no means be one-sided. It also heralded the downfall of the despicable Amin by undermining his domestic reputation for invincibility and thus encouraging the armed rebellion that was to topple him in 1975. All in all, the rescue at Entebbe was a near-perfect mission carried out in almost impossible circumstances.

The Dutch anti-terrorist unit, the BBE,★ is one of the most successful in the world. Their classic hostage rescue, always cited in professional manuals as an example of how to conduct anti-terrorist operations, took place between 23 May and 11 June 1977 on an inter-city train running between Rotterdam and Groenigen. Much of the background for this account is drawn from the diaries and interviews given to Frank Ochberg by the Dutch newspaper editor Gerard Vaders, who like every good journalist seems to have been in the right (or wrong, depending how you look at it) place at the right time. In December 1975 he had been on another train hijacked by the South Moluccans. These people had been part of the former Dutch colonial empire in Indonesia and had been among their most loyal subjects with large numbers of them supporting the Netherlands in their wars as soldiers. When the Dutch withdrew and Indonesia became independent, most of these men and their families had been shipped back to the Netherlands, partly for their own protection from the oppression of the dictatorial Indonesian leader, Sukarno. However, together with the South Moluccans who had remained in Indonesia, they longed for an independent homeland, South Molucca, of their own and believed that the Dutch should help them get it. The 1975 incident had been peacefully resolved by negotiation. This time Vaders was not so lucky.

He was almost jolted out of his seat on Monday 23 May when a South Moluccan girl pulled the emergency cord on the express as it passed through open countryside nearing the outskirts of Groenigen. No sooner had it ground to a halt than nine armed South Moluccans suddenly appeared out of the surrounding countryside and took over the train, despite the fact that the train driver and two hostages were shot (see pages 128-131). On this note, the 20-day siege began.

This second trainjacking was different from its predecessor in two major respects. Firstly, it had been timed to coincide with the seizure of a primary school, along with 105 children and five teachers at Bovensmilde, 25 kilometres from where the trainjacking was taking place, by four members of South

---

★ *The Bizondere Bystand Eenheid, the "Different Circumstances Unit", consists of two platoons of 33 men each. These are subdivided into five-man teams with a command control. One platoon is on a 90-minutes-to-action standby at all times. Their motto is: Semper Paratus Pro Justitia – Always Ready for Justice.*

Moluccans' Youth Movement. Secondly, it was much more carefully planned and ruthlessly carried out than the previous trainjack had been. As Vaders told Ochberg:

> The losers learn more than the victors. The victors fight the last war. The losers change and improve. For example, the Moluccans were quiet at the beginning this time. They gave a longer deadline. They had time for relaxation and for equilibrium. They took 54 hostages so they had more time to avoid personal relations. They were more rational and less emotional.[2]

They initially took nearly twice that number of hostages, but released 40 captives immediately and, as the incident neared the end of its second week, another two women and a man with heart problems. The hijackers were demanding the release of fellow countrymen who had been imprisoned for making similar hostage-taking forays and they repeated the perennial demand for South Moluccan independence. A 48-hour deadline was set, but, as is not uncommon, it passed without incident.

By 1977, the Dutch had had plenty of opportunities to develop a highly sophisticated response. Apart from the BBE, there was a small group of psychologists and psychoanalysts specializing in the psychology of hostage-takers who could be assembled quickly and through whom the negotiations were usually conducted. This differed from the British practice where the psychologists advised but did not negotiate. So although Prime Minister Joop den Uyl could make pronouncements to satisfy the public – "patience is the watchword, but we are prepared to use controlled violence if necessary" – neither he nor the Minister of Justice, to whom the captors asked to speak, was ever allowed to exchange a single word with the hijackers.

Dedicated phone lines were soon set up between the negotiators and the hijackers at both the train and the school. The South Moluccans were also allowed a direct telephone line between the train and the school. The purpose of this concession was threefold: in addition to the debriefing of released hostages, it would help the marines to monitor the movements and defence positions of the hijackers; it would enable the psychologists to analyse the captors' vocabulary, tone and other speech elements in order to predict their state of mind; and it would allow the skilled negotiators the opportunity to bring the incident to a peaceful conclusion in which no one got hurt. In the case of the trainjacking, it became steadily more apparent that, even though it had not involved the violence to hostages of the previous one, it was much less likely to be settled by negotiation. In any case, the Dutch response to any hostage incident always involves preparation from the very outset for an armed assault by the BBE and it was, in this case as always, ready to use "controlled violence" if need be. Such preparation centres initially on gathering as much intelligence as possible about the dispositions and arming of the captors and the distribution of the captives, so as to maximize the harm to the one and minimize it to the other.

The BBE built up this background information in unconventional ways as well as the usual ones. When the hijackers asked for food to be sent in, but insisted that the police who brought it were naked so that they could not conceal weapons, this became a bluff in the buff, as it were. Although they had to leave their clothes behind, these trained observers had not left behind their eyes and their wits and brought back much useful information. In a more orthodox fashion, a team of BBE frogmen used an adjoining dyke to swim close to the train to place highly sensitive listening and heat-seeking devices in close enough proximity to yield more necessary information. Because the train, being an inter-city express, was so long, points of attack based on this information would have to be particularly carefully chosen.

Early on the morning of 11 June, all this careful reconnaissance and analysis was put to the test. To distract and bemuse the hijackers at the critical split second before the attack, it was decided to decline the offer of stun grenades from the SAS, whose advice was being called on, and to use instead two F-104 Starfighters roaring over the train with after-burners going full blast. An unexpected bonus from this tactic was that the noise not only disorientated the captors, as had been intended, but so scared the captives that they threw themselves to the floor and were thus much less likely to find themselves in some marine's or hijacker's line of fire.*

Controlled explosions from wooden frames previously attached to selected doors enabled the rescuers to break into the train simultaneously at all the chosen points, firing their Heckler and Koch MP5 machineguns without any risk of shooting each other. Only one marine was wounded throughout the course of the whole attack, which was completed in under five minutes and saw six hijackers killed and three taken prisoner.

The only fault in this otherwise flawless operation came as a result of a misunderstanding by some of the marines giving the attacking party covering fire from outside the train. Two girls had decided to sleep out on the observation balcony at the end of the train to get away from the stifling heat inside. Because they were mistaken for hijackers they were killed by machinegun fire.

Just as the hijackings were carried out simultaneously at the two locations, so were the rescues, though ending the school seizure turned out to be relatively simple. The 15 South Moluccan children had been released

---

* *The success of this manoeuvre must particularly have gratified Henk van Breemen, the officer in command, who on being asked by a reluctant den Uyl if he couldn't do something "a little less military" had replied that he could. He could paint the aircraft white and put the word "police" in big letters on the side!*

immediately after the seizure. Three of the four South Moluccan captors soon struck up a good relationship with the children once the stress of the first harrowing day was over. They explained why they were doing what they doing and described the distant homeland they wanted to go back to and how their parents had loyally served the children's parents. By day two, the children were following something like their normal school routine of work and play and their captors would give a consoling cuddle to any child who became distressed.[3] At the request of the hostage-takers, sandwiches and cold drinks were sent in regularly by the police cordoning off the building. One child suffering from stomach cramps was sent home just as the deadline expired and here, as on the train, no big deal was made of its passing. While these human kindnesses were no excuse for the seizure, they were perhaps a mitigating factor.

By the fourth day all the children were suffering from a gastrointestinal disorder and were released together with one of their teachers. It was rumoured that an infection had been deliberately introduced via the sandwiches. That seems unlikely, for had any child died as a result it would have been a political disaster. The first sick child was, in all probability, the source of the illness and the infection spread rapidly in the confined and unhygienic siege conditions. The only other anxious moment came when a mentally disturbed woman ran into the school grounds and the captors insisted she be removed by policemen wearing nothing but their underpants.

When the co-ordinated BBE attack on the school was made, the four remaining teachers were released unharmed and the four South Moluccans were captured without casualties. But for the accidental killing of the two girls on the train, this rescue would, indeed, have been the copybook operation fulfilling all our rules bar the all important number ten: "Cause no hostage deaths, directly or indirectly." The same description, with the same proviso, could equally well be applied to the siege of the Iranian embassy that took place in London three years later.

In the brief interregnum between the fall of the Shah and the closing of Ayatollah Khomeini's absolute grip on Iran by early 1980, minorities all over the country had hoped for and expected a degree of freedom and autonomy they had not enjoyed for 30 years. Among them were the people of Khuzestan, a small, oil-rich region at the head of the Persian Gulf. They wanted an independent state of what they called Arabistan. Khomeini had absolutely no intention of surrendering such an important revenue-generating part of his new Islamic state. Nor had he any intention of giving in to the demand for the release of 91 Khuzestani prisoners in his jails made by their six young fellow countrymen when they took over the Iranian embassy in London's Princes Gate on 30 April 1980. They were to be disappointed. As one of the hostage-takers said: "The new leaders forgot all their promises to the people."

At 11.30 am that morning, a little later than usual, PC Trevor Lock of the Embassy Protection Unit took his usual short coffee break with the embassy concièrge in his cubby hole just inside the door. No sooner had he left his beat outside the embassy than "Salim" – his real name was Awn Ali Mohammed – and his five companions seized their moment and with it the embassy and 26 hostages. When Mr Trevor, as everyone came to call him, looked up from his cup, it was to stare into the barrel of a sub-machinegun. There was nothing he could do. Even if he could have drawn his own revolver from its underarm holster it would have been of little use against such odds.

Within a couple of minutes the embassy and those in it were under the gunmen's control. Among the hostages were four non-Iranians who would play major parts in the drama of the next six days. Sim Harris and Chris Cramer were BBC men who had come simply to pick up their visas for an assignment in Iran. Mustapha Karkouti was a Syrian journalist based in London who turned out to be both a linguist and a diplomatic intermediary, and Lock was the linchpin that held the hostages together and ensured they did nothing foolish. The fifth player and the only Iranian with a named part was Abbas Lavasani, a young, devout and fanatical disciple of the Ayatollah, whose intransigence would prove the catalyst for violence. When Prime Minister Margaret Thatcher's dogmatic determination never to deal with terrorists in any circumstances was added to this mix, violence was the inevitable and tragic outcome. Without these two elements it is quite possible that the police negotiator, DCI Max Vernon, might have brought the drama to a peaceful conclusion. As it was, by the "interval" he was, whether aware of it or not, only stringing the captors along while preparations for the assault were made.

Strategic and overall tactical control when situations such as this arose lay in the hands of COBRA, a small committee under the chairmanship of the Home Secretary, William Whitelaw, one of the few politicians ever to win the trust and friendship of Mrs Thatcher. COBRA took its name from the underground bunker in which it met – the Cabinet Office Operations Room – and had built up much experience in dealing with terrorism over the long years of conflict in Northern Ireland and its violent extension to the rest of Britain in a recent series of bombings, shootings and kidnappings. COBRA's instinct, like that of its namesake,* was to strike rather than negotiate.

In this case, the fangs were to be supplied by the Special Air Service (SAS). Hardened in Ireland, trained to perfection and always ready for action, the SAS had become a role model for anti-terrorist units the world over; its members were almost psychotically eager to put their deadly skills to the test. An SAS team had moved into the nearby Chelsea Barracks within hours of the embassy

---

* The King Cobra is one of the very few snakes that will attack a human being rather than get out of the way.

being taken over.

For the first three days the siege showed no signs of ending other than peacefully and, as so often happens, the first deadline had passed without the Khuzestanis carrying out their threat to kill the hostages if their demands were not met. Mr Trevor, Karkouti and Sim Harris had gradually established some kind of rapport with Salim. The Khuzestanis, though as part of the psychology of negotiation they always had to ask, were never refused their request for necessities such as food and drink and even cigarettes. Other more substantial demands were ostensibly conceded with no intention of carrying them out. The captors had asked that one of the ambassadors from Jordan, Algeria or Iraq be called in to mediate. Iraq was out of the question as it had almost certainly trained and equipped the gunmen for its own anti-Iranian ends as well as providing the brains behind the operation, "Sami", who had skipped the country before the incident began leaving his naive protégés high and dry. It is hard to see why this request was refused unless it had been pre-determined that a peaceful solution was to be avoided. The captors also demanded safe passage for themselves and the hostages out of the country. Until the last day of the incident, although increasingly frustrated and jumpy, they clearly believed they would be going home when it was all over. They had even been shopping in Harrods.

Throughout the siege, the police and SAS gradually built up a picture of what was happening inside the embassy and of the nature of the opposition they faced. Their first reliable information came with the release of Cramer on the second day. With considerable exercise of mind over matter, he turned a minor stomach complaint into an illness so apparently life-threatening that his captors let him go. Before he left, Lock had already briefed him on the exact inventory of their captors' weapons and explosives. One other hostage had already been released and three more were to be freed later. The last, on day five, was Mustapha Karkouti, whose linguistic and diplomatic skills had been so useful in bridging the gap between the captors and the captives.

When it seemed as if their services would be called on, the members of the SAS team gathered further information by dangling ultra-sensitive microphones down the chimneys and drilling into the walls to position others. The latter approach nearly gave the intended assault away, because although the holes were being made with hand drills, the noise was still picked up by the captors. Only fine histrionic performances from Mr Trevor and Sim Harris convinced the Khuzestanis that they were mistaken. Further drilling was only carried out when its sound was swamped by that of commercial aircraft flying over unusually low at the "request" of COBRA.

On the sixth day an incident occurred that would precipitate the final assault. Abbas Lavasani had been needling his captors, particularly the tough second-in-command, "Faisal", by proselytizing loudly and vehemently for the

Khomeini regime. Faisal's riposte was to scrawl insulting graffiti about the Ayatollah on the embassy walls. On seeing them, Lavasani began to rave and scream at Faisal and when threatened with his gun simply bared his chest and challenged him to shoot, declaring that he wished to die, he wished to be a martyr. Not long afterwards he got his wish. He was marched, rejoicing still in the prospect of death, downstairs to the hall where he was shot three times. The first shot was into the chest he had so brazenly exposed, the next two into his head. His body was left to lie in the hall until just after 6.30 pm when it was tossed into the street and a distraught Trevor Lock had to pass the message out of the window that in 45 minutes the next hostage would be shot. It was time for the SAS to go.

The final assault did not go quite as smoothly as planned. It was begun at 7.23 pm on the sixth evening by explosive charges being lowered through the skylights and simultaneously detonated to distract and confuse the captors. The intention was to blow the two large first-floor windows facing the street – and incidentally the focus of dozens of television cameras and hundreds of press photographers, the precursor of reality television as it were – and immediately after the initial explosions to enter the building at speed. One SAS man abseiling down the outer wall got stuck just above the burning window number one, which could not be blown till he was cut free. The rescuer outside window number two saw through a chink in the shutters that Sim Harris had rushed into the room in something of a panic to avoid the gunfire and could not detonate the charge until Sim had been persuaded to back away and lie on the floor.

From the moment the two windows were blown the rest of the attack went to plan, though it took 11 minutes to clear the building and secure the hostages, compared to the three it had taken at Entebbe. One of the rescuers would have been killed but for the quick thinking and courage of PC Lock, for which he was later awarded the George Cross.

When the windows blew Salim had positioned himself to shoot the first attacker to come through the door of the room where he had been talking to Mr Trevor. Throughout the siege, Lock had been racked by the dilemma of whether or not to use his gun, which had escaped the captors' cursory search. He could have fired only six shots before having to reload and there were six men to deal with. As a policeman, his first responsibility was to try to get everyone, including the captors, out alive and a gun battle was scarcely conducive to that end, but now the moment for action had come. As the lead SAS member prepared to jump through the opening, Lock hurled himself across the room, knocked a surprised Salim to the ground and held his revolver to the Khuzestani's head. He resisted the temptation to vent the pent-up anger of the past six days on his captive by pulling the trigger. His whole training was to restrain and arrest criminals for trial, not to kill them unless it was absolutely necessary. In contrast, the whole training of the SAS was to kill rather than restrain – unless absolutely necessary.

Trevor Lock was so astonished to hear himself addressed by name and shouted at to roll away from Salim that he obeyed instinctively. Salim was shot as he lay on the floor. The two Khuzestanis who held a dozen hostages in the telex room had started shooting them when the gun battle broke out. They had fired only a few rounds, killing one hostage and wounding two others, when they changed their minds, threw their weapons to the ground and placed their hands on their heads in a gesture of surrender. They were pushed up against a wall by the SAS and shot. A fourth captor was killed in an exchange of fire in another part of the building and a fifth, mingling with the hostages as they were bundled out of the burning building, was shot as he appeared to pull the pin from a grenade. Mrs Thatcher had made it clear that she wanted "no loose ends" and the SAS team was in no doubt that by this she meant no live terrorists to stand a publicity-bestowing trial. Unfortunately for her, she got one. Following standard practice, everyone was hustled out of the building, whoever they were. As each person emerged, he or she was spread-eagled face down on the ground with their hands handcuffed behind their backs. When the SAS came to count their prone catch there was one fish too many – 20 instead of 19. One captor had managed to hide himself among the captives who quickly and noisily identified him. As one SAS man began to drag away this particular "loose end" to be "tidied up", his colleagues realized that it would not have been a very good idea in front of half the world's television cameras and pulled him back. Fawzi Nejad was turned over to the police and eventually sentenced to life imprisonment for "this outrageous criminal enterprise". He is still in prison 23 years later.★

Everyone from Margaret Thatcher to the Ayatollah Khomeini was delighted and heaped praise on the police and the SAS. But were they right? With less intransigence on the British side, could the siege have been ended without bloodshed? We can never know, but as a rescue operation, apart from one hostage death, probably due to the delay in effecting entry, it was superbly executed.

★ *Home Office rules and the law prevent me from saying where.*

Chapter Nine

Negotiations

Negotiated solutions to political hostage-taking incidents cannot be treated in the same way as seizures and rescues. They cannot be divided into win, lose and draw categories. The whole point of negotiation is that there are seldom any absolute winners or losers, though the outcome may favour one party to a greater extent than the other. In a sense, the two categories of hostage incident considered so far are the outcome of failed negotiation, even if in most cases the failure consists of never having tried to negotiate in the first place. This definition tends to be adopted by those whose priority it is to get hostages out of an incident alive and, as far as possible, unharmed. On the other side of the definitional argument are those – women Prime Ministers prominent among them – who regard the very idea of negotiation with terrorists, let alone embarking on it, as a failure, unless it is merely being used as a ruse. For these people, negotiation consists of promises either made to be broken, or for use as a delaying tactic to render hostage-takers more vulnerable to an armed attack. They would argue that promises and concessions obtained by force or by the threat of force are binding neither morally nor legally. Intransigence is by no means confined to those on the side of the authorities. There have been numerous hostage-takers who have absolutely no wish to negotiate, but only to have their demands, often impossible ones, met in full or to die as martyrs.

In this chapter, I shall examine in detail five hostage incidents that were resolved by genuine negotiation, and touch upon nine others, in order to see if they have common characteristics. In the next chapter, I shall ask of what the art of negotiation consists and what are the qualities of a successful negotiator.

My first example occurred early in February 1945 which, strictly speaking, is just outside my chosen timeframe. However, it does exemplify many of the essential ingredients for successful hostage negotiation as well as being a stirring tale of derring-do. During the Second World War the Japanese had turned the University of Santo Tomas in Manila into an internment camp for some 4,000 civilian prisoners. A significant proportion of the internees were women and children and many were also American. The majority had been interned in harsh conditions since 1941. General Douglas MacArthur was worried that the retreating Japanese might kill them, but his own front line was still 100 miles from Manila. On 31 January, he ordered Brigadier General William C. Chase to lead a flying column to the Philippine capital and rescue the prisoners – just like that. He had chosen the right man. Chase's column consisted of elements of the 1st Cavalry, tanks and the small number of infantry that could be carried with them.

Incredibly, by the early evening of 3 February, Chase's column had gone through or round every obstacle and opposition and reached the outskirts of Manila. By 9.00 pm, the lead tank had broken into the camp and most of the prisoners had been freed. However, some of the retreating Japanese guards, unable to make their escape, had barricaded themselves into the Education Centre, taking several hundred prisoners with them as hostages. Any further assault would clearly have come at a heavy price in prisoner casualties. Moreover, such an attack might have sparked off the kamikaze spirit in which many Japanese soldiers chose death before dishonour and prompted them to kill themselves and their prisoners with them. It was then that Chase showed that as well as courage and military skill he had cool nerves and an instinctive grasp of the essential elements of negotiation.

The captors were demanding that they march out with their weapons, a demand to which Chase could not agree without endangering his own men, and were threatening to kill their American hostages if that demand were not met. Despite the fact that the US general was in the heart of enemy country and subject at any time to a counter-attack, he settled down to negotiate for three days, firstly to calm down the nervous hostage-takers and then to talk them out of their threats and demands. His opening move was to invest the building in such a way that the option of a fighting retreat was closed to the enemy. Then, step by step, he persuaded the Japanese officer in command to back off from his initial stance. On the first day, the Japanese permitted the delivery of food and Red Cross supplies. On the second day, they demanded that Chase draw his tanks back from the front gate. The general agreed to do so, provided the Japanese allowed the seriously ill to be removed and US medical teams to tend to the rest. At a crucial moment, Chase threatened to launch a full-scale attack if a single American was hurt and, on the third day, the Japanese released all the children. Finally, they agreed to release the rest of their prisoners in return for being allowed to disperse, unarmed, into the city of Manila. Chase agreed. Moreover, he kept his word and did not obstruct the unarmed flight of the Japanese soldiers. The American front was now only 13 miles away, so the flying column headed swiftly back with its freed captives. Throughout the whole operation, Chase did not suffer a single casualty, among either troops or civilians. For a modest concession he had successfully negotiated his way to all his objectives.[1]

The Philippines have seen both some of the least and most successful attempts to free hostages, but the most peculiar of them all must surely be the case of the holiday divers snatched from the Malaysian resort of Sipadan island.

Again, strictly speaking, this case falls outside my own definition of a purely political hostage-taking in that ostensibly it was just a matter of ransom, but it was about far more than the enormous sums of money involved and it had a significant impact on the politics of the Philippines. This hostage-taking incident was a paradox. In order to pursue a wider political aim, the coerced, Libya, was not only backing the captor, Abu Sayyah, but paying the ransom.

On 23 April 2000, a mixed group of tourists was relaxing after a day's diving when a group of armed men came running towards them along the beach from the side closest to the jungle. Before they knew what was happening, two Finns, two Frenchmen, three Germans, a Lebanese, nine Malaysians and two South Africans, together with the two Philippinos ministering to their needs at that moment, found themselves on board a boat heading for their captors' headquarters on Jolo island, an hour's journey away. There were to be no more leisurely cool drinks for a long five months.

Their abductors were members of Abu Sayyaf, "Bearer of the Sword" in Arabic, dubbed a criminal gang of mere extortionists by the Philippine government. While they were, indeed, past masters of extortion by kidnap, they were also part of the wider movement of militant Islam, which was seeking an independent Muslim state in the south of the Philippine archipelago. The movement's founder, Abduragak Abubakar Janjalani, fled in 1991 to the Philippines from the fighting in Afghanistan, where he was reputedly an associate of Osama bin Laden. United States intelligence still believes Abu Sayyaf to be connected with the wider Al Qaida movement, but whether this is based on paranoia or hard evidence there is no means of knowing. No proof has been published as far as I am aware.

Abu Sayyaf came into being as a splinter group from the Moro National Liberation Front. Although never more than 500 strong and the smallest of the three armed groups seeking to create an independent Islamic state, the extreme violence of its activities gave it an impact greater than its size. In 1998, Janjalani was killed in a gun battle with the army and, after a fierce internal struggle, his brother, Khadafy Janjalani, emerged as leader, though the Sipadan kidnapping was organized by another leading figure known as "Commander Robot".

The unfortunate hostages were endlessly herded on foot and by boat about the jungles and small islands of the southern Philippines, as their captors tried to keep one jump ahead of the army. Every time a few soldiers got near to them, they were hustled off to the next village. President Estrada made no serious attempt at significant military intervention until August and September, near the end of their ordeal, for fear of endangering the hostages' lives. Even though they were never actively maltreated, the captives endured considerable hardship and deprivation. At various stages the governments of Malaysia and France interfered in the negotiating process on behalf of their own citizens, thus further muddying the already murky waters of the Philippine government's own attempts, while Gaddafi waited for the right moment to intervene himself.

At first glance, it looked as if Gaddafi had been completely outmanoeuvred by the hostage-takers and parted with a huge sum of money for very little. In fact he had achieved a "triple whammy".

Libya, the erstwhile international pariah on account of its funding and support of terrorism – including the Abu Sayyaf gang – was suddenly widely publicized as the champion of liberty and the saviour of victims of an Islamic hostage-taking.

At the same time, Gaddafi was now able openly to give massive support, in cash and in kind, to a Muslim terrorist organization in the guise of ransom payments made on humanitarian grounds. The cash went to buy weapons to fight the central government more effectively. The investment in a large number of social projects, schools and medical facilities, housing and mosques in Abu Sayyaf's parish enhanced its standing in this part of the archipelago and turned already considerable autonomy into virtual independence, for a while at least.

Finally, the pragmatic approach of the French to the kidnapping of its citizens – get them back safe and sound by whatever means are best to hand – gave Libya a powerful European apologist to assist its campaign for the lifting of UN sanctions and gained it invitations to international events held on French soil.* If all this is confusing, imagine the bewilderment of the hostages at finding themselves in Tripoli being embraced by Gaddafi on their way home.

This must surely be the only case where the same entity is, in effect, both captor [by proxy] and coerced [nominally]. A political hostage-taking indeed, and one in which, whatever the captives may have felt about it, Abu Sayyaf and Libya, captor and coerced, emerged both highly and equally satisfied.

Though Americans are the victims of political hostage-taking all over the world, they very rarely have to cope with it in their own country. When incidents do take place on American soil they are usually by crazy crusaders,

---

* *France enjoys this diplomatic ploy, its most recent being its invitation to Mr Mugabe. It is also thought that France itself paid a ransom for its two citizens, using Libya as a channel.*

such as the Symbionese Liberation Army, or are domestically political in as much that they are carried out by minorities who feel themselves to be unjustly treated by the system. In the case of the Hanafi Muslims,* the objective of the hostage-takers was a mixture of the political and the personal. "The political motives were secondary to the personal, but the negotiating task in many ways resembled that arising from a purely political terrorist incident."[2]

At mid-morning on 9 March 1977, people were going about their usual business in the B'nai B'rith building, an Islamic centre in downtown Washington, when a group of what appeared to be guitar-carrying musicians entered the building. Synchronously, as if on a conductor's down beat, the musicians opened their instrument cases and, in the long tradition of American gangsters, produced a variety of guns and a crossbow. The conductor appeared to be a madman screaming imprecations at the Black Muslims, who had killed five of his children and shot at his wives four years earlier, and at the judicial system that had exacted insufficient revenge. Hamaas Abdul Khalis and his men rounded up the occupants of the building, forced them to lie face down with their hands bound behind their backs and threatened to shoot them one at a time unless his rather incoherent demands were met. "Now they will listen to us – or heads will roll," he shouted as the anger that had festered all this time found vent.

The demands, it eventually transpired, were an odd mixture of the socio-political and the personal. The personal was clearly his demand that the leader of the imprisoned Black Muslim group be brought to him, almost certainly so that in the tradition of the blood feud, homicidal revenge could be exacted. Conceeding this was never even contemplated. Khalis obviously also felt that the social and judicial ethos of the United States was loaded against black Muslims in general. At that time he was probably right. He wanted what he saw as the injustice of his $750 fine for contempt of court during the Black Muslim trial to be acknowledged by repaying the money to him. He also demanded the withdrawal of a film, *Mohammed, Messenger of God*, which he regarded as both blasphemous and offensive, which by Islamic criteria it was.

To enhance his leverage, Khalis had arranged for his Hanafi associates to take over two other Washington buildings and their occupants a couple of hours after his own seizure. At one of them, the City Hall on 14th Street, a young journalist was killed by a shotgun blast to the chest when the building was taken. This treble seizure not only made it trebly difficult for the Washington police to decide what to do best, but was further complicated by the killing, usually the trigger for an immediate armed response. Fortunately, the Chief of

---

* *The Hanafi (Sunni) school of Islamic jurisprudence was founded by Abu Hanifa, who died in Iraq in 767 AD. Abu Hanifa's interpretation of Muslim law was extremely tolerant of the differences within Muslim communities. He also thought belief more important than practice.*

Police, Maurice Cullinane, was a perspicacious man. He not only realized that an assault would result in a massive loss of life while Khalis was in such an unstable state, but that as a representative of the very forces against which the Hanafi leader was protesting, to try to negotiate would only inflame the situation further. Like all the best leaders, he knew the right time to break the rules and that what he needed was negotiators whom Khalis would deem sympathetic to his aims. With the aid of the State Department he found three Muslim ambassadors[3] who were willing to undertake the task – the Egyptian and Pakistani ambassadors to the United States, Ashraf Ghorbal and Sahabzada Yaqub Khan, and later the Iranian ambassador to France, Ardeshir Zahedi.

Initially, this tactful ploy had little effect and on first contact with the ambassadors Khalis continued to rant and rave. When the ambassadors spontaneously quoted the *Koran* at him, he angrily told them that he knew it better than they did. However, what these early exchanges did was very important to the eventual outcome, for they gave Khalis the opportunity to vent a lot of pent-up steam to people he believed would sympathize with his grievances.

At their second attempt the ambassadors chose their Koranic texts more carefully. "Let not the hatred of some people in once shutting you out of the mosque lead you to transgression ... Fear Allah, for Allah is strict in punishment." But Khalis demonstrated that his boast about his knowledge of the *Koran* was not a vain one, meeting every quote with an answering quote and homing in on the subject of retribution.* Again, common ground was being established and they were at least singing from the same hymn sheet, if not from the same line of music. Moreover, the tactic of dialogue, alternating with periods of total isolation in which Khalis was left to stew in his own juice, seemed to be lowering the tension and making him more reasonable. Two placatory, but for the authorities not very significant, gestures were made – his $750 was returned to him and the showing of the objectionable film was suspended.[4] The efficacy of these tactics was demonstrated when the following day, Khalis asked to meet with the Pakistani ambassador to continue negotiations.

The problem was how, who and where. Khalis was still suspicious and scathing when it was suggested that he might like to come out unarmed to meet Yaqub Khan. A compromise was soon reached. The American public, through the medium of television,[5] was about to be treated to the bizarre spectacle of three Islamic ambassadors and two unarmed police officers sitting at one side of a table, in the middle of the lobby of the B'nai B'rith building, with an unarmed Khalis and his son-in-law on the other. Bizarre, but it worked. Ghorbal, trying to find a way for Khalis to save all-important

---

* *The Bible, it seems, is not the only holy book where every quote can be matched by its opposite.*

face, suggested he let them have the 30 most vulnerable hostages. To everyone's astonishment – perhaps even his own – Khalis offered to release the lot provided he was allowed to go home and "put his affairs in order" before handing himself over to the police. On the advice of the psychiatrists* supporting his negotiation, Cullinane decided that the hostage-taker was now in a sufficiently stable state of mind for this to be acceptable. Both Khalis and Cullinane kept their word. His protest made spectacularly public by the mass media, Khalis called off his troops in all three of the buildings that had been taken, went home on bail and having "set his affairs in order" gave himself up to the police, and in due course to a 41-year prison sentence. The siege was over without further bloodshed. It is to be hoped that both he and his accomplices were not sent to the same penitentiary as the Black Muslims.

That a crisis created by Muslims had been resolved by the voluntary intervention of other impressive and distinguished Muslims, served to educate the American public a little to the virtues of the ambassadors' nations and religion. Although the ambassadors were essential to obtaining a peaceful outcome, all the ultimate decisions were taken by the Chief of Police.

Outsiders were also called in to help resolve the seizure by South Moluccans of a train in the Netherlands on 2 December 1975.** Although this crisis was solved via negotiation, two of the hostages were killed by their captors – in a similar event ended by force in 1977 (see pages 114–17), none of the hostages were killed.

Like most morning newspaper journalists, the editor of *Het Nieuwsblad van het Noorden*, Gerard Vaders, was not an early starter, so he was seated in the train to Amsterdam from Groenigen making notes for the day's work when just after 10.00 am the train was hijacked. Vaders continued to make notes for some time, but now of what was taking place. That moment of shock is best described in his own words.

> 10:07. Just past Beilen. Door slammed open. The barrels of a rifle and a sten gun are pointed inside. Shots are heard, hard and dry. In a reflex movement someone reaches for a gun barrel – an act of recklessness that goes unpunished. Another shot; it misses. The colours of the South Moluccan republic are stuck onto the gun butts: red, green, white and blue. The hijackers are extremely nervous. Black woollen balaclavas over their faces so that only the eyes and nose can be seen. A lot of shouting and some more shots.[7]

* *One suggested that he gave himself up because he could not bear to urinate and defecate in front of other people.[6]*
** *Two days later, the Indonesian consulate in Amsterdam was seized in a tandem operation by six other members of the same group. One hostage died jumping from a window. Since this seizure was ended peacefully five days after the one under discussion, I have not examined it here.*

The spectacular hostage incident in September 1970 that set off a spate of seizures, when the PFLP blew up three skyjacked planes simultaneously at Dawson's Field in Jordan. The hostages were not harmed.

A happy Leila Khaled, pioneer PFLP skyjacker in 1969. She was captured by the British when her part of the Dawson's Field operation went wrong, but was released a few days later when hostage lives were threatened.

A rare instance of face-to-face negotiation with hostage takers following the seizure of nine members of the Israeli Olympic team at Munich in September 1972

One of the Palestinian hostage takers in Munich

Abou Daoud (centre) who planned the Munich hostage taking

Patti Hearst, the media billionaire's daughter kidnapped in February 1974 by the Symbionese Liberation Army

The iconic picture that went in every revolutionary's pocket; Patti Hearst taking part in a raid on a San Francisco bank two months after her abduction

Carlos the Jackal (centre) in his new guise for one of the most high profile seizures ever in December 1975 when all the OPEC oil ministers were taken hostage in Vienna

The pilots who flew Israeli commandos two thousand miles to carry out a daring rescue in Entebbe, Uganda in July 1976 receive a hero's welcome home. Of the skyjacked Jewish passengers only three died – one possibly murdered by Uganda's dictator Idi Amin. The Commando leader, Jonathan Netenyahu, was killed and a sergeant badly wounded

Captain John Testrake giving an impromptu press conference in June 1985 with a little encouragement from one of his captors

The Dominican Embassy siege in February 1980 in which over, the course of two months, the ambassadors held hostage (including US Ambassador Asencio shown here) largely negotiated their own release.

Sim Harris makes his escape from the burning Iranian Embassy in London in April 1980 as the SAS stage an assault to rescue the hostages held there.

Happy to be back. John McCarthy in August 1991 after 64 months as a hostage in Lebanon

After almost four years in solitary, Terry Waite, the irrepressible negotiator taken hostage in Lebanon, is one of the last to come home in November 1991

The forty Chechens who took 700 people hostage in a Moscow Theatre in October 2001
threatened to blow them all up if Russia did not withdraw from Chechnya.
The veiled women are wearing explosive belts

All the hostage takers were killed after a well staged rescue at the Moscow theatre, but 129 hostages
died from the narcotic gas used because there was no medical back-up

The driver of the train tried to shut the hijackers out of his cab and was shot, first of all wounded and then taken to the luggage van where he was killed. Shortly afterwards, when the captors wished to convey the impression that they were carrying out their threat to execute hostages if their demands were not met, they threw his body out of the train. No sooner had the hijackers taken control than they made their captives tape up newspapers over the windows so that those outside could not see the disposition of the captors inside. This also had the effect of turning the inside of the carriage into a permanent twilight zone. On the penultimate day of the siege, the Moluccans rather gave the game away by putting up black plastic bin bags in the part of the train they had made their base. One of the lessons to be learned in hostage situations is that as often as not hostage-takers do not behave logically. They also put heavy chains and padlocks on all the door handles and attached to them what appeared to be sticks of explosive. The hostages realized that if any attempt were made to release them by force, their captors would have ample time to kill them first. They prayed that the police would exercise restraint and their prayers were answered, for exemplary restraint was exercised, even when the police go-between was given a sound thump or two almost every time he put in an appearance. As a final obstacle, the captors took Vaders himself as the first in a series of hostages who were spread-eagled and chained across the entrance to the carriage. The Moluccans were preparing for a long siege.

The coerced, too, prepared themselves for a long and patient wait, if that was what was needed to obtain a peaceful outcome. The first step was to persuade the captors to accept a police telephone on which they could make their demands and negotiate if they were so inclined. These exchanges would be carefully monitored for clues as to what was happening inside the train. At first, the captors refused to negotiate and simply stated their demands: the release of Moluccan prisoners in Dutch and Indonesian jails; changes in Dutch policy towards their bid for independence; safe passage out of the country; and, of course, publicity for their cause. If these demands were not met, hostages would be killed and the usual deadline was given and at first passed, as usual, without incident.

The Dutch, with the advice of psychologists, had perfected the art of making minor concessions with a great deal of fuss in order to break down gradually the determination and resistance of the captors while never yielding on the major concessions. The police allowed in food and drink, and later medicine, blankets and disinfectant, but never in sufficient quantities to satisfy fully the needs of either the captives or the captors. Vaders attributed this to incompetence,[8] but it is much more likely to have been a deliberate ploy. Combined with the cold in an unheated train and the lack of water other than the drinking water sent in by the police, this strategy helped to undermine the morale of the hostage-takers. This strategy can be a risky one, however, for the hostages must suffer, too. Captors may be driven to desperate measures and the deleterious effect on the health of hostages can be considerable. By the end of the 13-day siege, several of the passengers were quite ill, despite the heroic ministrations of "Dr" Hans Prins, who not only tended to them physically, but kept up everyone's spirits by his energy, cheerfulness and the bold face he put on their predicament.

Eventually the police tactic worked, but not before two hostages had been shot. Robert de Groot, a young family man, had been particularly argumentative and aggressive when made to tape up the carriage windows. He was, therefore, chosen as the first victim. He was shot and thrown from the train, but was not, in fact, dead and survived to tell the tale. The second victim was not so lucky. E.J. Bierling was an even younger family man and had never been intended as the next sacrifice. It was Vaders who had originally been selected for this role. He asked his captors whether, before he was shot, he could send a message to his family via another hostage and they agreed, though they listened in to make sure that he was not up to any tricks. It was this eavesdropping that saved him. Vaders spoke about the troubles in his marriage and family life and that he and his wife were having a difficult time with his stepdaughter. He sent messages of advice, regret and love that touched the hearts of his captors. He had ceased to be just "the clever bastard with the note book" and became a human being with the same sort of problems that his captors experienced in their own private lives. When he stood up to go to his death they could not bring themselves to kill him and selected the unfortunate Bierling instead.

The process of negotiation unfolded slowly in parallel with the violence. On the second day of the siege, the Moluccans sent messages via hostages, including a Chinese boy, to the farmhouse where the police had set up their headquarters. They accepted the police phone line, which they must have known would be tapped, and supplemented it with a megaphone through which they announced their demands again and warned anyone who approached the train too closely to keep back. Next, they asked to speak to the President of their own Moluccan Youth Organization, Mr Manusama, and to two pastors, whom they asked to deliver a statement they had written to the Dutch press and demand its publication. The demand was ignored, as was that for a new train driver and an escape plane at Schipol, so on the third day they shot Bierling.

After that killing there were no more hostage deaths and it was eventually the captors who asked to negotiate, demanding that two specific prominent members of their community act on behalf of the authorities. Although this was unorthodox, the police sensibly agreed. In the meantime, all the passengers in the poorly guarded rear of the train had escaped and others had been voluntarily released so that, of the 52 passengers initially taken, only 23 remained in captivity during the latter part of the siege. The Moluccans became more lax by the day, usually carrying no weapons by day and leaving only two sleepy sentries to keep an eye on the prisoners and the police at night. The captives considered the possibility of trying to overcome these two and escape, but they decided to do nothing.

Then on 14 December, the 13th day of the siege, the constant undermining of demands and the effects of the negotiators from their own community who understood their motives, resulted in the sudden collapse of the Moluccans' resistance. Their demands were now reduced only to surrendering themselves to Manusama before being handed over to the police. This request was granted and the siege came to an end. The captors had at least gained much of the publicity they sought through the media. Fifty of the 52 captives had emerged alive – probably many more than would have survived an assault. The coerced had made nothing but the most minor concessions and had the satisfaction of seeing the hijackers sent to prison for 17 years.

In a final irony, when Prins had asked one of the captors whether he ought not to deactivate the explosives before giving themselves up, the man had laughed and gave him one of the supposedly deadly charges as a souvenir. They were dummies made of fireworks.[9]

While the Beilen siege was in its closing stages, another siege in another country had been brought to a successful conclusion in six days. I regard this example as the epitome of successful hostage negotiation.

On Saturday 6 December 1975, Detective Superintendent Peter Imbert* was taking a well-earned snooze in front of the television when the news broke. For many weeks, he had been second-in-command of a Scotland Yard anti-terrorist team that had been analysing the pattern of the IRA unit which had been bombing and murdering in central London for the previous 18 months. This unit had already shot Ross McWhirter, one of the twin brothers behind the *Guinness Book of Records*; killed the children's cancer specialist, Gordon Hamilton-Fairley, by blowing up his car in mistake for another, and an army bomb disposal expert defusing one of its devices and the same men had left seven dead and many more injured by throwing bombs packed with nails and bolts into several pubs and restaurants in and around London, among them Scott's in Mayfair.

During this rampage, Imbert and his immediate boss, Detective Chief Superintendent Jim Neville, had gradually built up a picture of how the killers operated and, step by step, drawn a net more tightly round them. Although the police did not know exactly how many men were involved, they knew this

This account is based on an interview with Lord Imbert, who became, appropriately, Lord Lieutenant of the City of London.

gang always began an operation by stealing an old Ford Cortina. The gunmen did not make bomb attacks in wet weather because their explosives were detonated by electric batteries and they might have killed themselves if the rain had shorted the wiring. They struck in a limited radius from the centre of London between 7.30 pm and 10.30 pm, but apparently seldom at weekends. In other words, their attacks were meticulously planned. So, however, were the police countermeasures.

A cordon of eight personnel carriers with armed officers was set up in a circle with a one-mile radius during the high risk hours at points that gave rapid access to the centre of the city. Within the target area itself, 500 pairs of plainclothes policemen armed only with radios patrolled near the likely targets – even on Saturdays! One of these was Scott's.

Imbert had a hunch that, although this well-known restaurant had been bombed once before, the IRA would be unable to resist the implicit challenge of a "toffee-nosed" diner who had loudly declared after the first incident that he was damned if he would let the IRA drive him away from his favourite watering hole. Sure enough, Detective Inspector Henry Dowdswell and a constable colleague spotted an old Ford Cortina rounding the end of the road in the early evening of Saturday 6 Dcember 1975. They radioed New Scotland Yard with the details and the armed squads were activated. The IRA men opened fire on Scott's, then, realizing they had been spotted, raced off without damaging more than the long-suffering plate-glass window of the restaurant. Dowdswell and his colleague commandeered a taxi and set off in pursuit – the first time the police had been close enough to give chase in 18 months. The IRA members opened fire on the taxi, putting two shots through the windscreen. Undeterred, the driver, who later received an award for his bravery, stuck to his task. Caught in Alma Close, a cul-de-sac, and realizing they could not shake off their pursuers, the IRA men abandoned their vehicle and ran off on foot.

By now the armed officers had arrived and opened fire which was returned by the IRA men. Caught in the crossfire, Dowdswell* and his colleague prudently took cover. The gunmen, splitting into two groups, dashed down an alleyway eventually leading into Balcombe Street, and realizing the armed police were close behind, ran into a block of flats at number 22.

Hammering on a randomly chosen door on the first floor they grabbed Mrs Matthews when she answered it, and holding a gun to her head threatened to shoot her if the police did not back off. Her husband, Mr John Matthews, a retired postal worker, had gone out onto his balcony to see what all the hullaballoo was about, little realizing that he would be spending the next six days in his own front room as a hostage of the gunmen.

---

* Ironically, Dowdswell died a year later of a heart attack.

This was the situation that the television newsreader announced before the sleeping Imbert. His wife and sister-in-law discussed whether or not to wake the exhausted policeman, but their debate was cut short by Jim Neville's urgent telephone call for Imbert to hasten to the scene of the siege. On arrival, the young officer found himself landed with the unenviable task of acting as negotiator.

Little more than two months earlier, the police had brought the Spaghetti House siege in Knightsbridge, London, to a safe and successful conclusion. The three perpetrators, led by Frank Davies, a Nigerian purporting to belong to an organization called the Black Liberation Front, had held nine Italian waiters hostage for six days before releasing them all unharmed. However, though various political demands were made, Spaghetti House was a robbery gone wrong rather than a deliberate political hostage-taking. The only IRA hostage precedent Peter Imbert had to go on was the kidnapping of Dutch businessman Dr Tiede Herrema in County Limerick, Ireland, in October that year. Those captors had demanded the release of three colleagues from Portlaoise prison, but the Irish Justice Minister had turned them down flat, arguing that to accede to their demands would endanger the state. After a hunt of less than three weeks the Garda had traced the IRA unit and its hostage to an end-of-terrace house on an estate in County Kildare, where they were surrounded. Seventeen days later, the captors unexpectedly dropped their demands, freed their hostage and gave themselves up.

The Met anti-terrorist branch was quick to seek Garda advice, but could not gauge its relevance until the numerous uncertainties surrounding the Balcombe Street siege could be cleared up. Once the flat had been surrounded and the adjacent area cleared for public safety, the essential first step was to find out what was going on inside number 22.

How many hostages were there? Scotland Yard had misheard the captors' initial 999 call and thought at first that a child was involved — a mistake that was not remedied until several neighbours had been interviewed. How were the hostages coping with the situation? Mrs Matthews was known to be of a nervous disposition and there were fears that she might panic and make a foolish move. How many gunmen were there? Some witnesses had reported three men entering number 22, others five, still others four. How were the captors armed? Did they have automatic weapons, grenades or explosives as well as the handguns with which they had fired on the police?

Which rooms were they occupying and how aware were they of the nature and proximity of the forces that were besieging them? Was the initial demand for £20,000 and a getaway plane a genuine sticking point or a panicky opening bid like that at Spaghetti House in September? How mentally stable were the captors? Was psychosis, as well as political ideology, likely to play a part in their behaviour?

Imbert's first need was to establish communication with whichever of the captors was acting as spokesman and then to build trust by scrupulously fulfilling any promises made, however trivial they might seem.

On the Sunday morning Imbert spoke to Mrs Matthews and managed to reassure her that all would be well. So much so that O'Connel, the leader of the unit,* refused to let her speak to anyone again. In any case, as O'Connel had been using the house phone to call Scotland Yard and the press, it was cut off. Shortly afterwards a radio telephone was lowered from the flat above and taken in through the siege-flat window, thus putting all means of communication with the outside world in police hands. For three days, Imbert and O'Connel circled round each other conversationally like a pair of shy lovers. Soon they were using Christian names, though O'Connel did not use his real one, but called himself Tom. When Imbert asked him the names of the others in a rather obvious ploy to find out how many gunmen there were, he even managed to make a joke and replied "Tom, Dick and Paddy!"

Though not every approach yielded results, Imbert gradually filled in the picture inside the flat. That there were four captors was deduced from the sandwich order when food was eventually allowed in. This deduction was gradually confirmed from constant observation of all the windows in the flat. That the captors were using only the living room became apparent when O'Connel refused to go to the kitchen for water for Mrs Matthews because he believed it was occupied by police. In fact he was convinced that "your fellows are all over the place", although this was not the case, as any listening-in was being done from the contiguous flat. Bottled water was sent in much later as part of the process of creating control, dependency and trust.

All the time the two-way talk was being recorded and carefully analysed by Dr Peter Scott, the psychologist advising the police. This analysis was critical in assessing the state of mind of the gunmen and determining the best course of action. Were they weakening or were they getting hyped up to the point where they might act recklessly and kill their hostages?

By the third afternoon, O'Connel must have suspected something of the kind for he suddenly hurled the radio telephone out of the window. Imbert switched to the loudhailer and now began to use this much more public dialogue as a means of undermining the gunmen's morale by calling their actions "kids' stuff" and wondering aloud what the IRA Chief of Staff, Dathai O'Connel, would think of such a pathetic performance. Imbert was banking on the fact that this IRA unit was on the back foot for the first time and would be demoralized rather than infuriated. These men had never been pursued before, let alone fired on and driven to hole up on unprepared ground with random hostages who had little leverage value.

* *Martin O'Connel, Eddie Butler, Harry Duggan and Hugh Doherty.*

Imbert was only too well aware of the risk attached to this approach, a wrong word could provoke one of the gunmen into doing something desperate to assert his machismo, but in consultation with Scott it was decided that this would be the most fruitful line to pursue.

In any case, the SAS had been called in from the outset – a useful rehearsal, as it turned out, for the Iranian embassy siege 15 months later. Quartered at the nearby Chelsea barracks, they had already built a model of the flat at number 22. The Commissioner, with Home Office authorization, was ready to send them in at the first sign of impending violence or of the captors' morale being so low that their resistance would be ineffectual. It was, however, particularly important at this relatively early stage in the mainland terror campaign not only to save the lives of the hostages, but to secure prisoners who could be interrogated about the structure and tactics of the IRA units operating in Britain. A negotiated surrender was the aim. And this, on the sixth day, was achieved by a combination of factors.

The initial wrong-footing and the pressure imposed on the captors, the establishing of trust and dependency, the use of ego–diminishing dialogue, the constant pressure (Jim Neville took over from Imbert at night when things were quieter) and finally the realization by the captors that the SAS, who already had a formidable reputation, could storm the flat any moment, all contributed to O'Connel's decision to release the hostages and give themselves up.

The gunmen's awareness of the SAS threat came indirectly through a radio broadcast and was one of the relatively few instances when use by the media of information gleaned about the tactics of a siege benefited rather than endangered the hostages. It is hard to escape the suspicion, despite denials at the time, that the police, having established an open, mutually co-operative relationship with the media, used it to put pressure on the hostage-takers.

What of the outcome for the participants? The IRA men, having set out demanding ransom and transport, ended up with a square meal and a long stretch in prison. They spent 23 years of their life sentences in British jails before being transferred to Portlaoise in Ireland and were released as part of the "Peace Process" in April 1999. While in the Irish prison, they were let out for a day to attend a Sinn Fein conference where they received a hero's welcome. Imbert took all this philosophically as an inevitable element in the effort to find a solution to the violence in Northern Ireland though, as he said, "I would like to have shown the delegates pictures of the bodies of the people their heroes blew to bits. Perhaps they would not have clapped so loudly."

Much is rightly made of the traumatic effects of being held hostage, but we hear little of the effect on those responsible for trying to secure their release. Imbert's success at Balcombe Street propelled him to the highest ranks of Britain's police force, but he would find himself lying awake at night for many months afterwards replaying the negotiations in his head.

His wife tried to persuade him to relax and sleep, but it was a long time before he was able to dispel the acute awareness that something he had said to O'Connel might have triggered a fatal reaction rather than a positive one. As for the hostages whose release he secured, they eventually retired to Abingdon, but not before Mrs Matthews had expressed her dislike of Peter Imbert for "being much too kind to those men".

Other Negotiated Solutions with Interesting Implications:

28 September 1975, London	Three Nigerians of the Black Liberation Front seize nine Italian waiters in the Spaghetti House restaurant in Knightsbridge, London, and hold them in the basement for six days. They demand financial support for black schools and political groups and an aircraft to fly them out of Britain. Their demands are refused. Listening devices are inserted surreptitiously and psychologist Peter Scott analyse their mental state in their uncomfortable and claustrophobic hideout. False information is fed to them through a co-operative radio and press media. Demoralized, they surrender unconditionally on day six.
3 October 1975, Ireland	Dr Tiede Herrema, MD of a foreign-owned factory, is kidnapped by two IRA members at Castletroy on his way to work. On 21 October, both he and the hostage-takers are traced to a council house on Monasterevin estate. Herrema is being held in an upstairs bedroom. After 17 days of negotiation, Herrema is released and the captors surrendered. They are given 15- and 20-year prison sentences which Herrema says are too long.
May–October 1984, London–Libya	When police woman Yvonne Fletcher is shot on 17 April outside the Libyan embassy in London, a number of Libyans are arrested and charged with terrorist offences. In retaliation, Gaddafi takes four Englishmen, two engineers and two academics, hostage. Terry Waite, with

only the reluctant consent of the Archbishop of Cantebury, Dr Runcie, whose special envoy he is, goes to Libya in October 1984. In a series of meetings with Gaddafi as he tours his country, Waite manages to cross the Arabic-English language barrier and secure the release of the hostages. Part of the deal is better treatment for Libyans in Britain and, likewise, Britons in Libya.

November 1992, Brazil	After years of torture, murders and expropriations of their reserved territory by outsiders, the Guajajara Indians in the state of Maranhao take 82 hostages and set up roadblocks. They demand punishment for the murderers and that outsiders and an illegal settlement be removed from their lands. As previous promises have been broken, the Indians insist on an agreement being made with the national Minister of Justice to meet the demands within 30 days. The hostages are released after a week.
29 December 1992, Thailand	Four Black September members seize the Israeli embassy in Bangkok and six hostages, including the ambassador and two women. General Choonhavan surrounds the embassy with tanks and secures the release of the hostages without a fight after 19 hours.
18 March 1995, Sudan	An Ethiopian jet and 92 passengers are taken hostage by five gunmen. Negotiation consists of security forces saying that if they did not give in then force would be used. Twenty-four hours later, the gunmen surrender and release their hostages.
28 July 2000, Brazil	Some 50 members of the Caiapo tribe seize 16 Brazilian tourists sport-fishing in their reserve. They demand the resumption of demarcation and protection of their tribal lands. The hostages are released after a week's negotiation after the

	Justice Minister agreed to their demands. However, the mayor of a nearby town within the occupied land declared, "Who is the macho who's going to throw me out of here? I'm going to defend my land with bullets."
27 April 2001, Sudan	Ethiopian jet and 51 passengers hijacked. Hijackers surrender the same day after Interior Minister "extends to them alternatives, which are not very attractive". They are promised asylum rather than extradition to Ethiopia, but not immunity for their crime.
2 April 2002, Bethlehem, Israel	When is a hostage not a hostage? Some 200 Palestinians, 50 of them armed, are holed up in the Church of the Nativity. The Israeli army says they are wanted "terrorists" and are holding the priests as hostages. The Palestinians claim that most of the armed men inside the church were members of the Palestinian security forces who have taken refuge from Israeli troops with no intentions of holding hostages. Some of the Franciscans support the Israeli contention, others the Palestinian. The Franciscan leadership in Rome charge that the Israeli army was trying to legitimize an "imminent" attack on the Church of Nativity by declaring the friars inside as hostages. The Israelis claim that the Palestinians' action have turned the church "into a legitimate military objective and abused the immunity of sacred sites". After 37 days, everyone is free to leave. Twenty-six of the Palestinians are deported to Gaza and 13 are exiled to Europe.

Chapter Ten

Negotiating

hy negotiate with hostage-takers at all? There is a school of thought that believes it is wrong to do so under any circumstances, on moral rather than tactical grounds and regardless of any consequent loss of life.

> Negotiating with terrorists [instead of calling for their surrender] implies a relationship between equals that cannot be morally countenanced, unless one views terrorism as morally acceptable. In such negotiations the terrorist is given privileges ordinarily denied to law-abiding citizens, privileges like access to important officials and to the mass media. Honouring agreements reached with terrorists overlooks the glaring circumstance that the agreements were coerced, and so have no moral or legal validity. To keep faith with terrorists is to strengthen faith in terror.[1]

Subscribers to this belief regard eschewing violence and force as contemptibly weak and many police officers who have been trained and conditioned to apprehend criminals wherever possible, find negotiating, and perhaps releasing them, an almost insurmountably difficult change.[2] There is a subset of this school that permits ostensible negotiation, but only as a ruse to lull the captors into a false and temporary sense of security in which they will become easier prey for the rescuing forces. That captors and captives may both die in such an assault is treated as a by-product of policy. Even though the negotiator is responsible for preserving the lives of the hostages, he is primarily the agent of the coerced and, along with the Incident Commander, must ultimately act as such, whatever his personal preferences.

The followers of the no-negotiations school labour under a misapprehension. "To regard negotiating itself as a concession is mistakenly to equate talking with yielding."[3] Certainly, publicly to declare that there can be no negotiation, or to send a negotiator with nothing to concede is to condemn hostages to death, as Nixon did with his diplomats in Khartoum.[4]

However, it is not only the state that can be intransigent. Some hostage-takers have neither the desire nor the intention to negotiate, or even communicate. When that is the case there are two possibilities. The captors want to die, or at least to have expressed their willingness to die, in order to make a spectacular impact on behalf of their cause (or crazy ideology), or alternatively they want to make a gesture that will have the same effect before giving themselves up without resistance. It will usually become apparent within a few hours, a day or so at most, which of the two alternatives the coerced are faced with, for gestures are seldom prolonged. If the negotiator has death-wish captors to deal with, his task verges on the impossible.

> People who have decided to die do not feel threatened by death. They would rather die than live with what they think of as unbearable pain. They are difficult people to negotiate with because they have no need to live. Without the need to live, there is rarely something with which the negotiator can bargain.[5]

In these circumstances the negotiator has little option but to try to bargain for the release of as many hostages as possible – in exchange for publishing a manifesto, for example – and to use his skills to facilitate an assault. The problem he has is to decide if the apparently suicidal captors are bluffing or not. In the light of the spate of suicide bombings in the first two years of the 21st century, the probability that they are not bluffing has increased.

Setting aside ethical arguments, the fact remains that the great majority of sieges, whether political or criminal, are brought to an end by negotiation. Moreover, the proportion of hostages who meet their deaths at the hands of their captors in negotiated conclusions is a fraction of the proportion that do so at the hands of hostage-takers and rescuers in political incidents which are ended by force. Simply on humanitarian grounds then, it is probably worth attempting to negotiate in most hostage incidents. These fall into two categories – planned and accidental. Most political hostage-taking is planned and presupposes that the hostage-takers want something from the coerced. That something may not be apparent at first, as declared goals, or even minimal requirements, are quite often not the same thing as real aims.

An accidental hostage-taking occurs when the captor was intent on some other goal – a bombing or robbery, for example – and has been forced by unanticipated circumstances to abandon that goal and to take hostages as an impromptu means of trying to avoid either death or capture. Because both sides have been caught on the wrong foot in such situations, the tensions tend to be higher at first than in planned events, so one of the negotiator's initial tasks is to try to reduce that tension to a level where rational discussion can replace any instincts and emotions that may result in hostages being killed precipitately.

Regardless of whether the incident is planned or accidental, if negotiation is chosen as the means of resolution it will usually unfold in four phases: contact, bargaining, agreement and conclusion. The first is comparatively short, lasting a day or two and often less, though its unfinished tasks may run over into the second phase, which may vary from hours to months. The third and fourth phases normally last only a matter of minutes and should not only be kept quite distinct from each other, but also from phase two. In rare instances, there may be an anxious interval between agreement and conclusion, particularly if safe passage has been agreed and the arrangements for it are complicated.

The success of a negotiation will not only depend on how well these four phases are handled, but on how well they have been prepared for by any state that is a potential subject for coercion of this kind. The long-established British model, COBRA, is a good one and most developed countries, among which I include India and China, now have similar hostage and terrorist incident-planning bodies that can be activated in minutes and hours rather than in days. COBRA's role is purely strategic. It establishes a clear command and responsibility structure for each incident, while leaving the appointment of trained personnel and tactics to the organizations – usually the relevant police authority and special forces group that have been called in to deal with it. It lays down the policy parameters within which the negotiator and the Incident Commander must work and is the final arbiter if either wishes to depart for tactical reasons from the agreed procedure. It authorizes the necessary physical resources to manage the incident, but does not get involved in their detailed deployment unless that itself becomes contentious, if, for example, the police wish to try to continue to negotiate and the special forces feel that any further delay would make their "success" less likely. COBRA is headed by a politician, the Home Secretary, and so is likely to favour political priorities, to wish to be seen to "be doing something" rather than prolong the invisible process of negotiation. In the Netherlands, the chairman of the emergency committee is the Minister of Justice. In Germany and Israel, it is often the Chancellor or Prime Minister, but whoever chairs the committee, its tone is set by the highest political authority. As we saw at Princes Gate, it was Margaret Thatcher who dictated the "no prisoners" policy.

But if preparation by the highest authorities in the coerced country is one ingredient, there are other prerequisites to a successful outcome. The first, as we have seen above, is that the hostage-takers should wish to live and that the coerced should have sufficient force available to make it highly probable that they will die if force has to be used. Another is an acceptable means and mode of communication, a suitable communicator on the side of the coerced and a decision-maker willing to talk among the captors. Finally, each side needs to have something that the other wants and may be willing to exchange.

There is one further health warning before any so-called rules of engagement can be considered – there are no hard and fast rules! There is a substantial body of accumulated experience which suggests that certain conditions will obtain results more often than not and that certain actions will work more often than not, but there are no magic formulae that, if followed faithfully, will automatically yield the desired result. What may have worked in one case could easily precipitate a tragedy in another. There are only general principles against which specific tactics can be assessed and which may provide shortcuts to crisis analysis when time is short. A preconceived framework based on accumulated experience serves the same useful purpose as the pilot's pre-take-off checklist, which he should go through by means of a printed sheet rather than from memory. This ensures that nothing essential is overlooked in the pressure of the moment. Once airborne, the pilot may have to respond flexibly to emergencies and deviations from the norm – icing, engine failure and so on. The hostage negotiator is in a similar situation and a too-rigid adherence to prescribed theories of negotiation can equally lead to disaster.

Normal negotiation entails the recognition that all parties to it will gain more by negotiation than by confrontation and that to reach a solution some concessions will have to be made by each party. The process requires dialogue and an understanding of the other's point of view. The negotiator is like an actor who, while immersing himself in a role to carry conviction, must keep a part of himself sufficiently detached to exercise the stagecraft necessary to the mechanics of the play. The negotiator must empathize and understand, but not sympathize and identify with the captors if he is to be effective. He has to act in the belief that the negotiators from both sides are partners seeking to resolve a conflict rather than advance their own interests.[6] Because that approach is not always acceptable to either the captors or the coerced in a hostage situation for reasons of policy, diplomacy or ideology, normal negotiation may degenerate into abnormal negotiation.

An abnormal negotiation is one in which one or both parties have no intention under any circumstances of conceding anything from the outset. That this is the mode of negotiation in any given hostage situation may not be apparent for some time. In such negotiations one party, and sometimes both, would prefer self-destruction and the loss of everything to giving up anything. Such negotiation consists not of genuine dialogue, but of a series of parallel monologues that can never meet and which escalate both mutual resentment and misunderstanding until violence ensues. Donohue succinctly distinguished between the two modes of negotiation by describing normal negotiation as "moving together" and abnormal as "moving apart", the one conducive to co-operation and the other likely to lead to confrontation.[7]

To see hostage-taking as a plus-zero game where only the authorities or the hostage-takers can win is to reduce to a bloodbath a ritual that can otherwise work out in exchanging face and political symbols for human lives.[8]

These ritual and symbolic aspects are more important than the material in many cases. We should be prepared in a democracy with a free press to publish views with which we disagree or which we find immoral and reprehensible. Publication or broadcast is often all that is necessary to secure a peaceful surrender by the captors. We should always counter their arguments with our arguments rather than with the lives of hostages. From the various incoherent, long-winded and irrational captor manifestos I have read, that should not prove too difficult. As Milton said: "I cannot praise a fugitive and cloister'd virtue, unexercised and unbreathed, that sallies not out and sees her adversary."[9]

Every political hostage incident today will take place in the public eye through the distorting lens of the mass media. This will create an apparent conflict of interest between the impatient journalist who wants to get his story out fast and first and the patient negotiator who needs time and privacy to do his job properly. It is up to the Incident Commander or his spokesman to protect the negotiator from media pressure, while making as much use of the latter as he can. Throughout the preceding chapters we have seen how the press, radio and television – and now the Internet – can play a constructive or a destructive role in a hostage situation. If the Incident Commander can appreciate the needs of the media and give journalists as much as he can as soon as he can without jeopardizing the operation and promise a full story once the incident is over, he will find that 99 per cent of editors and producers will behave responsibly.

That hostage-takers themselves are often sophisticated, well-educated people who have made a careful study of the strategies and tactics employed by the coerced in previous incidents – their strengths and weaknesses - can be seen in many of the cases described in this book. It therefore behoves the negotiator and the Incident Commander to be flexible. If one tactic does not work, consider another. Alternatively, they may have to judge whether the chosen tactic, even if not working in obvious practical terms, may be having the desired psychological effect. Being prepared for an event does not necessarily entail being able to cope with it.[10] Those studying terrorist tactics or training hostage negotiators have to keep running if they want to stay ahead.

During the "contact" phase, the negotiator must establish who the hostage-takers are, who their spokesperson is, who their leader is and how much authority he has. (It is, fortunately, generally absolute.) What is his state of mind? What do the captors really want and to what lengths are they prepared to go to try to get it? How willing are they to communicate and negotiate? He

— it is still almost without exception a he — must convince the captors that negotiation is preferable to violence for both sides, but that if he has to he can bring an overwhelming force to bear. He should adopt a velvet-glove approach, because if the negotiation is to succeed he has to convince the captors that he is not only credible but trustworthy.

In practical terms and at the same time, the coerced, acting through an Incident Commander, must isolate the locus of the incident — building, aircraft, train etc — from any contact with the outside world except through the negotiator. The Commander must provide a high-quality and preferably unique channel through which this communication can be made, while at the same time cutting off all other possible means of communication — no megaphones allowed, as at Beilen, for instance. There have been many incidents in which the captors' ability to communicate separately with journalists, the families of captives and maverick politicians has made the task of negotiation much more difficult and sometimes impossible. It is very rare for a negotiator to be able to talk to captors face to face, so a separate police phone line that can be monitored and both activated and deactivated at the negotiator's will is ideal. The quality of the line is important, not only so that what the captor says can be accurately monitored, but so that the tone of voice can be interpreted by specialists in this field. They can often evaluate a captor's state of mind by his choice of vocabulary, pitch, tone, pace, breathing and so on and thus judge whether a negotiation is going well or if it is time for force to be used.[11] Correspondingly, the style of the negotiator's communication must be as close to the leading captor's in accent, vocabulary, language and cultural assumption as is possible without being perceived as patronizing. As we saw in the *Achille Lauro* and Testrake incidents, lack of a common language proved a serious obstacle to a peaceful solution. The choice of negotiator is critical. It would not be much use sending an Ulster Unionist to negotiate with the IRA or an Israeli with the PFLP, but it goes much further than that rather crude distinction. The ability of the negotiator to empathize with the captors should be an important consideration when choosing him. The professional negotiator is rarely a qualified psychologist, but that does not matter provided he has that expertise available to advise him, and has a reasonable knowledge of the political, religious and social context in which he is working.

There are two situations in which it may be neither practicable nor wise to have a trained negotiator in touch with the captors. The first tends to occur when a hostage incident is accidental. In this situation the captor may already have established a link with the person who happened to be on the spot — beat policeman, journalist or even a released hostage — before the professionals could reach the scene. If a sound rapport has been established between captors and ad hoc negotiator, it may be unwise to sever the link. It would be better just to put the professional at his shoulder to advise and guide.

It has long been an axiom of hostage negotiation theory that the negotiator and Incident Commander should never be the same person and that both should have been specifically selected and trained for the eventuality of hostage incidents. Negotiators should not command and Commanders should not negotiate. To surrender this division of responsibility forfeits a means of procrastination with which a captor may find it hard to argue. It also imposes intolerable stress on what are already two extremely stressful jobs. There are some situations where the dual or even triple role is unavoidable. For example, in an aircraft hijacking the captain is hostage, intermediary-negotiator and the commander responsible for the safety of his passengers. This difficulty does not arise in the seizure of a building or train unless, as was the case with the Dominican embassy seizure in Colombia in 1980 (see pages 68–70), one or more of the hostages are of sufficient authority for the captors to wish them to act as negotiators.

The other set of circumstances in which distinct boundaries between roles may have to be blurred is when the hostage-takers themselves will only speak to a particular person or the holder of a particular office. If such a demand is made, it should be refused, or rather evaded, as good negotiators try to avoid outright refusals. To grant this not only puts the politicians on the spot (a place they seem to find extremely uncomfortable), but greatly diminishes negotiating options.

If the request is simply to go through another respected member of the same ethnic group, or to speak to the ambassador of a particular nation whose language, religion and culture may be similar to the captors', then it should probably be granted. The exception would be if the ambassador in question would clearly be partisan, as the Iraqi ambassador, whose country armed the captors, would have been in the Princes Gate case. Unless the professional negotiator has a thorough knowledge and understanding of those three elements then he is unlikely to get as far with the captors as those non-professionals, even if he might not share UN negotiator Giandomenico Picco's rather extreme view that: "Nobody is a professional in these matters. There is no science to it, no assurances, no certainty of anything."[12]

Using an amateur negotiator is not without risk. We have seen in the case of the skyjacking in Malta (see pages 86–7), for example, what can happen when an unskilled person, even if he is prominent and distinguished, takes on the role of negotiator. However, in the cases studied in the previous chapter, outsiders were called in with some success either to negotiate or to mediate between negotiators and political hostage-takers. Those examples of such people show them all to have been men in whose normal occupations – diplomacy or politics – the ability to negotiate, to give and to take is a prerequisite for success. The Hanafi siege is a good example of where allowing the exception proved wise, especially as the Incident Commander still retained overall control of the situation. I believe that had COBRA wished to resolve Princes Gate peacefully it would have acceded to the captors' request to negotiate through the Jordanian or Algerian ambassador and that such a move might have worked.

All the problems described above have to be resolved as early as possible in phase one of a hostage incident and that is not easy. The negotiator is usually dealing with complete strangers whose names he does not even know. He is highly unlikely at the contact stage of a political case to have any psychological profile of any of the captors, though if properly trained he should at least have a general awareness of their likely political stance and the reasons for it. He should know whether members of the IRA, PFLP, Baader-Meinhof, Tupamaros or any other of the major hostage-taking groups are likely to be operating in his patch. There can, however, be no reasonable preparation for dealing with such obscure and confused political stances as those taken by the Khuzestanis or the Symbionese Liberation Army.

While he is negotiating, the negotiator must never forget that the mind games he is playing are deadly and can have fatal consequences for others. At the same time, he must not let that thought prey on his mind to the extent that he cannot negotiate with sufficient detachment. For this reason, if it becomes necessary to change a genuine negotiation into a time-gaining ruse, it is probably as well not to let the negotiator know any of the tactical details of the planned assault. That way he cannot give anything away inadvertently and can concentrate on distracting the captors. He must keep talking, lie to them about such matters as delays in transport or the distant release of prisoners that cannot be confirmed. This will be a difficult adjustment for him to make, for the essence of his exchanges with the captors, in phase one particularly, will have been to create credibility and trust by fulfilling his promises promptly and to the letter. The irony is that the more effectively he has done this the more convincing a liar he will be if the necessity for lies arises. A classic example of this is the transition in aims in the Princes Gate siege [see pages 117–21].[13]

In the initial contact phase, establishing who the captors are is rarely a problem for they inevitably announce this proudly or defiantly when making their demands. Establishing the true nature of those demands, however, is another matter. Negotiation, whether normal or abnormal, is a ritual in which both sides take positions as an initial ploy. The closer the negotiator's stated position is to his real one in some ways the better, though if too rigid it reduces his ability to make apparent concessions. The captor's initial demand will usually contain elements that even he must know cannot be met – such as a change of government – and others that are negotiable – such as prisoner release and safe passage from the country – and still others that should prove acceptable to the coerced without too much difficulty, such as the publication of a manifesto. The difficulty to start with is knowing whether the impossible demands are made simply as a bargaining move or are indicative of an absolute refusal to negotiate.

We have seen that most captor groups contain one or more members who are more or less psychotic personalities, but their leader may be perfectly rational. In any case, I rather like Schlosberg's dictum that there is "no such thing as a psycho". Rather, all behaviour is understandable, goal-oriented, pleasure-seeking and problem-solving in nature.[14] I do not, however, share the FBI's view[15] that political and criminal sieges do not differ in any important respect. They differ fundamentally on what the captors want and expect to get from them.

Finding out how many hostage-takers there are and how they are armed can also be hard at first. Well-managed dialogue helps, as do tricks like asking for a specific order from each hostage when food and drink is sent in. The best means of ascertaining weaponry is close observation, analysis of any previous fire-fight and the information provided by any observant hostages who may have been released.

Establishing these physical facts is the easier of the negotiator's tasks, getting into the mind of the captors, and particularly that of their leader, is far more difficult and in many ways more essential. In a planned incident, the negotiator needs constantly to bear in mind that the typical political captor, as Hacker puts it, "... appears normal ... He is neither a dummy nor a fool, a coward nor a weakling, but a professional – well trained, well prepared, and well disciplined in the habit of blind obedience."[16] To get into the mind of the decision-making captor the negotiator must:

(1)   Hear what he means as well as listen to what he says.

(2)   Understand what he feels as well as hear what he means.

(3)   Persuade him that understanding can lead to agreement.

(4)   Judge whether an agreement will hold till the incident is safely concluded.

Hearing what the captor means is much harder than listening to his words. It requires total concentration rather than what most of us do most of the time – listen with half an ear while we think about what we are going to say next. Hearing properly requires an ability to detect the slightest nuances of phraseology, to infer shifts in mood and intent from shifts in vocabulary and syntax – from effing and blinding to more specific terminology, from passive to active tense, for example. Then there are the changes in the physical aspects of speech to which we have already referred. Although the negotiator will probably have professional help to analyse these, in the course of a quick-fire, critical conversation he will have to use his own judgement without reference to the experts. As well as hearing what is said, he has to manage his own speech very carefully so as not to be misheard himself and to sustain a constructive dialogue. He must avoid giving offence or challenging, he must use "and" instead of "but", "how about" instead of "certainly not". His questions must be open ended so as to avoid yes or no answers and he must sense when to be informal and friendly and when to be formal and judicial – Geoffrey Jackson was a master of this. All these skills employed with tact will elicit informative responses from the captor.

Having elicited informative answers and carefully heard both the overt and the hidden in them, the negotiator must be able to put what he has heard in context if he is to understand. This requires awareness of cultural differences, for example, between those that are oblique and those that are direct. To speak too directly to someone in whose culture it is considered polite to deal in parable and metaphor is to appear crude and aggressive. To employ circumlocution and analogy to someone whose cultural norm is plain speaking will be to appear evasive and insincere. These differences can be acute between Western and Eastern nations. As Terry Waite pointed out to me:[17]

> You need to have a good appreciation and a good understanding of inter-cultural situations and inter-cultural communication and a certain degree of sensitivity to other people's feelings, an ability to understand another point of view without necessarily agreeing with it.

It was the repeated failure of the United States to appreciate the cultural context in which they and Khomeini's team were negotiating that made their attempts to gain the release of their hostages held in Iran in 1979–80 so fruitless.

The same tact is required in dealing with the matter of "loss of face". It is often suggested that people from eastern cultures are much more concerned about this than those from western cultures. I do not think this is true. It is simply that the form taken by that loss of face differs, but in both cases it is the loss of self-image, "the positive social identity in interaction with others" that is at stake.[18] Nor is it just individuals that get agitated about loss of face – the United States when tacitly admitting defeat over the Tehran and Lebanon hostages wanted to make a deal that was not seen as a deal[19] and Israel's release of prisoners had to be seen as a coincidence rather than as a consequence of pressure in Lebanon. These instances were nothing but a western mode of saving face. It was this same fear of loss of face that made the United States initially refuse to accept the release of some hostages in Lebanon if it could not have them all. This attitude nearly blew the whole negotiation, which was only salvaged by the intervention of Picco. It is usually wise in hostage situations to accept any offer to release some hostages – humanitarian grounds is often the captor's way of saving face – and hope for more later.

Prior to the Tehran embassy debacle, Waite's success in gaining the release of hostages held in Iran was not only down to his awareness of the political context, but "because of a willingness and an ability to form a personal, trusting relationship with one of the revolutionary guards who had access to those who had the key to unlocking the hostage situation".[20] The ability to empathize psychologically with the individual captor in control of his side of a hostage incident is the corollary to cultural awareness. While every individual is unique, it is unlikely that any one person, even a hostage-taker, will deviate much from his cultural norm, so the general perception of a person's culture can be used safely as a starting point, but only a starting point, in arriving at the psychological make-up of the particular individual with whom the negotiator is dealing.[21] Not until the negotiator has some idea of the psychology of the group with which he is dealing and of its leader, has been given a contained environment and controlled communication with the captors and has established at least the beginnings of mutual credibility and trust can he fruitfully move on to the next stage of the process – bargaining.

That is not to say that some minor deals may not already have been struck before this point – the supply of food in exchange for acceptance of a field telephone, for example. Each bargain struck and stuck to makes striking the next bargain much easier, even if that next bargain is only a tactical one from the point of view of the coerced. This applies as much to negotiation between states – when state-sponsored hostage-taking is involved – as it does to more individualized incidents. In both, a bargain struck and mucked up has the opposite effect. Giandomenico Picco, the UN negotiator, repeatedly complained[22] that the failure of the United States to keep its promises greatly increased his difficulties in negotiating with Iran and Syria for the release of the western hostages held in Lebanon.

Picco only succeeded eventually because he adhered to other elements of the hostage negotiator's code – never promise what you know you cannot deliver. Refusal to make such promises can actually increase trust between captor and negotiator. Picco's response when he was asked for a guarantee he could not give, was a classic example of how to respond, combining as it did, honesty, credibility and cultural awareness:

> Abdullah, guarantees are given only by God because he can do whatever he likes. What man can do is express his intentions to do the best he can. I will study how to make this announcement, but do not ask me for guarantees, because guarantees are given only by God.[23]

Whatever the negotiator gives, now or later, he must always make the concession on the condition that he gets something in return. In this way the negotiator exerts increasing control and diminishes the captor's own sense of control over the situation. The mind games certainly do not stop when the bargaining process begins, but they are now likely to play a secondary role to achieving concrete results. There is no predetermined length of time after which the negotiator can promise to have reached a definitive deal or after which he knows precisely what he is getting, what he must pay and whether or not he can trust the captor to deliver his side of the bargain. At best he can give approximate answers and a general indication as the negotiation develops about how long it will take him to reach a mutually satisfactory bargain.

There are two contradictory theories from the negotiator's point of view about the effect of the lapse of time on hostage incidents. The first argues that it is beneficial in that it allows captors and captives to develop the kind of relationship that transforms captives from commodities into people whom it is harder for their captors to kill. It also allows a situation in which the captors originally seized the initiative to develop into one in which the coerced increasingly have an advantage over isolated and contained captors. The longer the time that passes before an assault has to be launched, the longer the assault forces have to gather information about their target and to plan and rehearse their attack. If such an attack has been anticipated by the captors, their vigilance will increase, as will their instability and tension and that could be dangerous for the captives. The elapse of time, in slowing the tempo of events, reduces the level of the captors' anxiety and alertness, by what Schlosberg called "Dynamic Inactivity",[24] so that negotiation and rescue are both more likely to be successful.

The second theory opposes any delay in enforcing a choice between surrender and assault. It proposes that the elapse of time gives added media exposure and therefore greater success to the captors. It argues that the protracted frustration of the captors can either lead to the captives siding with them to oppose the coerced, or can tip the balance of the captors' behaviour from the rational to the irrational and lead to impulsive killing of hostages. This, in turn, may provoke an assault in which more hostages will probably be killed. Moreover, even if hostages do not die, the longer a siege lasts the greater the physical and psychological long-term damage they suffer will be. The correlation between increased cardiac, respiratory and gastrointestinal illness and Post-Traumatic Stress Disorder and the length of a siege has been well established.[25] Too little attention is paid by the authorities to the consequences of their siege conduct on the health of the captives, though there has been some improvement in post-incident debriefing,* counselling and psychiatric help.

Neither of these time-effect theories encompasses the whole truth, however. Different hostage situations require different approaches to delaying or speeding up the bargaining phase of negotiation. If negotiators are making good progress, then the first version should be followed, if they are not, the

---

* *"Although none of us were declared to be mentally ill, we benefited enormously from having the facilities of a good listener. Being able to tell your story before a good listener and thereby objectify it rather than suppress it inwardly helps speed up the return to normality."*[26]

second theory is more applicable. The decision on which process to apply rests entirely with the coerced.[27] The timing of the seizure is the only element of a hostage incident that lies within the determination of the captors. From the moment the seizure or abduction has been completed, the subsequent timescale of events, apart from a decision to surrender unconditionally, is outside of their control. Even when the captor tries to reassert control by threatening the death of a hostage or hostages if his conditions and deadlines are not met, he is reiterating his dependence on the reaction of the coerced.[28] If instead he kills a hostage without warning, he is still dependent on the coerced's decision whether to continue to negotiate, as in the Beilen train case, (see pages 128–31) or to launch an attack as at the Moscow theatre (see pages 91–5). This dependence probably explains why, in nearly every case that has been studied in this book, deadlines for killing hostages are either passed uneventfully or extended. Where they are acted upon, it tends to be only in relation to the first and perhaps second killing. Thereafter, the deadlines in these instances become more and more extended, as in the Testrake skyjacking (see pages 36–40) or the Egypt Air case (see pages 86–7). Whatever the timescale allowed for bargaining, the mind and motive probing of the contact phase will not end by any means during phase two, but it is now more likely to play a secondary role to getting concrete results.

Before you can complete a trading transaction, you have to know what you are buying and what you are paying for it. The process of defining[29] the transaction may take up most of the second phase of our four-part hostage negotiation. Equally gradual, and interdependent with definition, is the establishing of both trust and credibility between the parties. This will only develop as each party delivers on its promises, however small, punctually and precisely. The establishing of trust is not seen as a two-way process by many theoreticians, who envisage only the necessity for the negotiator to convince the captor that he is trustworthy. To me it seems no less important that the negotiator needs to establish whether he can trust the captors' leader before they shake hands metaphorically on phase three of the process – the agreement.

The best negotiators will often come out of a hostage situation with all the hostages alive and reasonably well and having conceded little of significance in return. They will know how and when to use the bargaining process itself to achieve some of their aims. For example, they will chose the right moment to start a discussion, not an argument, about the minutiae of some aspect of a possible concession, so that the captor becomes so absorbed in it that he overlooks the passing of a deadline. Every time they send in food, drink, medicine or make other humanitarian gestures they will want something in return, from the acceptance of a landline or a medical visit to the release of sick, old or vulnerable hostages. The captor will usually see the advantage to himself of making such concessions – less opprobrium, fewer awkward hostages to manage, a means of communicating his demands and so on. He may be less aware of the effect of other negotiating devices with which he goes along. One of the more subtle is to supply food, drink and medicine in bulk so that captors and captives have to co-operate in preparation or division and so enter into a normal humanizing relationship with each other for a few minutes. The hard school of negotiators, on the other hand, seems rather to favour making the environment more uncomfortable, supplying the minimum quantity of food, drink and medicine necessary to sustain life and keeping communication both infrequent and threatening in order to undermine captor morale, even if it does the same to the hostages. This approach has generally proved less successful than the more emollient one. The same can be said about the value of controlling and stretching the timetable of events during a hostage siege.

When a Turkish carpet is being bought in the bazaar both sides know that there is an element of ritual involved – it once took me three days and more coffee than I care to think about to conclude such a transaction. The outrageous opening demand is answered by the equally derisory opening offer, after which both parties get down to serious negotiation until, step by gradual step, a mutually satisfactory bargain is struck. It is the same in most hostage negotiations. In four cases out of five, the captor does not actually expect his more extreme demands to be met. The negotiator's difficulty, like that of the carpet buyer, is in deciding what is the absolute sticking point, the minimum below which negotiation will be broken off never to be resumed and, in the hostage case, that may result in the captor taking desperate measures. How well the negotiator makes this assessment depends more on how well he has got into the mind of the captor than on what he has to offer in exchange. He is, moreover, further handicapped in his negotiation by the fact that the coerced will have laid down beforehand what he is allowed to offer and he can only bargain within those limits. He may make concessions on basic human needs, transport and media access. Anything further, such as the introduction of outside negotiators or the release of prisoners, supplying alcohol, drugs, weapons or exchanging hostages for volunteers, has to be referred to a higher authority with all the advantage (but sometimes disadvantage) of delay that this brings. These demands are usually refused, though denying drugs or alcohol to a dependent captor may have dangerous psychological consequences.

Once the bargaining has been completed and both parties think they have arrived at a mutually acceptable deal, it is important that the negotiator defines the terms of that deal, clearly, concisely and quickly and ensures that this is also the understanding of the captors. This can be a dangerous moment for the negotiator. After all the stress he has experienced, perhaps for many days and with a minimum of relief, he will inevitably relax, thinking his part of the ordeal is over and that the rest can safely be left in the hands of the Incident

Commander. To a great extent it can, but he must be on stand-by to deal with any complications that might arise in the short time between agreement and the safe conclusion of the incident. A captor may start to change his mind or turn violent, a hostage may turn sassy or aggressive and provoke his captors to renege on the deal, a member of the Incident Commander's team may get over zealous and start shooting or otherwise disturbing the calm of the moment. All too often this is the time when the negotiator sees all of his painstaking work go up in smoke as the special forces are obliged to take over, but if he is alert to the warning signs he can sometimes still intervene to avert the calamity.

So, our hostage incident is over. The hostage-takers have gone off to prison and trial, the hostages have returned to their families to re-engage with them with the help of counsellors and psychiatrists. But what of the poor negotiator? Nancy Bohl has made a particular study of this aspect of hostage incidents[30] and is worth quoting at length:

> There may also be intrusive thoughts and flashbacks. These stress responses lead to increased anxiety because the negotiator begins to feel a loss of control over her or his thoughts. In particular, what is replayed in the mind of the negotiator is the ending of the incident. Although one would assume that the replay would involve imagining a more satisfactory ending, that is not what happens. Negotiators report that, when they replay the ending, they make it worse than what actually happened ... There are many sources of stress ... but the most important is fear of failure. To a negotiator, failure means that violence had to be used to end the confrontation. Although negotiators are chosen for their ability to withstand stress, they nevertheless experience powerful emotions associated with the incident – fear, anger, hostility, (and if the negotiation ends unsuccessfully) guilt, responsibility and self-blame. Several days later, post-traumatic stress symptoms, such as the inability to sleep, nightmares, intrusive thoughts, and flashbacks, may appear.

When talking to Lord Imbert, a man of considerable *sang froid*, about the Balcombe Street siege, I was particularly struck by his description of the nightmares, attention lapses and other signs of stress he experienced, despite having just successfully conducted a masterclass in negotiation.

The frequency with which words such as "almost", "usually", "normally", "sometimes" and the conditional form of verbs occur in this chapter will have conveyed the fact that the only rule in a hostage situation is that there are no rules, only guiding principles. We have spelt out the many qualities required of a good negotiator, but above all he must be flexible. This is one of the few things on which all commentators are agreed. "Trial and error is still the best way of reaching agreement..."[31] "Common sense and a good grasp of your particular circumstances should always be your guide..."[32] "A need for a contingent rather than a rule-based approach."[33] But perhaps Warren

Christopher put it best of all:

> We must never be prisoners of precedent. It is essential to keep the perspective of the opponent in mind, not to make concessions but to be able to frame unalterable principles in ways that also accommodate purposes of the other side.[34]

The fact of the matter is that the outcome of any given hostage incident is probably less dependent on the theories discussed in this chapter than on the nature of three unpredictable constituents: the captors, the captives and the coerced. They are the subject of the final part of this book.

Chapter Eleven

The Captors

What kind of people take hostages? Is political hostage-taking a perfectly logical and moral instrument of policy for the powerless to employ against the powerful, the have-nots against the haves? Or is it, together with other forms of terrorism, an aberration? Is it the result of mental disturbance so severe that it suppresses the normal restraints on the hammering out of political differences? Or is it a combination of the two, the strategy of the perfectly rational, highly intelligent mastermind – a Daoud, a Habbas, a Barayev – tactically expressed through the instrument of the resentful, the fanatical and the plain sick? Who are these hostage-takers and what are they like?

There are basically two main kinds of terrorist and hostage-taker. The majority of the foot soldiers are drawn from the ranks of the oppressed, the remainder, and most of their leaders, from those identifying emotionally and intellectually with a cause. The latter are usually from well-educated, middle-class families whose advantages they possess, but whose values they have rejected and who are not necessarily of the same nationality as the oppressed. They are themselves well educated, but often uncritical in their enthusiastic embrace of Marxism or anarchy. These educated hostage-takers probably became involved with the group they ultimately joined while they were still at university and many will have dropped out from their studies to become active participants.

Where the hostage-takers are drawn more directly from the oppressed in socially, economically and educationally deprived societies many reflect the shortcomings of the societies they have grown up in. Terrorists in rural Latin America, much of the Middle East, and even in Ireland with the IRA, are less likely to be well educated, but they are none the less dangerous for that. Research carried out by the FBI[1] suggests that the terrorists and hostage-takers of the 1980s and early '90s, particularly in the Middle East, were less well educated – and perhaps less thoughtful – than they had been in the 1970s. The paper describes them as having minimal operational and negotiation training, no formal education and little experience of working. It does not pause to ask why this might be so. The reason these people turn to terrorism is twofold. The first is a personal direct experience either of being falsely imprisoned, tortured or made homeless themselves, or of seeing those close to them not only suffer similar injustices but randomly slaughtered at the hands of an oppressor. State authority in their own countries in the shape of secret police, death squads and the military, frequently backed by the money, expertise and weaponry of the West, is the source of their misfortunes. Not surprisingly, that authority and its sponsors become the focus of a resentment and a hatred that knows no restraints.

The second factor that leads to the recruitment of terrorists and hostage-takers is their subjective perception of the inequalities and injustices they see in the world.

> The root causes of terrorism are not deprivation or oppression as such, but the perception and experience of injustice and the belief that such injustice is not natural or inevitable, but arbitrary, unnecessary and remediable ... They respond actively to what they perceive to be an intolerable injustice.[2]

As often as not, of course, they are right. The puzzle is, why are there not many more of them?

Hostage-taking, like its sibling, terrorism, is a predominantly male activity – roughly 80 per cent of terrorists are men.[3] Most of them are in their teens or early 20s. In Latin America and Africa, where the phenomenon of the child soldier is all too familiar, some are younger still. Their leaders are likely to be ten or 20 years older. When women are involved in hostage-taking, it tends to be in logistical and support roles and only as a small proportion of the total number of activists involved. There are exceptions – over half the members of Baader-Meinhof were women and they are also quite numerous in the Latin American groups. A few exceptional women have also been successful terrorist leaders: Leila Khaled (PFLP), Fusako Shigenobou (Japanese Red Army) and Gudrun Enslin (Baader-Meinhof), for example. Generally speaking, however, this particular form of uncivilized behaviour is a predominantly male preserve.

Lebanon hostage John McCarthy had a conversation with what he described as one of his paranoid and irrational guards which is illuminating:

> "I hate the West. I hate the British, the French, the Americans. I hate them all."
> The strength of his rage caught me like a blow between the eyes. It was useless to argue with him. Useless to ask how anyone could possibly hate whole nations. But I tried.
> "What else can we do?" he demanded.
> "You can use your intelligence. You can put your case before the world. Every time you use violence against the innocent you turn more and more people against you."

"We have tried. No one listens."

There is truth in what he says. Injustices go on and on, and few pay attention until they overflow into violence and further injustice.[4]

For the hostage negotiator, however, it is not enough just to know who the captors he is dealing with are and where they are coming from, he must also probe into their minds and hearts. What will he find when he gets there?

"They must be mad," is a not uncommon reaction of law-abiding citizens to the more bizarre and suicidal acts of hijacking and seizure committed by hostage-takers, but in a strictly medical sense are they obviously so? Not according to Hoffman. "I have been studying terrorism for more than 20 years yet I am always struck by how 'normal' most terrorists seem when one actually sits down and talks to them."[5] And, of course, a great many of them are just that – normal people who have been driven by abnormal circumstances to join in an abnormal act. It would be hard, for example, to find a more normal bunch of people than those who hijacked TWA355. Although the ringleader's wife, Julie Busic, called her autobiography *Lovers and Madmen*, the hijackers' only madness was a patriotism so intense that they were prepared, like millions have been before them, to suffer and die for it. But they were also so "normal" that they went to great lengths to minimize the fear and discomfort of their hostages to whom they carefully explained their cause, hurt or abused no one and the only death for which they were responsible was due to the fact that their safety instructions were ignored by the New York police.

Although individual captors have been the subject of both psychoanalysis and treatment, too many have been killed or locked up as criminals in high security prisons to have formed a sufficiently large and coherent cohort for formal scientific study of the kind needed to answer such a general question.

We can answer it partially, in an unscientific way, by collating the numerous observations of those who have been most directly affected by the hostage-takers' mental attitudes – their captives. In assessing their opinions, two caveats must be entered. With very few exceptions none of the hostages were psychologically or even medically qualified and also, since being held hostage is an aberrant state, those responsible for imposing and sustaining it were likely to be seen as aberrant by their victims. Nevertheless, what captives have observed, particularly about obsessional behaviour, is enlightening.

The most obvious example of a nervous tic, a child's comforter syndrome, is the way captive after captive refers to his guards' obsession[6] with their guns. They are forever cleaning them, practising with them, playing with them, fondling them, talking about them, showing them off to their captives and making empty threats with them. The threats, of course, do not always prove to be empty, which is what makes them so terrifying. Tom Sutherland, one of the

Lebanon hostages, had an explanation: "For years we were chained to a wall or radiator, but they were chained to their guns; futile symbols of power, not power itself. This was something these men could never know …"

Such obsessive behaviour may well be the result of unbearable temporary stress and anxiety rather than innate mental disturbance, but the same cannot be said of the religious justification that many hostage-takers put forward for what they are doing. Christianity in Latin America, Islam in the Middle East or Chechnya, for example, is often cited as sufficient justification for terrorist acts. However, since religious explanations for what people think, say and do that may be objectionable to others are common in everyday life, offering them as a reason or excuse for hostage-taking cannot be described as a symptom of mental disorder, except by those who consider religion itself to be a surrender of reason. In the case of the captors in my assemblage of hostage incidents, it does seem to indicate that the dividing line between genuine devout observance and psychotic obsession is a thin one.

Another behavioural oddity noticed by many captives is the obvious fear displayed by their captors. By this they do not mean the natural fear of being killed or captured during the course of a rescue or reprisal, but fear, manifest in sweaty hands and faces and shallow, rapid and irregular breathing, and guilt about what they are doing, have done or are about to do to their captives. This is seen by the hostages to be quite different from the signs of sexual or sadistic excitement brought on by their captors' various physical assaults. What they note is simply the fear induced and the guilty conscience that both stem from their recognition of the violence within them from depriving another human being of liberty and all that goes with it.

Captors also experience a different kind of fear, particularly during and immediately after the seizure of a building or a hijacking, one that Keneally describes as "the exaltation of fright, that revolutionary intent, that fixity of will".[7] This is the fear that accompanies those acts of courage often performed by hostage-takers and which in an orthodox military situation would probably be described as heroic. Whether suicidal acts that deliberately court death are courageous or cowardly is another matter. Jackson saw the death wish in his young guards as neither, but as a sad progression from the admirable to the deplorable:

> I could distinguish a familiar mixture, admirable as long as contained within wholesome limits, of fatalism with human dignity. Only when the fatalism began to assume the manifestation of an addiction did its inherent morbidity take command of the personality. The addiction, it seemed to me, was to violence, to destruction, to negation and thence, by ineluctable extension, to death.[8]

There seem to me to be three quite distinct versions of a so-called death wish. The first group consists of the adrenaline junkies, the thrill seekers, who while lacking the nerve or the degree of self-contempt necessary for suicide, nevertheless court death at the hands of others. They may do this to impress their peers or to compensate for their own sense of non-entity, emasculation and lack of control over their own lives and destinies. To end it, or rather to invite the very forces they so despise to end it, is to re-exert control over life for the few moments during which it is deliberately abandoned without sacrificing the captor's belief in himself as both a martyr and a hero. This is particularly true among those adherents of religious beliefs, such as Shia Muslims, who set great store by martyrdom and promise those who suffer it great rewards in a next life. For such hostage-takers, skyjacking, especially, is the ultimate trip, in both senses of the phrase, for in it the prospect of captors and captives dying spectacularly together is at its greatest.

A second group, while reconciled to the fact that what they are doing may entail being killed by the coerced, do not actively seek to die. Martyrdom, honourable and principled failure, is not sought by these captors who "are idealistically inspired. They seek, not personal gain, but prestige and power for a collective goal; they believe that they act in the service a higher cause."[9] They would like to survive the incident, but if they do not, so be it.

My third group consists of those often loud-mouthed captors who insist on their readiness to die for their cause rather than surrender their hostages without something substantial in return, but do not really mean it. In reality, they cannot wait to be offered some face-saving reason to live. As Khalis obviously concluded in deciding to end the Hannafi siege "the thought of one's own death grows tasteless when one has chewed on it for 38 hours".[10]

The negotiator's problem is to decide to which of these superficially identical groups his particular hostage-takers belong if he is to prescribe the appropriate blend of pressure, flattery and concession that will persuade them to surrender. He also has to assess how likely they are to kill, as well as how ready they are to die in an environment where the triggers to both responses may lie outside of his control.

Violence and occasionally killing is a common factor in the initial stage of any act of kidnapping or seizure in which hostage-takers not only have to overcome security measures, but also have to deal with hostages who resist or refuse to co-operate in ways that imperil the planned take-over. Violence is also used in the next stage to instil fear and compel obedience and it is a short step from there to killing hostages as a means of exerting pressure on the coerced.

The terrorist leader Abou Abbas emphasized that: "The purpose of armed struggle is not simply to kill ... its purpose is to reach a political goal."[11] Many of the groups studied contained at least one member with sadistic or homicidal tendencies who was eager, or at least willing, to carry out beatings and murders. Frank Ochberg has described such a person as "a finely tuned animal unfettered by reason [and] dangerously coiled and ready to spring."[12]

More surprisingly, perhaps, there are as many hostage-takers for whom killing and torturing are repugnant and who argue against their use. It has been suggested[13] that one of the reasons why diplomats form such a high proportion of hostages – one author thought 20 per cent in the 1970s[14] – is because as the privileged representatives of oppressive authority they are less conscience-disturbing to kill than some randomly taken ordinary citizen. The distinction between the two does not work, however, in countries where so many innocents die at the hands of the authorities that the killing of other innocents presents no moral problem.[15] In any case, I suspect that the real reason diplomats are a popular target – and most of them are representatives of nations foreign to the captors – is that they represent the most effective human lever with which to move the coerced. Another way in which captors toughen their resolve against their captives is to whittle the group down to a manageable core consisting entirely of those towards whom the hostage-takers already feel a high degree of animosity – Jews and Americans, for example. They release the others on "humanitarian" grounds or in exchange for material support or lesser concessions.

Many of the more scrupulous captors who are reluctant to kill their captives are simply behaving rationally, since such murders are the most common trigger to an assault in which they can expect to be killed or, at best, imprisoned for life if they are captured. Conversely, for those who seek to die, but are afraid to kill themselves, the knowledge that they are more likely to achieve their death wish second-hand from the bullet of a sky marshal, a soldier or a policeman if they commit murder is an added incentive to do so.[16] The prospect of death or lifelong imprisonment is seen by the hawks among national leaders of the coerced as the best means of deterring further attacks. This is a fallacy. There is no evidence such threats work. "Military force creates martyrs."[17] Why else does Israel's policy of strikes aimed at terrorists from Hammas and other extremist groups, but which kill far more civilians, so conspicuously fail to deter suicide bombing? And why does Hammas' indiscriminate and outrageous slaughter of innocent civilians so conspicuously fail to persuade Israel to stop its strikes and abandon its expansionist policy?

So why do so many hostage-takers maltreat, torture and kill their hostages when this cannot work towards their avowed ends? The ever-perceptive Geoffrey Jackson, reflecting on the savage beating of the captive in his neighbouring cage, made this pertinent observation:

> The lesson ... was that of the essential ferocity of our captors. Force differs from violence, not only by measurable degree but in moral quality; and raw violence ... cannot simply be switched on by human beings without the added forced-draught of

naked ferocity ... I have, therefore, concluded ... that ferocity, far more than precise ideology, was the main single and common component of my captors' assorted personalities. Where it had not existed, or had been only latent, it had to be learned, or to emerge, for its host to live in consistency with himself.[18]

The experiments of Miligam at Yale, and many others since, in which the participants have grown increasingly willing to inflict ever more severe, and in some cases almost lethal, pain on each other, shows that such cruelty and ferocity is latent in nearly all of us. In most hostage-takers and other terrorists it is nearer the surface and, worse from the hostage's point of view, the restraints they have been taught diminish in some captors with time. Tom Sutherland, experienced this with one guard in particular:

When it got hot and the power went out, he would come in with a large sheet of cardboard and fan us. But as time went on, he tired of this and ultimately became one of the most vindictive of all the guards. This somehow turned out to be a fairly standard behaviour pattern. When a guard first arrived on the scene and saw fellow human beings locked up, and even chained to the wall, they were very sympathetic, and to ease our situation, tried to do what they could – bringing us coffee, candy, lots of Kleenex, water on request, longer periods in the toilet, etc. After a few weeks, however, they all became hardened to the situation.[19]

We have all experienced a degree of passionate and largely unthinking support for something or someone – a rugby team or a political party, a pop star or a footballer – but only when our partisanship goes beyond the limits of reason and conscience does it become dangerous. Fighting football fans are a good example of this in everyday life and I have found myself embarrassed in retrospect at the vehemence with which I have supported the Welsh rugby team and recognized the seeds of something worse than mere partisanship. An excess of moral righteousness, a belief that who is not with us is against us, or that it is permissible to inflict death and suffering on the innocent in the overriding interest of a "righteous cause", typify the mindset of the terrorist, be he a President or a Palestinian. Anyone in that frame of mind is ready to be recruited as a hostage-taker.[20]

Arguably, it is we who are ill mentally, or at least spiritually. The ever-popular and age-old human obsession with gossip, sex and violence has gone, by means of the mass media, far beyond the parish pump and the village shop. Moreover, it has now been supplemented by the worship of celebrity rather than of more enduring fame. In their relentless eagerness to increase profit through reaching more people and the advertising revenue they bring, television, radio, the tabloid press and sometimes even the broadsheets and serious journals, happily pander to the lowest common denominator. Hostage incidents provide prime examples of the cult of instant and transient celebrity to which tens of millions of television viewers world-wide are addicted in the shape of "reality television". A hostage incident can provide enthralling reality television on very low production costs, tabloid entertainment with catharsis not provided by simulating pity and fear, but by providing real terror and bloodshed.

The clever hostage-taker knows just how to exploit this media greed and is himself frequently on the temporary high that celebrity can bring and which assuages his sense of inferiority. But, kicks apart, his main purpose is to wage "psychological war ... an aggressive technique, based on the direct or indirect use of mass means of communication and news transmitted orally in order to demoralize the government".[21] Often he will do this by presenting himself in a role – bereft parent, tortured student – that he knows, if augmented by the media, will get a sympathetic response from the public and thus put pressure on the coerced. He is usually canny enough not to go too far and arouse its opposite, outrage, and thus give the coerced an excuse to deal harshly with him.

It would be foolish to assume that because many hostage-takers with minor psychological problems have chosen to join a terrorist or hostage-taking group as a means of indulging their inclinations, or because a few captors are seriously disturbed, that they will all act irrationally in their dealings with both their captives and the coerced. We have seen repeatedly in previous chapters the ingenuity with which captors not only foil the attempts of the coerced during a rescue attempt, but also with which they control the psychology of their relationship with their captives.

The list of tricks captors have come up with in order to thwart would-be rescuers is a long one. In skyjacking, hopping from airport to airport not only makes preparing a warm reception difficult, but also constitutes a serious technical and diplomatic challenge to any special services group tailing the captors – as Delta Force found to its embarrassment in the Mediterranean. Once an aircraft is finally on the ground, hostage-takers constantly change their positions in it. They may swop clothes with hostages and force them to show themselves holding empty weapons in windows and doorways. If that does not look confusing enough, they may simply disperse their hostages about a friendly territory, as they did in the Testrake incident in 1985 or move them repeatedly round their own patch. Noticeably one of the few deterrents to have had some effect is the reduction in the number of those friendly territories willing to accept hostage-takers unconditionally. This has been increasingly evident since the break-up of the Soviet Union and the growing desire of countries such as Cuba, Algeria and Libya to be welcomed back into the international fold.

Urban terrorists will pick their ground for an attack or a seizure so that, while they know every alleyway and sewer, safe house and place for ambuscade, most of those sent against them will find the chosen battleground unfamiliar and dangerous territory. Even when hostage-takers play away from home, they have learned to put obstacles in the way of potential attackers. Stairwells are blocked with debris, the area inside windows is strewn with furniture to hamper a swift entry, doors on a train are chained up and in all these situations real or dummy explosives and booby traps will be used to make an assault more hazardous for the hostages as well as for the attackers. Once the siege is under way, hostage-takers, suspicious since opiates were successfully used in captor's food in several instances, have been demanding that is sealed and often sent in bulk so that it cannot be tampered with. The corollary of this is that for a few moments, while it is being prepared or divided up, it helps to create a bond, often referred to as the Stockholm Syndrome, between captor and captive.

Hostage-takers are fully aware of all the implications of the Stockholm Syndrome and can either try to cultivate or block it according to circumstances. There is a variety of tactics employed by captors to prevent empathetic bonds being forged between captives and guards who may later have to torture or kill them. Nor do they want to expose their own rigid and narrow view of life to the doubt that a friendly relationship with an unjustly imprisoned person of very different views and outlook can raise. Some of the more intelligent captors are sufficiently confident of their ability to hold their ground in an argument with their captives on matters of politics and religion, but the majority of the rank and file would be incapable of doing so and must be protected against any corruption of their beliefs. Sometimes the differences in religion were even encouraged. Three of the American hostages in Lebanon who shared a cell were committed Christians, one of them a pastor. These captives held regular daily services in their cell, which they dubbed "The Church of the Locked Door". Their Muslim guards, who themselves faithfully observed the five daily commitments to prayer required in Islam, far from objecting or obstructing them, commended them, as people of the Book, for their devotion and provided them with a Bible and Prayer Book.

Such concessions were the exception for the arm's length school of hostage-takers who wanted to make sure their captives remained commodities to be traded rather than people to be respected. To this end, in Lebanon and Latin America particularly, guards were frequently masked and were frequently changed and conversation or any kind of fraternization with captives was forbidden. In the Dozier case (see pages 103–04), the hostage was not only chained to his cot and never spoken to by his masked guards, but was kept inside a tent in the room in which he was being held. The problem for the leaders who wished to impose this approach on their subordinates was the residual milk of human kindness, occasionally even vestiges of a troubled conscience, that could be found in some of even the most disciplined guards.

In kidnap cases, evidence abounds in the personal accounts of many hostages of the conflict in some guards between natural instincts of compassion, amounting now and then to affection, and the necessity dictated by their role to make their captives afraid of them. This conflict diminishes after a few weeks, but seems to return in an aggravated form when incidents last for many months or even years, as we have seen in the cases of Asencio, Jackson and many of the Lebanese hostages. Some of these captives became skilful in manipulating this dichotomy for their own survival. Keneally put the contradictions vividly in his novel *Flying Hero Class*: "They want to be at the same time the saviours and the executioners of their victims. A cross between a gangster and a goddam social worker."[22]

In Lebanon, guards would give a prisoner a birthday party, show photographs of their own children and newspaper articles and pictures about the hostage's family and friends and their attempts to secure their release. We have already seen how the guards would loosen chains or bring in extra rations. Captors would show actual physical affection that was not overtly homosexual in intent, particularly after they, or one of their fellow guards, had just administered a beating for some trivial offence, such as allowing a blindfold to slip, or for no reason at all. As Lebanon hostage Keenan, a perceptive observer, recognized, these were the only signs of contrition and a guilty conscience permitted to captors. He described one of them as: "A man more confused than the man in chains, a man more hurt and anguished than the man he had just beaten." The world of the captor is as unreal as the world of the captive. If hostages in kidnap cases are held captive by their captors, in a more subtle way, captors are held hostage by their captives.[23]

In siege situations, hostage-takers show a fierce loyalty unto death towards each other, even to comrades of whose violent conduct they disapprove. The bonding effect of "us against the world" is very powerful when it is reinforced by a shared fear or a common ideology, religious zeal or hatred for the enemy. It is more powerful if all three are combined, as they are in many hostage incidents. Attempts to wean individual captors from their loyalty in such situations are fruitless. Even offers of lighter sentences for turning king's evidence do not seem to find many takers. Nor is this from fear of the consequences of reneging or betraying. As we saw with Baader-Meinhof, however, it is far easier to join such a group than it is to leave it and live.

The other school of thought – we shall examine it in greater detail when we consider the psychology of captives – held that if the hostages could be won over to sympathize with their captives and develop friendly relations with them there would be two advantages. It would be very much harder for the coerced to mount an assault without risking hostage lives. Also, if the hostage-takers did decide to surrender or were arrested their captives would not only serve as a human shield against marksmen, but might come to their defence in court. We saw how this applied in the TWA355 hijacking in 1976 and the original Stockholm incident (see p173-175) after which the syndrome takes its name.

Ultimately, I find it difficult to come down definitively on one side or other in the debate about whether mental disturbance or idealism is the predominant factor in the kind of people who become hostage-takers. It might be wise in the circumstances to conclude this chapter with the admonition of that doyen of experts on terrorism, F.J. Hacker.[24]

> Acts of terrorism are incomprehensible if we look at only their political motivations and effects and ignore their psychological basis. On the other hand, to attempt to explain terrorism by considering only the personality structure or psychodynamics of the terrorist is to fall prey to reductionism that conceals or distorts the impact of terrorist acts.

Chapter Twelve

The Captives

Why me? The question every hostage asks himself sooner or later. Some can honestly answer "because of my job". I represent my country or one of the means of influencing my country's public and therefore my capture provides a lever. Another can say I am a valuable asset or my wealthy family loves me and so good money will be paid for my release. Or, like Schleyer, Anderson or Jackson, because I did not take the preventative measures I was advised to. But even when all those diplomats* and media men, businessmen and relatives of the rich are added together, it still leaves over half of all political hostages unaccounted for. The majority of captives, particularly in sieges, have been taken quite at random. They were in the wrong place – building, train, ship or aircraft – at the wrong time. As individuals rather than trading units, they have no personal value initially to their captors whatsoever. It is this de-personalized unpredictability that is so disconcerting.

Hostage-taking, like other forms of terrorism, depends precisely on that randomness of the violence and the violation for its effect.[1] Its most effective weapon is fear. One in seven airline passengers, for example, thinks it likely that he will be involved in a skyjacking. Even at the peak of the skyjack epidemic in the 1970s and early 1980s the odds against becoming a captive in this way were one in 100,000.[2] In 1985, one of the worst years, there were ten million take-offs and only 20 skyjackings; of a billion passengers only 68 were killed, and 57 of those were accounted for by the abortive rescue attempt at Luqa airport [see pages 86–7]. Even those who accept the possibility of being kidnapped as part of their job description are thrown completely when it actually happens to them. One minute a diplomat or a senior business executive is in a position of authority, "having men under him. I say do this and he doeth

* *Approximately 20 per cent of political hostages in the late 1970s and early 1980s, less subsequently.*

it," and the next they can do absolutely nothing without the express permission of a complete stranger – even to the point of using the lavatory.[3]

Whether they were targeted or accidental captives, every one of them, at some stage or other once a few hours have passed, will go through roughly similar stages as his ordeal unfolds. Phase one is a state of shock and denial – "this can't be happening to me" – and a flight or fight reaction which rarely lasts more than a few seconds until realization dawns that neither option is available. If you have not made a successful bolt for it, as did some of the youngsters at Ma'a lot (see p84), in those first split seconds, or shot the hijackers (see p86) then it will be unlikely, but not impossible,* that the chance arises again. In phase two, hostages divide roughly into two groups – those who experience a paralysis of will and those who have already set their resistance and survival mechanisms into operation. At this stage, waiting patiently can be a more survival-orientated course of action than behaving in an impulsive or an ill-considered manner. The third phase is the one in which the situation is rationalized and, to a greater or lesser extent, adapted to in a variety of ways.

It is useful when considering hostage behaviour to try to imagine what the captive's experience has been like. Try an experiment.** Get someone, preferably a stranger, to lock you into a small room in which a bright, naked bulb is permanently on. Get him to block out all natural light, but ask him to install a video camera that covers much of the space. If it is winter, turn any heating off; if it is summer turn it up. Get your stranger to chain you to a radiator, or any other immovable fixture, by your hands and feet, blindfold you and put a thin mattress on the floor before locking you in for 48 hours. After the first 24 hours you may use the lavatory for five minutes, but you are not allowed to use toilet paper. You may wash your hands and face in cold water for a minute once a day, but there will be no towel. Twice a day, at irregular intervals, someone will inch open the door, shove in some plain food – unleavened bread, rice, maybe a hard-boiled egg – and immediately lock you in again. He will not speak to you and if you try to speak to him he will hit you.

Because you know when you will get out and that you will not be shunted from pillar to post, beaten and possibly killed, the experiment is not a very realistic one, but it might give you a tiny insight into a fraction of what a typical kidnap hostage has to endure. I would be surprised if, when you are let out by your captor, you do not greet him with effusive pleasure. (That feeling is the first-minute infective virus of the Stockholm Syndrome, the self-preserving reaction that I shall consider later.) Brian Jenkins, one of the

* *Trevor Lock using his gun after six days of concealing it at Princes Gate [see page 120], the hostages who escaped when slackly guarded at the Moscow theatre [see page 92] and the Dutch Train in 1977 [see page 130].*

** *The author and publisher disclaim all responsibility for anyone carrying out this experiment which they do entirely at their own risk.*

pioneers of hostage studies, describes the captive's experience thus:

> One of the most harrowing experiences a person can be subjected to. No matter how short the period of captivity, it may be worse than the lengthy imprisonment of a convict. The sentence of the hostage is indefinite; it may end in release or death – the outcome is unknown, even whimsical, beyond the control of the hostage. No prescribed set of rules can be followed to avoid punishment or execution. A hostage has no final hour to prepare for mentally as the condemned prisoner has. Nor, typically, is the hostage a member of an organized group as is the prisoner of war. Most often, he is alone. It is not simply a matter of being deprived of one's freedom for a few days; it is an agonizing game of mental Russian roulette.[4]

So who gets to survive this game of Russian roulette relatively unscathed and who finds, metaphorically speaking, that it has blown part of his brain away? There are three groups of factors that determine the answer to this question for each individual in a political hostage-taking. The first consists of three factors over which the captive has little or no control: who he is at the time of capture and who his captors are; how he is treated; and the actions of governments and law enforcement agencies. The second has three factors over which the captive has partial control: his relationship with his fellow hostages; his relationship with his captors; and his physical condition. The third has two factors over which the captive can exercise virtually total control if he so chooses: what he believes in; and his attitude to others.

It does matter who you are. A diplomat, a politician or a senior businessman has a high trading value and because the goods are valuable they tend to be treated more carefully. If they are damaged, the hostage-taker has less to trade and will be faced with an angry and probably vengeful customer. In siege situations, valuable hostages are not shot. However, the captive has no control over any of this. Once he has decided on a career and implemented such security precautions as his employers or advisers prescribe, the die is cast and he can do no more. The same goes for the anonymous man on the Clapham omnibus. If the omnibus is hijacked so is he and to the hostage-taker he becomes just one item in a package of trade goods worth only whatever fraction he represents of the total number of passengers seized.

What the captor in both cases will be unaware of is the hidden qualities of his goods, the background and upbringing that make him an active element in the bargaining between the captor and the coerced. On those hidden values much may depend. Considerable research[5] shows that older men, of good education and disciplined upbringing and occupational habits, being of similar ethnic, linguistic, religious or cultural background to their captors, are not only more likely to be released, but to survive the ordeal of captivity better than younger men (and particularly women) of poor education and who are unaccustomed to hardship and discipline or self-discipline. Additionally, as one hostage[6] observed of his numerous fellows in adversity, those with personal or family problems cracked up much sooner than those with good family relationships and secure and satisfying jobs. Obviously, if a hostage's captors are innately hostile to him because of his colour, race, sex, religion, economic status or any other obvious distinguishing characteristic, there is little he can do but try to avoid behaving stereotypically. In Iran and Lebanon, those with military training, the harsher the better, seemed both to endure captivity and to recover afterwards better than most. The experience of hardship, discipline and routine, of being abused and shouted at were all good training and no doubt also accounted for the relative resilience of English public school boy John McCarthy, who would have experienced much the same! The corollary was that they were more likely to be chosen as victims of torture and murder, especially if they were thought to be involved with the CIA. Language skills also help a hostage to survive. Only two of the Lebanon hostages, Weir and Carton, spoke fluent Arabic and the 12 Frenchmen had the advantage that French is the second language of the country. On the whole these 14 received better treatment than the other hostages. A prime example of the combination of survival characteristics listed above was the Lebanon hostage Jackie Mann. This 75-year-old former Battle of Britain fighter pilot was held in solitary for two years, frequently and severely beaten and in poor health. Nevertheless, he was described by a fellow hostage as "so relaxed about himself that outside influences, however foul, couldn't touch his inner serenity".[7] One other group of natural survivors must be mentioned. The Dutch psychologist, Dr Wilhem van Dijk, studying and debriefing the captives from the various train and school seizures of the 1970s, found that the significant proportion of farmers and rural workers among them, inured to hardship and dependent on self-discipline to make a living, seemed barely to have been touched by the experience they had undergone.[8] Captors who are taken in large groups, where numbers bestow a degree of individual anonymity on all who choose to behave discretley and take advantage of it, emerge on the whole less disturbed than captives who have been the sole, or almost sole, focus of their captors' attention. This is particularly true where hostages are being selected one at a time to be killed – the protection of the flock offers a sense of security from the wolf, illusory for the unfortunate individual, but inherently sound in terms of the survival of the rest of the group. It has also been observed in mass hostage situations that the greater the homogeneity of the captive group, the greater that sense of security and individual strength becomes. Moreover, it is apparent that in most cases it is the intensity and unpredictability of the experience rather than its duration that most effect the outcome for the hostage in terms of psychological trauma. The intensity of the experience is, in turn, determined by how the captors choose to treat their hostages.

Some captors are more abusive than others, some ignore their hostages and try to minimize contact, some are friendly, some execute or threaten to execute them one at a time, some allow food and clothing to be delivered, whereas others do not. What are the effects of different treatment on stress levels and coping strategies?[9]

First let us consider the fate of the kidnap captive.

Ill-treatment comes in a wide variety of forms from murder to mild abuse, but the most common, and in many ways the most damaging, is the combination of deprivation of freedom and confinement in a small space. The Nazis perfected this form of torture by putting the captive in a space so small, the Stehbunker, that he could not stand up, lie down or sit.[10] Though none of the cages or cells in this study were quite that small, they were frequently not a great deal larger. The thin mattress filled the floor space in a single cell and a tall man, such as Terry Waite at six foot seven, could not stand erect. There would seldom be room to take more than a pace or two and even that was denied to those chained to the wall. Sharing a larger cell with one or two other hostages, as happened quite frequently in Lebanon, could not only have psychological advantages, but with a degree of co-operation and organization could allow space for some exercise.

The effects of such restrictive confinement were exacerbated for some by solitary confinement and minimal communication, even with the guards. Waite, who endured it for almost four years, mastered the effects by rationalizing that "only the body was captive in solitary, as there were limitless intellectual nooks and crannies into which I could retreat and find stimulation, entertainment, comfort and distance. This mentally ... was in some ways not as difficult as it might have been."[11]

Extreme physical forms of traditional torture are rare for hostages – the "don't damage the goods" necessity again – and are mainly confined to beatings of which the indignity and unpredictability were as hurtful as all but the most severe blows of the bastinado and the rifle butt. Other physical suffering was imposed indirectly by denying the hostage control of his bodily functions. If taken ill gastrically, a captive might be obliged to defecate in front of his cell-mate on a torn-out sheet of a magazine, which he could dispose of in the lavatory later, or simply foul himself. The opportunity to go to the lavatory was infrequent and brief, which was both degrading and noisome. The opportunity for a change of clothing and a trim of either the beard or hair was even rarer. The cell was poorly ventilated and constantly illuminated artificially, had a peep-hole or cctv camera to spy on the captive and rarely would a chink allowing daylight into the room be found. A cage was even more exposed. Possessions, sanity-saving photographs of loved ones or other keepsakes, painstakingly home-made games of chess or cards, would be arbitrarily removed and just as arbitrarily restored. In the early days of their captivity, kidnap hostages were usually subjected to intensive and lengthy interrogation, especially if they were suspected, however absurdly, of possessing intelligence or of being connected with the CIA. As Jackson found, it is hard to convey to others "the depth of weariness and nervous and physical exhaustion with which so strange an experience leaves its participant".[12]

The heartening element in all of this is that the majority of kidnap hostages surmounted the squalor, the physical deprivation, the pain and the abuse to survive, sometimes even to emerge as better and stronger people than they were before their captivity. The better survivors were those who struck the best balance between the compliance necessary for survival and the resistance necessary to maintain self-respect. Many were able to do this by recognizing with Keenan that their captors and guards "needed our fear to become the men they wanted to be. We would not give it. Nor did they know how to abstract it. They were the prisoners of our resistance." Sadly, for others, the worst effects of their ill-treatment did not show themselves until the ordeal was over.

Hostages in a siege have different pressures to overcome and different experiences from those who have been kidnapped. Their ordeal is usually much shorter, but their fear of imminent death at the hands of their captors or the agents of the coerced is much more intense and unrelenting. Sieges tend to be measured in days or in months with very little in between. The hostages rarely suffer anything like the same degree of deprivation or physical abuse as those who have been kidnapped. Indeed, when a siege is protracted, captors and coerced alike often make considerable efforts to see that hostages get food, drinks, medicines and even toiletries and games. They usually have a degree of movement within the confines of the captor's fortress, in accordance with his notions of security. Fear is the siege captive's most severe source of torture.

In both types of hostage incident, the mood of the captors, and the consequent treatment of the captives, is largely determined not just by the actions of the besiegers in the immediate vicinity, but by events in the wider world. A bombing of Tripoli or a shelling of Beirut can cost hostages not only their comforts, but their lives. The response of the authorities and their negotiators in tone and substance to the hostage-takers' demands can either trigger anger and violence or induce a relaxation of attitude and a more humane treatment of the hostages. These external events represent the third factor which is entirely outside the control of the captive and, in the next chapter, I shall consider the rationale by which various governments arrive at their policies in response to hostage-taking.

Of the three factors over which the hostage has partial control, the one most closely related to his captors' treatment of him is his own physical condition. Obviously the more restrictive the conditions of confinement, the deprivation of sustenance and the severity of abuse the harder it is to maintain physical health. While much attention is given to the hostage's mental state, the physical aspect is one that is often neglected by many of the authorities dealing with hostage situations both during and after their captivity. Those captives who recognize the significance of maintaining their health and physical fitness as best as they are able are usually the ones who emerge from the ordeal in the best condition, but to do so requires both ingenuity and self-discipline. Keeping a healthy body certainly helps to maintain a healthy mind under such stressful circumstances where even the most stoic of hostages can doubt his own sanity. The shock of being kidnapped or besieged, often in a violent manner, will induce stress – the non-specific response of the body to demands made on the whole being – as will the fear, suffering and deprivation that the captive is subjected to during the captivity itself. By working to maintain his physical well-being, as far as circumstances permit, the captive can regain some control over that stress.

Captives have devised many ways to exercise regularly, from carrying out Canadian air force drills to reducing anaerobic tension (which arises from lack of free oxygen) from practising callisthenics to converting an eight-foot cell into an opportunity to take an eight-kilometre walk by taking two strides at a time. The alternative is to see one's lung and muscle capacity diminish even more rapidly than it will do naturally during a lengthy captivity. This debilitation can manifest itself in everything from cramps to erectile dysfunction and a fall in energy levels to the point where lethargy, despair and hypochondria take over. That can often be the path to madness and possibly death, though the mortality rate from stress-related illness and natural causes in captivity is remarkably low among this largely middle-aged population.

Other health hazards range from the lack of medicines to treat both casual illness and chronic cardiac, respiratory or renal disease to the poor hygiene and nutrition the captive is confronted with, even in the shortest sieges. The survival-conscious captive will wash himself and wash and change his clothes whenever the infrequent opportunity arises. He will eat whatever food is put before him, however strange and unpalatable. He will chew it slowly and thoroughly not only to aid an impaired digestion, but also to help pass the time. The arrival of each meal will help mark out the day, for in most cultures meals are taken at more or less set times, even though those times may be different from the ones he is used to. All these measures will help to slow the inevitable decline that a harsh and unexpected captivity entails. Because this decline in long-term hostages may be gradual, it is easy for them not to be aware of how much they have deteriorated physically. The absence of mirrors and the disappearance of familiar features behind hair and grime makes self-assessment of one's physical condition that much more difficult.

To some extent a captive's ability to ensure his own survival depends on the second factor that is only partially under his control – the co-operation and encouragement of his fellow captives. The sample is too small to be significant, but it is curious that in Lebanon, the British and French hostages from the older civilizations so despised by Mr Rumsfeld got on together with more mutual tolerance and understanding than the Americans whose social mores were brash and competitive. One of the latter, Tom Sutherland, got on better with the Frenchmen with whom he shared a cell than with his fellow Americans. Who a captive's all-too-close companions may be is not within his power to determine, though when a building is seized there is a strong possibility that he will be acquainted with some of them and may find himself among friends and colleagues. The person a captive sits next to on a plane or a train will almost certainly be a complete stranger with whom he will have to share a most stressful ordeal. The ability to establish a mutually supportive relationship quickly will be a significant factor in his own ability to cope. Incarcerated with other frightened and harassed captives whose ways may irritate and exasperate him, he would do well to bear in mind Terry Waite's admonition.

> You have somehow to learn that every individual has his own unique way of surviving and his way of surviving might not be yours. And somehow you have to understand that and learn to respect that, and that's easier said than done when you're chained against somebody day and night for year after year.[13]

Or as Keenan, another Lebanon hostage, recognized: "Our captivity was the great leveller by which position, status, intellect or ability ceased to be self-possessions. They became the common goods of all."

The alternative to this co-operation and pooling of mental and material resources can be both destructive and, in some instances, fatal. Several of the supposedly mature diplomatic hostages in the Dominican embassy siege [see pages 68–70] bickered and squabbled fiercely and interminably. In doing so, they impaired their judgement, damaged their health and absorbed much of the time and energy of their more level-headed fellow hostages in keeping the peace – energy which should have been devoted to dealing with their common situation. In such antagonistic circumstances "how quickly frightened people blame their fellow victims because they dare not blame their oppressors".[14] And how tempted they are to offer up others to death when a victim is to be chosen. Whether or not his death is on the agenda may depend on the captive's personal relationship with his captors and is the third and most fascinating factor that again is only partially in the captive's control. The relationship between captive and captor has been the subject of numerous studies and one aspect of it more than any other has intrigued those researchers – the Stockholm Syndrome, as it was later named by Swedish criminologist, Nils Bejerot. This process of identification takes its name from one particular incident.

On 23 August 1973, Jan Olsson took three women and a man hostage in the

Sveriges Kreditbank in Stockholm and threatened to kill his hostages if his friend, Clark Olofsson, was not released from prison. The authorities agreed to his demand in order to establish a communication link with both the hostages and Olsson. Olsson also demanded guns, protective equipment, three million Swedish Kroner (about $2m in 2003) and a fast getaway car. The two men (Clark Olofsson had joined his friend after being released from prison) held their hostages for six days. During this time an unexpected transformation in the relationship of captors and captives took place. The two men were kind to their captives. This, coupled with the relief and gratitude at not being killed by two known criminals, generated a dependency, even affection in the captives toward their captors, and these feelings appear to have been reciprocated. Indeed, the affection between one captive and one captor is reputed to have led to intimate physical caresses and possibly more. Voluntary sexual intercourse is not unheard of between captor and captive: it is, after all, the ultimate form of protective bonding. Rape, of course, is the opposite. In both sets of circumstances many hostages have been ashamed or reluctant to admit to it afterwards.[15] The opposite of reluctance was shown by one of the women hostages, Kristin Ehnemark, who embraced Olofsson as he was being led away under arrest after being forced out of the building by a gas attack on 28 August. She shouted after him, "Clark, I'll see you again," but she did not marry him – that is one of the myths attached to this event. They remained friends and the original kidnapper, Jan Olsson, later married one of the many female admirers that the publicity surrounding the incident won him.

An example of a captor being similarly affected occurred after the ending of the 13-day siege of the Indonesian consulate in the Hague in December 1975. One of the hostage-takers wrote a farewell message of regret on the T-shirt of a girl he had seized at gunpoint when the siege began. "We are like two trees. Fate separates us. The road runs between us, but our hands reach across it."[16]

Stockholm Syndrome can overwhelm a large proportion of kidnap hostages, especially those who experience any kindness or consideration at the hands of their captors. This syndrome is even more prevalent in siege situations, where the feeling of dependency, of having your life controlled by someone else, is supplemented by the fear of being killed by those assaulting your hideout, or by your captors out of revenge for such an assault or attempt. Whether that assault is primarily to release you or to kill or capture your captors is quite immaterial to you.

While held in the bank, the hostages protested vehemently whenever the police intimated that a rescue might be under consideration that might harm their captors. They huddled round the two convicts to protect them from possible sniper fire and when they finally emerged from the bank, they all refused to testify against their captors at their trial and even raised money for their defence. Such previously unrecorded and unscrutinized, if not unprecedented, behaviour intrigued psychiatrists and law enforcement authorities more and more as it became apparent that such behaviour was quite common in other political and criminal cases. Although the eponymous event was a criminal hostage-taking, its implications for the political kind are too important for it to be ignored.

A number of explanations have been offered as to why Stockholm Syndrome develops. The most common is that it reawakens the dependency that most of us experience in childhood – traumatic infantilism and pathological transference.[17] In layman's language

> The mind of the child is filled with awe at the omnipotence of his parents. His heart is full of terror at the possibility that a displeased parent will abandon or punish him. These fears cause children to be obedient to parent figures and willing to acquire their ways … It is through "identification with the aggressor" … that children are woven into the social fabric.[18]

I am not qualified to comment on the psychological explanations, but the reversion to childhood interpretation provides a useful analogy when discussing Stockholm Syndrome. It would be interesting to study the childhoods of those, such as Brockman, Bourgeois and Claustre,*[19] who not only did not succumb to it, but actively rejected all that it implied. As we saw in Brockman's case (see page 35) the language used to express this rejection can be extreme, almost hysterically self-justifying. In Bourgeois' own words:

> The zeal deployed by most of the hostages to be on good terms with the kidnappers makes me wonder … their diligence comes close to being indecent. I have not the least inclination to fraternize with such monsters … What a repugnant servility! This time it really makes me sick. Sure, the terrorists revel in it, improvise songs to their own glory, and the hostages go one better, adding refrains damning the government … so much the worse if I distinguish myself by not playing the game. I prefer to "kick the bucket" rather than to be ashamed of myself.[20]

Perhaps the unloved orphans of the Third World would prove immune – or perhaps doubly vulnerable. Moreover, an Israeli seized by the PFLP, or a Palestinian by the IDF, would almost certainly be immunized by prejudice. It would be amusing, and perhaps enlightening in this context, to examine the political allegiances and attitudes towards captors and their ideology that hostages held before they were captured and correlate it with their experience of Stockholm Syndrone and any subsequent change in beliefs. Are Democrats more

---

* *Je n'étais nullement atteint par le syndrome de Stockholm; un syndrome d'ailleurs bien pratique pour culpabiliser les otages que leur experience a pu amener a réfléchir sur certaines réalités déplaisantes de toute politique extérieure.*

susceptible than Republicans, Liberals and Social Democrats than Conservatives?

It is certainly offered as an explanation that Stockholm Syndrome is experienced by those who already share or sympathize with the ideals or cause of the captor and reject the ethos and practice of the authorities against whom he has taken hostages. I do not think that this theory has been empirically tested, but my guess is that if it was, it might show the hostage less critical of the captor, but it would not account for the incapacitating and protective response of the true Stockholm Syndrome case.

Yet a third explanation is that the harsh conditions of captivity and the constant repetition of the captors' ideological or political reasons for what they are doing amount to a form of brainwashing that makes the hostage feel guilty and, therefore, placatory. I concur with Crayton[21] in rejecting this aetiology on grounds of common sense. Crayton suggests more plausibly that the abrupt and traumatic severance of all his normal reference points destroys the hostage's sense of self to such an extent that he seeks to create new reference points from his new circumstances. In so far as a sense of self is generated by our relationships with others, that seems reasonable.

So what are the determinants of Stockholm Syndrome? In a comprehensive case the hostage needs to feel empathy with the captor and hostility towards the authorities trying to kill or capture him. Some analysts feel that it also requires the captor to have positive feelings towards his hostage.[22] I disagree. Stockholm Syndrome can manifest itself when the captor treats his captive harshly or with indifference, in the same way that a child, however ambivalently, can love and depend on a strict and even cruel parent. Where the feeling of concern is mutual, I think of the captor as presenting a Reciprocal Stockholm Syndrome. We have seen in previous chapters how captives, such as Jackson and Asencio, set about generating that reciprocity in a controlled way for their own benefit and protection. The child–parent analogy can be extended to include a parental reluctance by the captor to harm his hostage–child.

The first of the Stockholm Syndrome determinants can be augmented by intellectual and emotional sympathy for the captor's cause or indignation at what they see as his wrongful treatment. The Croatian skyjacking of TWA355 [see pages 31–6] is a case in point. The second is frequently increased by the fear that in the process of achieving their aims vis-à-vis the captor the authorities may ignore the well-being of the captives who are also likely to be killed or wounded in any shoot-out. In the light of the statistics this is both perfectly logical and understandable.

The length of a captivity is not a significant factor in determining whether the Stockholm Syndrome manifests itself. The shortest incident of hostage-taking I have come across where this empathy has occurred was in Nicaragua and lasted only six-and-a-half hours; in other instances it has taken months to develop fully. Nor does the size or composition of the hostage group seem important, though it does seem less likely to occur where a significant number of captors or guards are female, which might seem to contradict the child-parent explanation.

Reciprocal Stockholm Syndrome tends to occur when the hostage has become a sympathetic personality rather than a bargaining counter in the eyes of his captor. The Gerard Vaders case is the classic example [see pages 128–31]. This protective obligation can be augmented by the overt co-operation and sympathy of the captive – the obedient and affectionate child. There is no doubt that the captive does wish to placate his captor, but this is a matter of self-preservation of the kind most people experience to a lesser degree in the workplace, at home and on social occasions. We have all bitten our tongues and suppressed our natural instincts in such situations, perhaps even been a little ingratiating in order to avoid any unpleasant consequences. When confronted by a highly strung, trigger-happy hostage-taker, the need not to offend becomes paramount and may best be ensured by following instinct and developing positive thoughts and feelings for the captor and submitting entirely to his will.

As we have seen again and again in the cases studied here, hostages will deliberately submit themselves to the rigours of their captor's regime rather than risk offending them. Captives will re-chain themselves to the wall, draw the guards' attention to an unlocked door or an unattended weapon. One captive asked for his radio to be taken away lest he inadvertently hear the local news he was forbidden to listen to. Another, whose ears had been filled with wax to prevent her hearing distant sounds told her captor it was coming out. She got a ruptured eardrum for her pains. In the same vein, captives often try to excuse to themselves their captors' unacceptable or cruel behaviour. The beating must have been a mistake, the absence of food mere forgetfulness. Not to make such excuses would be to have to face the inescapable reality that the captor's power to do to the captive whatever he likes, even murder him, is absolute, just as a parent's power over an infant is absolute.

There have been many cases in which the captive feels that the interference of the authorities has jeopardized his development of a "safe" relationship with his captor. As one hostage put it: "There were moments when we established an equilibrium and I believed that things would work out. Whenever outside forces interfered with that equilibrium it all had to be redone."[23]

Clearly if siding with the hostage-taker against the authorities will save your life then that is what you are going to do, even if it means being misunderstood and abused by those authorities upon your release. The good negotiator, unless he actually wishes to encourage Stockholm Syndrome to develop in order to enhance the safety of the captive, takes care not to force the hostage into this choice by the way he deals with the captor. As Strenz sensibly observed: "A hostile hostage is the price that law enforcement must pay for a living hostage. Anti-law enforcement feelings are not new to the police ... However, a human life is an irreplaceable treasure and worth some hostility."[24] Whether or not he is hostile towards the police is up to the rational hostage. His attitude and his beliefs are the two aspects of his captivity that remain entirely within his own control, though exercising that control may require considerable self-discipline.

Resistance is normally essential to survival, but it does not have to be confrontational to succeed. The question each captive has to ask himself is twofold: what form of resistance best suits my character and psychological needs and how can I best resist within that context without endangering my survival and that of my fellow hostages? There are as many answers to those questions as there are captives and circumstances of captivity.

Those, like Lavasani at Princes Gate [see pages 117–21], de Groot on the Beilen train [see pages 128–31] and Klinghoffer on the *Achille Lauro* [see pages 49–53], who challenge their captors aggressively and argumentatively over co-operation, religion or political ideology are signing their own death warrants when it comes to choosing an individual hostage as the next victim for a demonstration killing. Conversely, a number of FBI studies have shown that to be unduly subservient is also to stand out from the crowd, to be labelled a wimp, and will increase your chances of being selected for killing. Such an attitude can also have a deleterious long-term effect on a captive who survives, in that after his release he may well feel guilty for not having resisted and may suffer a lowering of self-esteem.

At one level down from fatal confrontation are the naturally abrasive hostages, like Keenan and Anderson, who found it necessary to challenge their captors openly in order to bolster their own self-esteem, even though doing so earned them numerous, and occasionally severe, beatings. Others, such as McCarthy and Waite, were equally stubborn, but in a more passive way. It is an interesting example of mutual transference of survival behaviour that McCarthy and Keenan, very different characters, one very English the other proudly Irish, who shared a cell for much of the four-and-a-half years they were in captivity together, not only respected each other's very different attitudes, but adapted some of them for their own use until the best balance in their approach to effective resistance was struck.

> Even blindfolded, I was ready to fight, and that I could still fight and hurt them. I learned that as long as it was done sparingly and calmly, keeping the guards a little edgy was a valuable asset, if only to maintain our own confidence.[25]

At the opposite end of the scale to the confrontational are those special, but few, captives who are able to retreat completely into the castle of self, pull up the mental drawbridge connecting them to the outside world and withstand the siege regardless of the physical battering the castle walls are subjected to. Their's is the strength of the ascetic and the hermit, effective but not very endearing to fellow captives. To find a more healthy attitude I revert, as so often, to Sir Geoffrey Jackson, who struck "a balance between too much hope constantly deferred and too little leading to despondency".

There are other qualities of attitude common to most of those who survive a hostage captivity with the least psychological damage. They keep themselves active and flexible mentally and physically. They retain the ability to laugh both at themselves and at their adversity. The hostages whose accounts I have read or to whom I have spoken almost without exception recommend a sense of humour as a great salve to the wounds of humiliation inflicted by their captivity. They all seem to be able to …

> … accept each day as it comes. You don't think in terms of how long, you think in terms of each day. And you just go on, you just go on, and after a while you don't worry about that, you just keep going. If you're going to survive in a situation of extremity, you've got to have belief in something, even if it's only yourself or the cause for which you are enduring what you're enduring.[26]

Is it coincidence that the extroverts, such as Waite or Sutherland, seem to have suffered fewer long-term effects and less relationship stress than the introverts such as McCarthy, Keenan or Reed? Perhaps because the former had the opportunity to develop some missing aspect of their personalities while the latter, by nature of their isolation in captivity, did not? But all of them, as well as a stubborn and positive attitude, drew deeply on more abstract inner resources, a belief in themselves and a belief in some certainty beyond themselves.

Self-belief starts with being confident of who you are, where you fit into the scheme of things and being satisfied with the place in it you have managed to attain. If a lifetime's accumulated experience provides the map to that self, then memories are the co-ordinates by which the journey is traced. Remembering plays a big part in the grounding of those captives who best survive, but only if it is done with relish rather than regret. But how do we select the memories we choose to review? Is the selection based on a conscious matching with the needs of the moment or do the memories spring uninvited to the mind? A bit of both, I suspect, though even the uninvited may be the selections of the subconscious mind.

Terry Waite gave much thought to the workings of his memory in captivity and acquired a deal of self-knowledge in the process. For such an ebullient character, and he remains such, he showed unusual humility in assessing his place in the scheme of things. He asked himself the question: "If you have no one else to impress with your recollections of achievements past, do you still select them to impress yourself and bolster your self-confidence?"[27] When he finally came out of solitary and joined some of the other hostages in comparably comfortable circumstances, his self-important anecdotes amused some and irritated others. One of his companions was astute enough to see that while he was reinflating his ego after so long without an audience, he was also sending himself up more than he was puffing himself up – something I doubt if he would have had the courage and wit to do before his captivity. Significantly, confronted after so long with the stresses and strains of relating again to others, his asthma, and the hyperventilation that accompanied it, became severe and disturbing. Although Anderson helped him to calm down and control his breathing, the other hostages quickly became exasperated with him – an indication of how thin the capacity for tolerance had worn outside the deep-rutted routines the hostages had established for themselves after such a long period in captivity.

Waite was but one of many hostages who suffered longer-term kidnaps to talk about the importance of memories in coping with the loss of freedom. Jackie Mann had more of them and explained it better than any of the other hostages:

> I had no outside stimulation or occupation, but inside my head there was 75 years of memories, stories and experiences locked away. It was a mental library, to which I could go and select an incident, and play it back like a film; and most importantly, it was a library which no one, not even my captors, could take from me.[28]

But if reminiscing reinforces faith in oneself, then looking forward positively stimulates hope. This process of looking forward can take the form of something as simple as imagining a walk, or a meal, or talking to a friend, or it can rocket off into fantasy of the wildest kind. It is, of course, also possible to fantasize retrospectively, to amend our memories so as to give ourselves a more glorious role than that to which in fact we were properly entitled. Many a hostage admitted to "remembering, with advantages, the deeds he did that day." (*Henry V,* Act IV, Scene III). And finding that, too, a comfort.

Self-belief in hostile conditions also depends on a ruthless maintenance of one's integrity, of doing and saying nothing of which the captive need be ashamed at the time or later. A refusal to save oneself a beating or procure a clandestine listen to the radio by lying; a refusal to kowtow or to pay lip-service to views one finds repugnant or arguments one believes to be wrong, whether expressed by one's captors or one's fellow captives; a refusal to steal food off another hostage or to have sex with a captor in order to secure an earlier release; all these are the marks of integrity and all were refusals made by hostages included in this study. Sustaining personal integrity also consists of refusing to accept blame or feel guilt for the situation in which the captive finds himself, or for the often-desperate and forgivable circumstances that may have driven his captors to seize him. The corollary of these negative elements of hostage integrity is the courage to look out beyond himself at precisely those issues that have brought about his captivity with an objective eye and an open mind, to become more, not less, aware of the world from which he has been severed. Pierre Claustre saw this clearly when, during the three years of his captivity in Chad, he dwelt upon the events that had brought it about and concluded that it was simply because he was a Frenchman. He is worth quoting at length:

> I became aware that the undeserved violence to which we had been subjected had its origins and its justification in a greater and even less deserved injustice inflicted on a whole population without good reason ... The only crime of these mountain people, against whom France had intervened militarily, was to want to live in freedom, in whatever way seemed right to them, and to reject an authority imposed upon them which they did not want ... The date groves and villages torched by Tombalbaye's soldiers, the massacre of the civilian population of Zoui by the soldiers of Malloum, the fighters killed or wounded by our helicopters and our fighter bombers were all events for which I, as a Frenchman, was directly responsible.[29]

Not, perhaps, in quite such a grand manner as Claustre, but nearly all hostages castigate themselves for their sins of omission and vow to be better people if they can only be spared and freed from their captivity. They promise to be nicer to their wives and children, kinder to their colleagues and friends, more forgiving to their enemies, more tolerant, charitable, generous, considerate and hard-working. They assure themselves that when they return to normal life they will truly appreciate the little things of which they have been deprived during their captivity and whose importance has only now been brought home to them. Since many of these vows are recorded in biographies and autobiographies, psychiatric reports and media interviews, it would be interesting to visit former hostages five, ten, and 20 years after their liberation to see how well they have kept the promises they made to themselves or their gods under the duress of despair. All hostages are changed by their experience. "For some it was a re-humanization, an affirmation of something lost or forgotten. For others it was loss — a turning away from oneself in awe, in horror and in fear."[30]

Even those philosophical and determined hostages who emerged positively from captivity experienced failures of self-belief in various ways, at various times and to varying degrees, but what is baffling is that all but a handful failed in one respect all the time — they made no serious attempt to escape, let alone succeeded in doing so. Of the kidnapped captives in this study, just two, or perhaps three with a generous interpretation of escape, managed to break free of their captives, and then only in the early minutes of their captivity. Only at the second Dutch train siege and at the Moscow theatre did hostages take the opportunity offered by lax or overstretched guards and get away, and the flight crew of one skyjacked aircraft escaped because the skyjackers did not know the cockpit was not at the front of the aircraft and rushed to the wrong place.

Crayton[31] made a study of 40 sieges involving 363 hostages and of these only four genuinely escaped unaided, though 21 others did so because their seizure was incidental to the captors' main objective.

Most hostages thought about escape and talked about it and planned it endlessly, but when it came to the crunch their nerve failed and they put it off to another time, and then another and another ... Apart from those made by Jackie Mann, who at the age of 75 perhaps felt as though he had little to lose, I know of no other serious (non-suicidal) attempts even by those who were convinced their captors were going to kill them anyway. This failure of nerve applied equally to civilian hostages and those from the military or with a previous military background who, if they had been captured in battle, would have been breaking out at every possible opportunity. It was not as though opportunities did not present themselves – doors were left unlocked, fetters were unsecured, loaded weapons were left lying around, guards were AWOL, asleep, or alone and inattentive. The excuses for inaction were legion – reluctance to kill, not knowing the language or the whereabouts of the place of captivity, not wishing to endanger or desert fellow hostages and many others equally specious. But why?

I think there are two possible explanations. In battle you know you stand a good chance of being killed or captured and although you are still afraid you are at least forewarned and prepared. You also know that if captured, under the Geneva Convention on the treatment of prisoners of war, you are unlikely to be killed out of hand for no reason or tortured. In contrast, the unexpected shock of being taken hostage has a temporary paralysing effect on all but the most highly trained and resilient.[32] Once incarcerated, ill-treatment, deprivation and close confinement sap, and sometimes completely break, the will. "The 'breaking' process is both a physical and a psychological procedure that renders it mentally harder for the prisoner to resist and makes it physically harder to escape should the opportunity present itself – or just to survive."[33] In fact that concentration on day-to-day survival absorbed most of the energy and effort of every captive leaving little to spare for the more dangerous challenge of an escape bid in which he might be killed.

The other explanation is that deep down the captive believed it was up to someone – or something – else to get him out and that external element would not let him down if only he could survive for long enough. Believing, Daniel-like, in divine deliverance, praying for rescue or release were for some a substitute for taking personal responsibility for restoring their freedom. It is easy to mock, but the inescapable fact remains that those who did have strong religious beliefs, or less frequently some other outside reference point from which to draw strength, did survive better and longer than those who were, in the widest sense, faithless.

Even the most self-confident people need a stable source of validation beyond themselves be it a god, the devotion of a loved one or a belief in a cause. However illusory that belief may turn out to be, however false the god, however disloyal the loved one, however flawed the cause, at the time it serves the purpose of motivating survival. Nor does it much matter in what outside force the believer believes, as Terry Waite reminded me:

> I don't necessarily think that religious belief per se has a higher claim than other forms of belief, though I do think you've got to have belief in something … I think religion comes into its own when you are able to face, as far as you can, the stark reality of being a human being, with all its joys and sorrows, pain and happiness.[34]

Once more it is Geoffrey Jackson who comes up with the best formula – a profound belief in God and a devoted wife, who went home as instructed when he was captured and repainted the house in colours they had previously agreed, so that he could imagine her doing it. No wonder he emerged an even stronger man than the one he had been when he was taken hostage.

The outside world assumes that when a hostage is released his ordeal is over and he can be forgotten about. This is far from the case. For a lucky few the aftermath lasts only a few weeks, for many it lives with them for years and for some a lifetime. The aftermath normally consists of three phases – the return, the reaction and the recovery – which are partially sequential and partially overlapping. There is a fourth phase, too, a full return to normality, which some unfortunates never attain.

The return subdivides into two parts, emergence and celebrity. Because the physical signs of confinement, ill-treatment and deprivation are the most obvious – sores, cuts, bruises, emaciation, pallor and being dirty and unshaven – officialdom may concentrate upon them when it first receives a hostage into its safekeeping. While this medical attention is both necessary and welcome, it can overlay and obscure the deeper injuries, mental as well as the long-term physical ones, that the hostage has sustained. When a hostage steps from the isolation of captivity more or less straight into the limelight of cameras and microphones thrust at him by a horde of reporters, he moves from the complete nonentity of his captivity to instant celebrity. The second phase of the return is inevitably euphoric as he moves out of the dark world, in which he did not know if he would be alive the next day, into the limelight. The fewer hostages released at one time the greater the intensity of that transition. Some old media hands, such as Waite or the experienced reporters in Lebanon, knew what to expect, though its intensity still came as a shock, others were overwhelmed. Some thrived on the publicity – Tom Sutherland's daughter pronounced the exposure the best possible therapy for him – others found it as daunting as their confinement had been and could not cope. If the authorities had negotiated a release, or pulled off a rescue, they wanted to milk the situation to the last drop and did not always put the welfare of the hostage first. Others, whose return was ignored by press, public and governments alike, built up a great head of self-destructive resentment, especially towards those government agencies they felt had made an insufficient effort to secure their release. This indifference seemed to undermine their already shaky sense of self. For the majority, however, there was a healing power in the instant fame and fortune,[35] though fortune depended to a great extent on nationality and the ability to exploit the experience in print and on-screen. European governments may sometimes have paid large ransoms under the table, but they did not generally compensate former hostages financially, rather taking the view that the individual should not have been so foolish as to have been taken hostage in the first place. The American Lebanon hostages were reputed to have received very large sums, as much as $120m in one case, but I have come across no hard evidence for this. Whatever the hostage's nationality, the care and generosity shown towards them by complete strangers during their captivity and in the immediate aftermath were moving. Letters, postcards and gifts – the majority of which never reached them – showed the extent of public concern. During his captivity, Terry Waite received only one postcard, from a complete stranger, a picture of a stained glass window showing John Bunyan in his prison, but the boost it gave his morale was enormous.

Celebrity, like sympathy, tends to be an ephemeral thing and nearly all this generosity evaporated once the hostage's 15 minutes, or 15 days, in the limelight had passed. This phase, in which the former hostage suddenly finds himself a celebrity, may last for only a few hours or a few weeks, but seldom longer before the let-down of the second phase. This period, in which the former hostage tries to come to terms with the trauma of his experience, can last for a few weeks or for years depending not just on his resilience, but on the severity and length of his captivity and on the efficacy of the rehabilitation he receives.* Some never emerged from these phases, others only did so partially. Former employers, whether in the public or the private sector, tended to look askance at these reminders to the rest of the employees of what the price of serving them might be.[36] The let-down after being the focus of so much attention could be painful for some hostages, almost as if they were being returned to the obscurity of their captivity. This ego-reducing experience was usually coupled with the erosion of ties with all those former fellow hostages with whom interdependence had been so important during captivity. The consequences of this relapse into obscurity, compounding that of captivity, could be serious – depression, chronic anxiety, sleep disorders, unexplained flashbacks, guilt, anger and difficulty in concentrating.[37] Those captives whose

---

* *There is disagreement among the experts about which is the more important – Hauber opts for duration, Campbell for severity. The interaction of the two may be a better guide.*

former lives were less orientated towards worldly success sometimes experienced an almost total detachment from the concerns of the world, an inertia similar to that which they had used to protect themselves in captivity. Ernst Fischler, a German hostage released in China in 1930 wrote: "The world has grown strange to us, how poor and trivial its hollow superficiality and its preoccupations with outward things seems to us now."[38] These new stresses, coupled with the physical and emotional trauma of the captivity itself, may well lead to heart disease, kidney problems, failure of the immune system and cancer.[39] The physical consequences were not always so serious, but the trivial ones, though the cause of considerable amusement, could be frustrating for the newly released hostage. John McCarthy found it "hard to walk without overbalancing and to co-ordinate generally with so much space. Can- and bottle-openers left me feeling completely kack-handed. Any sort of knife, even a potato peeler, left my fingers cut and bleeding. A simple process like making a cup of coffee seemed to have limitless pitfalls." As Jill Morell – McCarthy's girlfriend when he was in captivity – realized this was because "for years, he had never looked further than ten feet in front of him and that perspective was now something to be rediscovered".

The damage to the psyche may be greater than that to the body and can lead to serious difficulties in personal and social relationships; an inability to settle back into the routines and disciplines of employment or work of any kind, broken marriages and engagements and difficulties in relating to children, parents and friends.

It is sometimes forgotten that the families and close friends of long-term hostages suffer greatly, too, albeit not in a directly physical way. They may not know whether their loved ones are dead or alive, what they are suffering, what kind of mental and physical shape they will be in when they return – if they ever do. Will the bonds of love be able to survive their attenuation? All the time the hostage has been frozen in time, living from day to day in a miniature world in which less happens in 100 days than in 100 hours in the outside world, his family has had to get on with ordinary living. Domestic and social patterns have changed for the to all intents and purposes "deserted" wife or partner; children will have passed through schools, universities and jobs; grandchildren will have been born; lovers will have found other loves – all these people will have moved on while the hostage, in their terms, will have stood still. Sometimes the distance travelled is too great for its steps to be retraced. Sometimes those left wondering kept the road open by campaigning furiously, in some cases literally furiously, for their governments to do more to get the hostages returned.

The hostages themselves tried to bridge this gap in different ways. Some turned to autobiography, others to fiction and philosophy – Kaufmann wrote of "his urgent need to write". Some blocked out the worst part of their experiences. Others embroidered them to make their own role in captivity less undignified and more heroic than it actually was, yet others talked about them, but as though they had happened to someone else. Some found talking helpful, some distressing. All long-term hostages were confronted with the problem of having to recreate their relationships with those closest to them – an experience many families found similarly difficult or impossible after the long absences of servicemen during the Second World War with its subsequent high divorce rate. Waite was given a room in Trinity Hall in which to write his book during the week and eased himself gradually back into family life at weekends.

> I came back into the family step-by-step, piecemeal, rather than coming back, whoosh, like that and doing everything at once, and that was wise. They got a breather. And they'd moved on, I mean they're different, they've had other experiences, so they've moved on just as I have moved on and you have to take that gently and slowly.[40]

Jackie Mann and his wife found that despite, or perhaps because of, the length of their relationship, "The air was never cleared" because both were afraid of arguing, having spent the last three years longing for each other." Their expectations of a textbook happy ending had risen so high, neither would admit the possibility of disagreement. Some did manage to talk it through, but many family members were too frightened to hear about such painful experiences and afraid to complain about their own tribulations lest they awaken disturbing memories on either side. Some hostages found it hard to express the gratitude they felt for that intangible support that came from knowing that someone out their loved them and waited for them. Several expressed their feelings in other people's words, as in this poem by Konstantin Simonov which was sent to Jill Morell.

> They will never understand that in the midst of death
> You with your waiting saved me.
> Only you and I know how I survived.
> It's because you waited as no one else did.

A hostage's prospects of recovery also depend on the quality of the debriefing and rehabilitation he receives immediately after his release. It is an astonishing thing that America, a nation obsessed with psychoanalysis and panaceas of every kind, provided only tea and orange juice for its embassy staff after their 444 days of captivity in Tehran before plunging them back into everyday life in 1981. Ten years later, when the last of the British hostages was freed from Lebanon, Britain had become the emulated world leader in the psychology of returning captives to normal life. When Jackie Mann, John McCarthy and Terry Waite returned to England, long and careful preparation had already been made to ease them back into a normal existence.[41] By this time, three significant advances had been made on earlier hostage debriefing techniques. The extent, pace and timing of the debriefing and adjustment were entirely determined by the hostage rather than by either the psychologists or the secular authorities. The psychologists sat in from the outset on the intelligence service's debriefing so that the hostage did not have to go through his painful basic story twice. It was also recognized that the primary psychological team could become so involved in the stress and trauma of the hostage that a back-up team of fellow professionals, which never saw the hostage, was needed. This was so that the primary interlocutors could both unburden and seek second opinions about their conclusions and their proposals.

When the hostages arrived back in England, they and their families were given comfortable accommodation at an RAF base before any contact was made with the world beyond, access from which was carefully controlled. The hostages thus had their first, and therapeutic, choice of deciding how much exposure to the media they should have. At the outset of earlier returns, often before they had even seen members of their own families, hostages were plunged straight into a press conference. They were thus tempted to pour forth their stories to the world before they told it to those who cared or knew how to handle it. This could tempt them into making statements and striking attitudes from which they later found it hard to draw back, however much they wanted to.

At every stage a rapport was built up between the hostage and the psychiatrist by giving the hostage confidence that no line of questioning would be pursued that he did not consent to. It was a priority to restore the captive's sense of control★ of events after so long with none. Another way in which this sense of being in control was cultivated was to show the captives compilation videos of the events that had taken place while they were absent.

The approach used in dealing with hostages in the 1980s and '90s had begun to be developed in resettling prisoners of war and followed two, usually parallel, lines of enquiry. The first was to establish accurately what actually happened to provide a cognitive framework within which the hostage could re-orientate himself. The other aimed at establishing what the hostage felt about these events so that he could express his reactions "non-cathartically" and give them emotional meaning.

Those in Britain who passed through this careful process, or similar ones in other countries, generally adapted to everyday life more quickly and more thoroughly than those simply plunged straight back into it. These, like Tom Sutherland, were able to turn the appalling negative into the positive:

No matter how much I recount the negative in cell horrors or tales of chains or

★ *I wonder if, once home, hostages became control freaks, for a while at least, or went to the opposite extreme and wanted all decisions made for them as they had been in captivity.*

travelling taped up under the bed of a truck or dark holes or a terrible beating or three suicide attempts, the positive of the experience comes through in the end – for that is how it translated itself.[42]

But however fully they recovered, as Diane Cole wrote of the Tehran embassy hostages, "Let no one be deceived; some part of each one will remain in that embassy forever."[43] That so many hostages remained so long in captivity was largely due to the policies of the coerced, the United States and other governments, and that is the subject of the next chapter.

Chapter Thirteen

The Coerced

Political hostage-taking is one of the more insidious forms of blackmail in that there are instances in which making a deal, or even giving in completely, can be less damaging than putting the matter in the hands of the law-enforcement authorities. It can create a situation in which morality and pragmatism are placed in direct conflict with one another. Morality says that hostage-taking, like any other form of blackmail, should always be resisted and priority given to catching or killing the perpetrator.

Pragmatism, on the other hand, argues that in the unconditional pursuit of retribution, both the primary victim – the hostage – and the secondary victim – the coerced (usually the state) – can be damaged more than if they had given in or at least negotiated. In a criminal blackmail case, the pursuit of the criminal may ruin the life and reputation of the victim, but in a political hostage-taking it could not only cost him his life, but do serious damage to the ethos of the state.

Clearly the state that allows little or no civil liberty to its citizens and regards their lives as expendable in furtherance of national policy has little to fear from the hostage-taker. In doing the research for this book, I have come across no case of political hostage-taking against the state in modern China or North Korea, Myanmar (Burma) or Zimbabwe. On the contrary, in such countries it is the state that takes its citizens hostage as a guarantee of their compliant behaviour.

It is noticeable that the price paid by the nations of the former Soviet Union and eastern Europe for their emergence into varying degrees of civil freedom has been the return, in some cases the spectacular return, of the scourge of political hostage-taking. This been so extensive in some cases that they have been tempted to revert to the secretive and oppressive methods of their totalitarian past, to the halcyon days of the 1970s when, at the height of the hostage-taking epidemic, the Soviet Union was not only immune, but actively encouraging the practice elsewhere.

There is a second small group of third rank,* as opposed to Third World, states, usually in the grip of a single, autocratic leader. These, as well as severely restricting the liberty of their own citizens, have, in the period covered by this study, actively and sometimes openly sponsored terrorism of all kinds, including hostage-taking. They may well, if more discreetly, still be doing so. For Iran, Syria, Iraq and Libya, the various guerrilla and terrorist groups were the mercenaries of the 20th century through whom they could fight their proxy wars against opponents who were too powerful to confront directly.[1] For them it is solely a question of did hostage-taking work in the past and will it continue to work in the future? Arguably it enabled them to punch consistently above their weight internationally with only the occasional bloody nose. Equally, it has failed to win them any of their major political objectives.

However, for the great majority of nation states the dilemma remains – how to respond most effectively to hostage-taking without jeopardizing the civilized standards they purport to uphold. These nations fall into two main categories. The first consists of those that talk tough and declare that they will have no dealings with hostage-takers under any circumstances. The leading members of this category are Britain, Israel, Russia and the United States. A second batch of less powerful intransigent states – Argentina, Colombia, Egypt, Jordan, Uruguay and Saudi Arabia – are probably the noisiest of those following this course. The quietest are the countries of eastern Europe and the former Soviet Union, who have kept the postures, if not the power, of former times. The question can reasonably be asked: "Do the tough-talking countries suffer less from hostage-taking than others?"

The second category consists of the pragmatists, of which France is the prime example, with Germany, Italy, the Netherlands and Sweden close behind. These openly deploy force, negotiation and surrender as seems most appropriate to the circumstances. I can think of no country that gives in consistently as a matter of policy, however hidden the agenda.

The legal situation for all nations, on paper at least, is reasonably clear. International law, confirmed in domestic law at least nominally by the majority of states, lays down the obligation *aut dedere, aut judicare* – give them up (to extradition) or try them. In practice it is not always so simple. How should democratic governments treat cases of skyjacking in which no deaths occur and in which the skyjackers' sole motive is to escape from an oppressive regime from which their lives are at risk, as in the case of the Stansted Afghans? The classic case is that of the Greek dissident from the rule of the colonels in 1981, who seized a commercial flight and flew it to Sweden. At first this liberal nation

---

* *There is only one truly first-rank nation in the world today, the United States. In the second rank I place Britain, the larger countries of Western Europe, China, India and Russia.*

welcomed him as a hero and only later, in the wake of international protests, did it change its mind and prosecute.[2] Similar cases are to be found in the United States where, at one stage, Cuban dissidents who hijacked planes or boats and fled from Castro's regime to Florida were granted asylum rather than prosecuted or extradited.[3] Later, when the trickle became a flood, the question arose as to whether they should be treated as illegal immigrants or not.

Schreiber[4] asks the pertinent question of whether the countries which grant asylum to those fleeing from tyrannous regimes who arrive legally should then prosecute similar cases whose flight has entailed a non-violent, but unlawful, seizure of their means of transport. If so, with what should they be charged and how should they be punished? The argument is sometimes used that in cases in which, since no one was killed or injured, it is not a terrorist offence. But however worthy the intentions of political hijackers and kidnappers there can be no doubt that even in situations such as the ones cited above, or in the Croatian seizure of TWA355 [see pages 31–6], the captives have been terrified, that is to say terrorized.[5]

So much for the law, but the "tough" states have no compunction in ignoring it when it suits them if their citizens are held hostage in countries that fail to secure their release, or condone or abet their detention. Israel claimed a higher moral law at Entebbe and when the United States staged Eagle Claw to widespread international outrage in the Third World, it argued, and won the argument in the International Court, that Iran had forfeited the right to be protected by international law because it had failed to carry out its obligations under that law to protect diplomats and that, in any case, the US was acting in self-defence. There can be much sympathy for the two countries, both for the circumstances in which they found themselves and for their arguments. However, where both countries are concerned, there does seem to be a distinctive pattern in which they go along with international law or United Nations mandates when these endorse their own views and where they ignore them without exception when they do not.[6] Nor is this convenience a purely passive one. Most of the "tough" states have carried out quite unjustifiable actions when it has suited their domestic policy to do so. In 1986, the United States claimed the right under its War Powers Act to bomb Libya in retaliation for what it believed to be a Libyan-backed bomb attack on a West German night club in which two US servicemen were killed and many more were injured. The bombing of two Libyan cities in attacks launched from bases in Britain resulted in the deaths of 93 civilians, including Gadaffi's three-year-old adopted daughter. The US raid could not be interpreted as "reasonable response" by any measure. The disproportion, though not the immorality, was much less apparent when, following the bombing of the US embassies in Kenya and Tanzania in 1998, which resulted in a massive loss of civilian lives, the US launched rocket attacks on Afghanistan and the Sudan. Whatever indications the CIA may have had that these countries were behind the atrocities, the fact remains that the US retaliation, in which many more unconnected people were killed without any due judicial process, can only be interpreted as revenge rather than justice. President Clinton made it clear where his administration stood. "There … will be times when law enforcement and diplomatic tools are simply not enough, when our very national security is challenged … when we must take extraordinary steps to protect the safety of our citizens."[7]

There are perfectly honourable reasons for refusing extradition when the request is from a state where the captor's human rights are almost certain to be abused by extra-judicial imprisonment, torture or murder. The question of extradition is also a thorny one between states, such as the US and Britain, who differ about whether it is humane and civilized to inflict capital punishment on anyone, however heinous the crime of which he has been convicted. Less honourably, there are plenty of instances where the *aut dedere, aut judicare* obligation is ignored out of sympathy for the cause of the hostage-taker.

Finally there are those cases, like that of Abou Daoud in Italy after the *Achille Lauro* affair, where the domestic prosecution service feels there is not enough evidence to prosecute and therefore not enough evidence to extradite. Though these excuses are often proffered for not prosecuting, the far more common, if unacknowledged, one is the fear that once a hostage-taker has been convicted and imprisoned, there will be further incidents of hostage-taking by his comrades or sympathizers aimed at securing his release by blackmail. There are numerous ways in which this chain of events can be avoided other than ignoring the offence.

The first is not to capture the captors in the first place, but to make sure that safe passage out of the country is conceded as part of the negotiations. The captors will then usually be flown to some country that is generally less scrupulous about terrorism. This solution is not only pusillanimous, but increasingly difficult to resort to now that there are far fewer countries willing to accept hostage-takers as a matter of policy.

A second way is to prosecute, convict and then either pardon, commute most of the sentence, or release the prisoner on a parole from which the authorities know perfectly well he will not return. These can be useful face-saving devices when extradition has been denied to another friendly state as much from national pride and refusal to be bullied as from any legal nicety.

Then there is the Thatcher-Fujimori solution – avoid serious negotiation and make sure all the captors are killed during a rescue assault. As this usually involves cold-blooded murder by the assault force, it reduces the state that indulges in it to the level of the hostage-takers. Moreover, it does not always work and one or more of the captors may survive amidst the captives, as was the case at Princes Gate, who then has to be tried and imprisoned. The involuntary release of these is admittedly rare. Nevertheless, there are several instances, even among the "tough" states, in which a convicted hostage-taker has been released as a result of pressure brought to bear in a subsequent hostage-taking. British Prime Minister Edward Heath had little choice but to release Leila Khaled after Skyjack Sunday and Chancellor Schmidt chose similarly to give in to Baader-Meinhof in the Peter Lorenz affair.

In this respect, there is clearly a distinction between hostage-taking and other forms of terrorism. It has been a long-established practice, at least since the 19th century, for the great powers to use force to secure the release of their citizens held hostage in the territory of another sovereign state if that state will not take the necessary action itself. This was done with or without the co-operation of the country in whose territory the hostages were held. The trouble with "wars on terrorism", whether declared in the 19th or the 21st century, is that they turn the attacks of terrorists from being criminal offences into legitimate acts of war, and not just in the eyes of their perpetrators.

The two principal modern practitioners of the doctrine of justifiable revenge, Israel and the United States, have cloaked their actions in the emperor-like clothes of domestic laws that have created the entirely new category of "combatants without prisoner of war status".

This is in straight contradiction of the 1949 Geneva Convention on the treatment of prisoners of war and has no standing whatsoever in international law. Those held in this way without trial are not allowed legal advice or representation, cannot communicate with their families other than through rare and reluctantly conceded visits from the Red Cross, and are subjected to treatment the use of which, however psychological and sophisticated the methods used, amounts to torture. Yet this non-POW status is the rationalization in the two most notorious instances in recent times among democracies of long-term detention without trial, and amounts as much to hostage-taking as the past actions of Iran or Libya, of Hizbollah or the Red Brigades.

The justification given by the United States is that the detention of suspected Taliban fighters at Guantanamo is the only way in which its intelligence agencies can obtain valuable and essential information about the organization of terrorist networks and their plans for further atrocities. It will be 50 years, if at all, before official documents reveal whether this makes such detentions valid in at least pragmatic terms, even if it cannot be vindicated in legal ones.

The Israelis are more bluntly defiant in their actions and explanations. In response to an Israeli Supreme Court judgement that detentions of this kind were illegal under their own laws, the government of Ariel Sharon changed the law. On 1 March 2000 the Knesset enacted a retrospective law making such detentions legal. Detention is solely at the discretion of the army Chief of Staff and release at that of the Minister of Defence. Trials are held *in camera* and the accused may be denied knowledge of the evidence against him. The reason given by the government, as by its predecessors, was that it was the best way to find out what had happened to the small number of Israelis who had been kidnapped or disappeared.[8] One official formerly responsible for responding to hostage situations put this gloss on his country's tactics: "Playing the hostage game is like playing a game of chess. You make a move, and then you must work out what the other person's move will be. If we are honest, no one has any idea how to deal with hostage-taking."[9]

A purely condemnatory reaction is not helpful. Israel and America are principal targets of terrorist attacks and their citizens of killing and kidnap. But their governments need to ask themselves whether to some extent they have not brought this plague upon themselves. Is it simply a matter of unreasonable envy or is it because the one has been bullying its neighbours, the other the rest of the world? They need to ask whether the satisfaction they derive from this kind of response is sufficient compensation for undermining the international community's sometimes slow and clumsy development of a system of international law to combat terrorism? Above all, they have to ask themselves, does it work? Are the tough nations less prone to hostage-taking and other forms of terrorism than those that adopt a more flexible and pragmatic approach?

The decision to adopt such a policy is not taken in a political vacuum. In a democratic society with a free press, public opinion is largely moulded by what people read, hear and see on their television screens. The sight of children held at gunpoint will tug more heart-strings than the prospect of some elderly diplomat shut up below ground as a hostage. Politicians, with some exceptions, are heavily influenced in what they say and do by that same public opinion. Apart from the small section of the democratic world's media that is financed directly or indirectly from public funds, profitability depends on advertising and payments for access. These, in turn, depend on the number and purchasing power of those who want that access. For 90 per cent of the media, and that must now include the Internet, attracting those numbers of consumers depends on the amount of sensation, scandal and sex on offer. Hostage-taking incidents seen out of perspective are an excellent source of the first two, even if they rarely involve the third. And so the cycle revolves with the great majority of hostage-takers well aware that the publicity they so desperately seek can be secured by exploiting the media's appetites. The families of the hostages share the same objective, in that the greater the media exposure, the more likely the government will feel obliged to negotiate rather than ignore his plight or resort to force that may imperil his or her life.

Until the late 1980s even democratic governments used to be able to limit, more or less effectively, the access the hostage-taker may have to such sources of publicity. However, if they chose that course they confronted the dilemma of how to do so without stifling the access to the information and freedom of debate essential to the health of a free society. This may mean having to tolerate such rabid comments as appeared in the *New York Post* of 30 April 2002. "Americans [must] understand how much they need to fear and loathe Militant Islam," or, "It's time to call the true enemy what it is: Militant Islam. To hell with political correctness." To suppress such comments, deny liberal values, curtail personal freedom "for the sake of order is to fall into the error of the terrorists themselves, the folly of believing the end justifies the means."[10] There are plenty to point out the corollary: "If the state truly wishes to protect itself from the threat and destruction of terror violence, then social order must be strengthened at the expense of individual freedom."[11] The confident democracy is the one that can strike a balance between order and liberty, security and openness.

Sometimes the media co-operated, sometimes it made the task of the authorities in dealing with a particular hostage-taking incident more difficult. By the concluding date of this study, it had become virtually impossible, in an age of satellite broadcasting and the Internet, to take the suppressive option. Even those totalitarian regimes in which all the traditional media were under strict government control were finding an increasing number of ever larger gaps in their information *cordon sanitaire*. Nor in the age of the mobile phone can access to the scene of a hostage incident be denied by cutting off physical and telecommunication access to its location. Whereas in the 1970s autocratic regimes were virtually immune from hostage-taking, as a result of their ability to deny publicity as much as their willingness to act ruthlessly, they are now driven to a sole reliance on ruthlessness. For the martyr-complex hostage-taker, as the Russians and the Israelis have discovered, this alone is no deterrent. Now democratic governments are more or less obliged to do what the wisest of them always did – supply as much information as possible as soon as possible to the media, together with a believable promise of the whole story later.

Governments are also generally at a disadvantage in confronting hostage-takers by virtue of the very nature of their intelligence work and counter-terrorism measures. Terrorists can pick both target and timing, but governments cannot protect every likely target or every potential hostage victim 24 hours a day. Noticeably, those with a high degree of personal protection are never kidnapped. On top of this, there are hundreds of vague warnings every day, but very few concrete ones. The background noise from which the pertinent signal has to be picked out can be overwhelming, something not always appreciated by those who complain after the event that one of these generalized warnings was not acted on. Where intelligence services succeed, as they do most of the time, in anticipating, preventing and thwarting hostage-taking and other terrorist attacks by good intelligence work and clandestine precautions, they are precluded from claiming credit publicly because they need to use those same channels and methods again. When they fail and a kidnapping or a siege takes place, it does so in the full glare of adverse publicity. Then the effectiveness of both government and security services will be judged solely on their ability to deal with that particular situation. Hence the temptation to react forcefully rather than more subtly and to make it clear, both loudly and publicly, that this is their intention.

> The US government will make no concessions to individuals or groups holding official or private US citizens hostage. The United States will use every appropriate resource to gain the safe return of American citizens held hostage. At the same time it is US government policy to deny hostage-takers any benefits of ransom, prisoner releases, policy changes, or other acts of concession.

Thus a reiteration of the official policy of the United States as promulgated from Washington in February 2002, and it has given birth to some tortuous footnotes. One State Department official told Miller, "We will talk but we will not negotiate." Negotiation in this context means a bartering of hostages for tangible demands, while talking means an inquiry into the well-being of the hostages and appeals on humanitarian grounds for their release.[12]

In practice, events through history have worked out rather differently, as a sequence of Presidents found their tough talk having to give way to the demands of Real Politik and electoral survival. Nixon, at least, was consistent in ignoring this fact, although his rather too public and aggressive hostility towards Black September cost the lives of his diplomats in Khartoum.

Truman blustered at the Chinese about the seizure of his consulate in Mukden and fumed at his inability to bomb or blockade them. He only got his people released by quiet diplomacy; Lyndon Johnson got nowhere with threats in persuading the North Koreans to return the crew of the spy ship *Pueblo* which they held hostage in 1969. He succeeded by admitting US guilt in the matter and apologizing; Jimmy Carter fell sharply in public estimation for failing to get the US diplomats held in Tehran freed through Eagle Claw and its aborted progeny. He succeeded by unfreezing Iranian assets, but too late to save himself from electoral defeat. The most successful hostage release in Carter's term was in the Hanafi siege – secured by negotiation;[13] Ronald Reagan made more tough-guy B-movie noises than most of his predecessors, but they did not get him back his hostages in Lebanon. He succeeded because he was something of a softy at heart as well as passionately anti-Communist, so sold weapons to Iran to get his people out and to finance Oliver North's illegal subsidy of the Contras in Nicaragua.

Nor was United States' policy any more successful in achieving its declared aims when sticking to the no-deals approach and employing, or attempting to employ, force. The armed rescue of the *Mayaguez* in 1975 cost 41 US marines their lives at a time when the crew was being voluntarily returned. Forcing the Egypt Air plane carrying the *Achille Lauro* hijackers to land at a NATO base in Italy and demanding their handover only provoked Italy into refusing to extradite and possibly conniving at their escape after conviction. The bombing of Libya in 1986 has been justified by claiming a reduction in Libyan-sponsored terrorism. In fact, it resulted in further revenge bombings, more taking of American hostages in Lebanon and in Gaddafi being more subtle and discreet in his sponsorship, as was the case in Indonesia. The attack on Libya did little more than demonstrate that US toughness would only be exercised against those states which were not important in US foreign policy terms. It would not be applied against those, such as Syria and Iran, which were useful, nor against China or the Soviet Union, which were too powerful to provoke safely. It would only be fair to the much-maligned CIA to point out that it advised against most of these wild adventures.

These double standards did little to endear the United States to even its allies. One French former hostage scathingly observed that, in the name of Real Politik, Reagan not only welcomed his captor, Hassan Habre, who was once described as the Pinochet of Chad, to the White House on 4 July 1987, but had him stand alongside him during the 14 July parade while behind "*une brochette de ministres*" (lovely metaphor) banged on about not dealing with hostage-takers. Cynically he asks whether the hostages in Lebanon, whose governments "played the hero" in refusing to negotiate with their captors, would live to see those same captors given a full state welcome in Paris, London, Bonn and Washington.[14]

It would seem that the United States' northern neighbour had more success in adopting the get-tough policy when Canada's Prime Minister, Pierre Trudeau, was confronted by a situation in which the francophone separatist movement in Quebec province kidnapped one of his ministers, Pierre Laporte, and a British commissioner, Jasper Cross. "There's a lot of bleeding hearts around who just don't like to see people with helmets and guns. All I can say is go on and bleed, but it is more important to keep law and order in society than to be worried about weak-kneed people."[15] Trudeau's tough speech on television, when he declared a state of apprehended insurrection on 16 October 1970, initially drew considerable support, among the English-speaking majority at least. After two months in which there were thousands of arrests and searches without warrant by police backed by large numbers of troops, that uncritical support had evaporated. By that time, Laporte had been found dead and Cross had been released. It is true that there were no more kidnappings or assassinations by FLQ, but perhaps the eventual erosion of popular support that was to turn Trudeau from the universally acclaimed, do-no-wrong good guy into an increasingly unpopular leader of the opposition can be traced to this event.

But what of America's protégé in the Middle East? Literally besieged on all sides, even from the sea, and with its very existence threatened by the Arab world, Israel was more belligerent in its stance and more vehement in its protestations of no deals on hostages than any other country. At the same time, it had itself become one of the most ruthless of state hostage-takers, holding hundreds of Lebanese and Palestinians, without trial or prospect of release and in harsh conditions, as a bargaining counter in its conflict with the PLO, Hizbollah, Islamic Jihad and the other Islamic militant groups. Yet Israel, too, was compelled to give up its own hostages on several occasions, not so much from fear of its enemies or their counter pressures, as from the pressure applied by the United States, the patron and ally that it could not afford, literally, to offend by refusing. No one, least of all the Palestinians, was taken in by protestations of "coincidence" or "purely humanitarian reasons" when prisoners were released from Israeli jails.

The third member of the top division tough team, Britain, turned out only to be tough when it had a tough Prime Minister – a Margaret Thatcher or a Tony Blair. Edward Heath, a civilized man, had felt obliged to release Leila Khaled rather than see scores of Britons murdered; John Major, a weak but kindly man, was accused of encouraging renewed IRA activity by his conciliatory approach. Admittedly the Iron Lady's tough, "I want no loose ends" approach had been eminently successful within the limited terms of the Princes Gate siege, but her support of Reagan over the bombing of Libya and her refusal to allow even much-needed dialysis machines to be traded for Collet's life, resulted only in the death of British hostages in Lebanon and the Lockerbie disaster without any discernible furtherance of British foreign policy in the Middle East. Thatcher's attitude to the human shields held in Kuwait by Saddam in 1991 is more understandable, but to the families who felt themselves to be in the middle of the firing line of anxiety, her manner indicated that she "had been rushing to chuck kerosene over us".[16]

The Soviet Union once belonged to this group, but the successor states, while making the same threatening noises, have at least edged a little towards the pragmatic. Russia readily launched bloody counter-attacks on Chechens when they seized an aircraft, a hospital and a theatre, but was also capable of turning the other cheek when it was more expedient than sticking out its jaw. In December 1988, when an airliner was hijacked by a number of Jews, the Russians allowed both it and the hostages to be flown to Israel rather than storming it. Perhaps they guessed that the Israelis would return both the plane and the hostages once the captors had arrived safely, and this they did. As for the second division tough guys, it is only necessary to recite their names again to indicate just how unsuccessful their policy has been in preventing further hostage-taking – Argentina, Colombia, Egypt, Saudi Arabia and Uruguay.

The tough states might reasonably riposte that, although any one individual reaction may not have had the desired outcome, the general policy of no deals has acted as a deterrent to other would-be hostage-takers. It is, of course, impossible to prove a negative hypothesis, but there are two problems with it. In the first place there is no empirical evidence to support such a claim, not a single proven case of a hostage-taking organization admitting that it refrained from a particular target because of the threat of retaliation.[17] In the second, no democratic state, not even Israel, has been able to pursue such a policy with the 100 per cent ruthless adherence that alone could substantiate the proposition. It might be argued that, in the past, totalitarian states have demonstrated its effectiveness, but there is no way of knowing what failures there may have been in such closed societies. In any case, the events of the past two years should be sufficient proof to the contrary.

Contrast the unproductive stance of the tough group with the highly successful one, in human terms at least, of the pragmatists of western Europe. By the mid-1970s, the French were quick to realize that different hostage situations demanded different responses and that to take up rigid positions in advance would mean either loss of face or loss of flexibility. For example, the government of President Mitterand came to a convenient arrangement with Iran whereby its investment in a French uranium enrichment firm was reimbursed in return for the release of the last French hostages in Lebanon on 4 May 1988. This was only four days before Mitterand defeated challenger Chirac in the final round of the presidential election.[18] In other instances, ransom was paid for the release of prisoners in a more direct manner, but no hostage-takers could count on France giving in tamely on every occasion. In Djibouti and Marseilles, no hesitation was shown by the GIGN in forcefully rescuing hostages with very low casualty levels among hostages and assault troops and 90 per cent fatalities among the hostage-takers. So effective was the GIGN that its services were greatly in demand and happily furnished to countries with which France hoped to do military business, such as Egypt and Saudi Arabia.

The other major countries of western Europe have displayed similar, if not so consummately skilful and successful, pragmatism, sometimes hitting back, as in Mogadishu, Stockholm in 1975 or the Dozier case, sometimes giving in and sometimes negotiating. Germany, for example, prevaricated and procrastinated for the first six months of 1987, when the United States sought to extradite the Hamedi brothers, responsible for the hijacking of TWA847. Immediately after their arrest, two Germans were taken hostage in Lebanon and it was made clear that if the Hamedis were turned over they would be killed. In the end, Germany tried and convicted the brothers itself, only to find itself under pressure to release them. It compromised in the end by easing their conditions of imprisonment.

Even Britain once belonged to this pragmatic group. During Britain's mandate in Iraq in the 1920s, when any tribal area became too troublesome, the British would issue a warning to the recalcitrant village. When all the inhabitants had left, taking all their furniture and possessions with them, the RAF would bomb the mud-built houses flat. The inhabitants would then return and rebuild while the British took as hostage for future good behaviour some economically insignificant person, such as a boy goatherd. These hostages had such a good time that soon everyone was clamouring to be taken when the opportunity arose.[19]

The inescapable fact remains that although sieges in Europe last three times longer on average than in the rest of the world and involve twice as many hostages, although kidnappings are more short-lived, there is a smaller proportion of hostages that are either harmed or killed – between three and four per cent of deaths in rescue missions – and fewer captors achieve their demands for safe conduct out of the country than in any other region of the world.[20]

In the second half of the 20th century, 20 countries accounted for some three-quarters of all political hostage-taking, ten for over half. Governments were three times more likely to give in to a hostage-taker who kidnapped – out of the public eye – than to one who staged a siege, who only achieved his aims one time in five. Corporations gave in nearly three-quarters of the time and over 90 per cent if only ransom were demanded, which might suggest that companies value the lives of their employees more highly than countries value those of their citizens![21]

It is possible to draw some general inferences from the incidents examined in the preceding chapters. Hostage-taking usually succeeds if the captors choose to strike on familiar ground in a carefully planned and coolly executed way. The captors most likely to get what they demand are those who are prepared to die for their cause, but would prefer not to do so, and who limit their genuine demands, as opposed to their opening bids, to those things the coerced can politically afford to concede.

The captives who have survived have been those with a strong infusion of the same qualities that enable people to survive other extreme physical, emotional and mental crises – belief in themselves, something to live for and the will to survive at any cost. In terms of saving hostage lives, negotiation is many times more effective than rescue attempts by force, in which roughly ten times as many hostages die as are killed in cold blood by their captors. Rescues only succeed when, like seizures, they have been meticulously planned, fully rehearsed and ruthlessly carried out by specialist forces trained for the job.

The most effective weapons with which to combat hostage-takers, or any other terrorists, are effective security measures in vulnerable places and for vulnerable people and good counter-terrorist intelligence. Such intelligence is best obtained from human sources rather than satellites, but requires skilful filtering and analysis if the few diamonds are to be sorted from the many tonnes of earth. The biggest obstacle to effective intelligence gathering is intellectual and national arrogance and the ignorance of other cultures that it can breed. The most likely way to recover hostages from a state, or state-sponsored, hostage-taker is to understand and work with those elements within that state who have the strongest political and economic motives for releasing them. The lesson, above all, is that half a century of hostage-taking has demonstrated that there are no solutions that always work, no theories that always apply and no rules that can never be broken. But all these are the criteria that apply to the past. Will they be equally applicable to the future?

Chapter Fourteen

Tomorrow's Hostages

Since the heyday of political hostage-taking in the 1970s and earlier 1980s, there has been a declining trend in this activity, interrupted by occasional mini-surges and spectacular one-off events, mostly in Russia. There have also been fewer cross-border international incidents and a number of countries that used to feature regularly in the top of the cops top ten now no longer do so – Lebanon, Britain and Germany, for example. On the other hand, the number of violent acts of terrorism has increased considerably over the past five years.[1] Among the world's militant dissidents, hostage-taking is no longer a favoured choice as a means of securing their ends. Will the decline in its popularity continue on down to zero? Will it cease to be a valid lever for the powerless to use on the powerful? Or will it change its nature and re-emerge in a different form?

There are a number of reasons for the decline and for the changing emphasis of terror in recent years. With the notable exceptions of Chechnya, Kashmir and Palestine, most of the smaller ethnic groups seeking independence have either found it peacefully by political means, as they have to a degree in Scotland and Wales, have seen the fervour for independence dwindle, as in the Basque country, Corsica or Quebec, or are fighting it out in bloody tribal wars as in Afghanistan, Africa and parts of southeast Asia. Where once stability behind arbitrarily drawn colonial borders depended on the arbitrary, but regulated, conduct of colonial policemen and soldiers, chaos now reigns. In none of these situations is political hostage-taking likely to be an appropriate or effective weapon. After all, who is to be taken and who is to be coerced?

A combination of developments has diminished the value placed on human life and, therefore, of the bargaining leverage of threatening to kill a hostage. The multitudinousness of mankind – six-and-a-quarter billion of us at the last count – and the rash of lethal conflicts across the globe (or rather the ability of a global media to bring their brutality to our attention), have diminished the perceived importance of any one individual life other than our own and that of our nearest and dearest. The media, with its daily diet of unimaginative fictional mayhem and the supposedly objective reporting of all-too-real mayhem in the world at large, has fed an appetite for the ever more shocking and bloody that has dulled our sensibilities to such a degree that horrors have to be ever more horrific to awaken them. They can thus be more easily traded off for political reasons without too many pangs of national conscience. Our sympathy for the plight of others decreases in length and strength proportionately to the increasing demands made on it. The media, anxious to titillate at every turn, allows no catastrophe to hold its attention, or ours, for long before pushing it aside with the next. It is doubtful if those tenacious and wide-reaching campaigns of the 1970s and '80s for the release of individual hostages would be possible to sustain in media terms today.* On top of that is the modern obsession with thinking of people in purely economic and statistical terms – producers, voters, pensioners, consumers, unemployed and so on – that reduce them to the same dehumanizing trade goods status in which the hostage-taker thinks of them.

It has also dawned gradually on the advocates of hostage-taking as a lever for political coercion that it has actually achieved very little in the past 30 years – the release of a few hundred imprisoned comrades, usually the payment of modest ransoms, the occasional publication of some incomprehensible manifesto. What it did achieve was much greater awareness of the causes on behalf of which it was undertaken. We were made more sharply aware of individual instances of injustice, oppression or thwarted legitimate aspirations to nationhood. But so what? That awareness has led to the overthrow of no government, the creation of no new state in Palestine or Papua New Guinea, Kashmir or Chechnya. If we can no longer, as Neville Chamberlain did, ignore "a quarrel in a far away country between people of whom we know nothing",[2] we do not feel we can do much about it. Nor is this greater awareness a one-way traffic. The people of "far away countries" are in turn increasingly aware, by means of the global media, of the discrepancies in power, wealth and social justice between us. They see no reason to tolerate that difference either between nations or within their own. "In a world accustomed to placing more value on ends than means the terrorist is the supreme pragmatist."[3] It used to be true that "terrorists wanted a lot of people watching not a lot of people dead",[4] but if those watching treat what they see as just another television thriller and their governments, in consequence, are

* During the captivity of the US diplomats in Tehran one US television programme signed off every evening with a reminder of how many days they had been held.

even more disinclined to make concessions than they were before, then traditional, small-scale hostage-taking will be abandoned for something more forceful. If common hostage-taking is the crime of the greedy, then political hostage-taking was the crime of the hopeful. It was based on the belief that in return for the lives of hostages, meaningful concessions would be made sufficiently often by the coerced to make the risks worthwhile. But experience has gradually seen that hope evaporate leaving a residue of despair and the destructive hate that goes with it. Thus we see all those young suicide bombers – and they are always young for the ambitious old men behind them will not sacrifice their own lives – who have everything to live for save hope, so they prefer to die. When Islamic Jihad was challenged on its use of this despicable tactic, its spokesman grimly replied: "We have nothing with which to repel killing and thuggery against us except the weapon of martyrdom. It is easy and costs us only our lives. Human bombs cannot be defeated, not even by nuclear bombs."[5]

But nor can human bombs on the scale employed by Hamas, Al Aqsa, Martyrs Brigade or the Chechens – though the latter have upped the ante with their suicide raids in the past couple of years – do anything to change policy in Israel or Russia, or indeed do anything but go up another rung on the ladder of violence such states are only too ready to climb. So what can the frustrated militant do now to attract the attention of the media or influence a stubborn government? With the switch that appears to have taken place from wishing to influence your enemy, to wishing only to destroy him, the importance of hostage-taking will continue to diminish, but it will also change in nature rather than disappear altogether.

The hostage-taker is likely to depart from his traditional patterns in one of three ways. Other than for criminal purposes only two people and one group of people of genuine prominence have been encountered in this study who have been taken hostage – Juan Fangio and Aldo Moro - the one held briefly as a gesture, the other murdered as a consequence of party infighting among Italy's politicians and the OPEC Oil Ministers. The really high-profile leaders in a modern state, the Presidents and premiers and senior ministers are well, but not infallibly, protected. The leading lights in the sporting, entertainment and business worlds, who have often been the targets of purely criminal abduction, may hire private bodyguards, but they cannot provide absolute protection. It seems highly probable to me that within the next five to ten years some hostage-taker more ingenious or bold than his fellows, will succeed in seizing a Michael Schumacher or a Michael Jordan, a Putin or a Sharon, and that major concessions will have to be made to get them back alive.

The second way that hostage-takers may restore the length of their shrinking lever is to emphasize the vulnerability of the targets they chose – a clinic full of babies and pregnant women, a hospital for the handicapped or the elderly infirm. We have already seen the precursors of such seizures in the schools at Ma'alot and Bovensmilde and the thousands of hospital patients held hostage by the Chechens in 1995 and 1996 in the Russian towns of Budyonnovsk and Kizlyar. Seizures of a few hundred hostages at a time have hitherto been thought of as large-scale,[6]* but they will be considered but a handful when tens of thousands are taken at Old Trafford or the Yankee Stadium, the San Siro or the new Olympic Stadium in Athens. Strictly speaking, hostage-taking on this scale is more akin to extortion, but the boundaries between acts that involve a trade-off of some kind are blurred and even those I have just suggested will be small fry to what is possible.

Donald Rumsfeld chose to describe the people of Iraq as hostages in order to justify the United States "doing what is right" in invading that country. But he may not have paused to consider that the tables might be turned, that those he dubs "terrorists" might decide to take a whole American city hostage by the simple expedient of plausibly threatening it with devastation from a dirty nuclear bomb or an e-bomb, from a biological or chemical weapon. The device need not even exist for the panic and fear that would totally disrupt normal life to set in. Those[7] who argue that there is a limit to the scale of catastrophe the terrorist can usefully bring about, and therefore to the nature and range of the weapons he employs, make the fallacious assumption that all terrorists, like hostage-takers, are in the business of bargaining and that a peaceful, negotiated outcome of most incidents is still possible. For some it still may be, but for others who have given up any hope of what they regard as justice, only hate and the desire to bring down the pillars of the temple with them remain. Such a terrorist will gladly see thousands die for no better reason than that he wants thousands dead. Of the various options that in practical, rather than James Bond-style, terms are at his disposal, the cheapest and easiest to obtain and deploy is a biological weapon of some kind.

The biological threat is a particularly insidious one for it promises to invade and take over our bodies, perhaps slowly, perhaps painfully, perhaps inexorably and maybe over many weeks. Even though there has been an increase in the number of threats of bio-terrorism – the FBI reported an increase in the United States from 37 cases a year in 1996 to 300 in 2001 – the fear has become disproportionate to the risk. In the anthrax letters episode of October 2001 in America, only five people were killed, but the panic at all levels reached epidemic proportions. Fear is the deadliest weapon to have replaced conventional hostage-taking, because it induces not only a pleasure-destroying paranoia in the general population – as places of entertainment and holiday resorts are already finding – but it also gradually paralyses the normal social

* *The one truly big seizure so far was that at the Grand Mosque in Mecca [see pages 89–91] when as many as 50,000 worshippers were at risk.*

intercourse and interpersonal exchanges on which the smooth running of a free society depends. Take skyjacking for the purpose of taking hostages, for example. More effective security measures and greater success in negotiation and rescue had largely restored people's faith in air travel, so that although some were still apprehensive, the fear was manageable and prevented very few travellers from flying. Along comes a single attempt to shoot down a commercial jet with a ground-to-air missile in Kenya, or the turning of aircraft themselves into missiles on 9/11 and fear again dominates as people realize that some of the new terrorists would rather kill than capture. One effect of 9/11 was to bring about a staggering, and economically damaging, drop in the number of passengers flying, especially for tourism – an essential part of the economy to many poorer countries. Flights in and out of the United States in the week after 9/11 fell by 79 per cent and world-wide by 19 per cent[8] and took six months to return to normal. Clearly a sequence of such events could have a crippling effect on international travel and, therefore, on the world economy generally.

There is a greater consensus today than for a long time about what constitutes an act of terrorism, as countries of every kind, from dictatorships to democracies, find themselves the victims of a less political, more anarchic or religious, kind of terrorism. The consequence is that a fearful populace makes less and less protest at the loss of fundamental liberties which states of all creeds and colours are imposing in the name of "the war against terrorism". Those concerned to reduce the violence of terrorism have first to be concerned with reducing the subtler violence of legitimate power.[9] We are witnessing an increase of what might be called privatized terrorism, based not on any collective desire to negotiate concessions or fulfil national aspirations, but on an obsessive belief in some supposed religious or philosophical absolute that requires that those who do not subscribe to it be despatched to hell as soon as possible. Perhaps this is a passing phase, as was the anarchism which frightened Europe in the late 19th and early 20th centuries. Perhaps the severity of acts of terror will escalate to the point where their devastation becomes so great that for all but the profoundly psychotic it becomes futile. Or perhaps it will evolve under the influence of such blinkered men as Bush and Rumsfeld on the one hand and Osama bin Laden and his like on the other into a crusade between the bigoted evangelism of right-wing America and the bigoted militancy of Islam. Both are travesties of the true teaching of the religions they claim to espouse, but between them they are capable of bringing about the Armageddon which fanatics on both sides seem willing to welcome.

If we do not take careful thought and make a balanced response to all forms of terrorism, then there will be three casualties at least as serious as loss of life and destruction of property – the loss of peace of mind, the destruction of the rule of law in favour of the rule of the arbitrary strike, and the loss of the freedom of action and expression which we have only fully enjoyed for a little over a century. We are already seeing this process in train with the introduction of indefinite imprisonment without even an appearance before a magistrate for suspected terrorists, increased surveillance of our private lives – the Data Protection Act seems something of a joke in this context – and an ever-increasing tendency among law-enforcement and security organizations to shoot first and ask questions afterwards. Turning the prevention of terrorism into a war on terrorism in this way plays into the hands of the terrorist. It not only gives him a spuriously honourable status, but it obscures the nature of modern terrorism and the best way to deal with it. The driving force behind many contemporary acts of terror is a charismatic, if obsessional, individual with the ability to strike both indiscriminately and asymmetrically. Perhaps the age of liberal democracy is drawing to a close. But that need not be so.

Medieval man in western Europe lived with the constant knowledge that he could be ridden down at any moment by any one of the four horsemen of the Apocalypse* and believed in the imminence of Armageddon. Yet he got on with his daily life despite these fears and in stoic acceptance of the prospect of early death, while hoping that it would wait until another day. These same fears and this attitude of mind are still familiar to some two-thirds of the world's population. Talk to them about the possibility of a terrorist cataclysm and they will shrug their shoulders with indifference and get on with the more pressing task of getting enough to eat or walking to a distant well. To combat the worst excesses of modern terrorism we may have to adopt a similar attitude of mind, rendering it less effective by refusing to allow our lives to be significantly altered or to be warped by fear. We may even look back on the hostage-taking of the past 30 years as a golden age.

---

* *War, pestilence, famine and death in every other guise, followed by Hell.*

Appendix One

Post-Second World War Chronology

Note: This Chronology of the principal events considered in this study draws largely on data from the Rand Corporation, The Memorial Institute for the Prevention of Terrorism Oaklahoma City, and numerous individual sources. There are sometimes considerable discrepancies in figures for killed, wounded, number of hostages and dates as between sources. For consistency we have taken the UK source from St Andrews University as definitive and I am grateful to the members of the Centre for the Study of Terrorism and Political Violence for their help. The chronology will be refined in future editions.

Hostage taking incidents are indicated by (H) terrorist incidents which I believe to have some bearing on the hostage story by (T). Similarly significant general political events are also included. Entries marked ★ are dealt with at greater length in the main text. The hostage taking in the Lebanon is listed separately at the end of the chronology.

1945

31 January★	General Chase set out to free US hostages held by the Japanese in Manilla and succeeded by negotiation (H)
31 October	Jewish terrorist offensive against British rule in Palestine began. (T)

1947

12 July	Jewish Irgun terrorists kidnapped and then hanged two British Army sergeants. The terrorists were trying to secure the release of three Irgun members who had been sentenced to death by the British authorities in Palestine. (H)

1948

30 January   Indian independence leader and statesman Mahatma Gandhi shot dead. (T)

9 April   Jewish Irgun terrorist group attacked Deir Yassin, Palestine, murdering 254 Arab women and children captured in the remains of the village. (T)

14 May   State of Israel came into being.

17 September   United Nations mediator in Palestine, Swedish Count Folke Bernadotte, murdered by Jewish Stern gang member in Jerusalem, Palestine, who fired at point blank range through window of his official car. (T)

20 November   US consulate in Manchuria at Mukden seized. Several Americans were held in areas of China recently overrun by armies of the Chinese Communist Party. (H)

1952

10 March   Fulgencio Batista 2nd coup in Cuba. (1st 4 September 1933)

1953   Castro's first revolt against Batista failed

1955

1 April   Greek Cypriot EOKA terrorist campaign for independence began. (T)

15 May   Batista released Castro from prison

20 August   Several dozen French civilians killed in Algiers by FLN guerrillas. French security forces attacked Algerian civilians in retaliation. (T)

1956

*2 December**   The Castros and Guevara slipped back into Cuba and staged successful coup in 1957

1957

27 September   Political prisoners being flown from Santa Cruz to La Paz, Bolivia, took over the aircraft and forced it to fly to Argentina, where they were granted political asylum. (T)

1958

*24 February**   Argentine motor racing champion Juan Manuel Fangio kidnapped from a hotel lobby in Havana, Cuba, by Twenty Sixth of July Movement to stop him taking part in a race and to embarrass the Cuban government. (H)

7 June   A US Army helicopter strayed across the border into East Germany and was forced to land. After surrendering, the crew of nine Americans was turned over to Soviet Army officials. The Soviet Union insisted that the United States recognize the East German Communist government by negotiating with it directly for the release of the hostages that Washington recognized the regime in East Berlin as the legal government. In July the East German government put the nine airmen on public display at a restricted news conference. The servicemen complained that they were being held as political hostages. They were released later that month. (H)

*27 June**   27 US Marines kidnapped by Castro's guerrillas on Cuba, near the US naval base at Guantanamo Bay. All were eventually released unharmed. (H)

1961

22 January   Cruise liner *Santa Maria* and some 600 passengers seized by Portuguese rebels. US and Brazilian warships intercepted the ship and hostages were released in Brazil February 2. (H)

1 May   First ever United States aircraft hijacked and forced to fly to Cuba. Captor given asylum, but jailed for twenty years when he returned to Maimi in 1975. (T)

1962

22 August   OAS staged unsuccessful machine gun attack on car of French President Charles de Gaulle. (T)

1963

22 November   US President JF Kennedy assassinated in mysterious circumstances

7 December   Bolivia . Tin miners seized four Americans and other foreigners as hostages in an attempt to obtain the release of imprisoned union leaders. Bolivian troops surrounded their place of detention. Captives freed after nine days. (H)

1965

21 February   Black power leader Malcolm X shot dead during a public meeting in Auboadan ballroom, in Harlem, New York City. (T)

25 May   Three Israeli civilians killed in Al Fatah Palestinian attack on Jewish settlement at Ramat Hakovash, Israel. (T)

1966

26 September   El Condor nationalists hijacked Argentine aircraft from Buenos Aires to British occupied Falklands in a bid to bring attention to Argentina's claim to the islands. They eventually surrendered their hostages and were returned to Argentina by the British authorities. (H)

1967

23 March   Six government soldiers killed in Bolivia by Communist guerillas led by Cuban Che Guevara. Seven months later he was tracked down by government troops and killed.

30 June   Aircraft carrying Katangan rebel leader Moïse Tshombe hijacked en route to Ibiza and forced to land in Algeria in a bid to extradite him to his native Congo. The Algerians kept him under house arrest until he died two years later. (H)

1968

23 January   Two North Korean submarine chasers and four torpedo boats surrounded the USS *Pueblo*, an intelligence ship engaged in electronic espionage roughly three miles outside North Korean territorial waters. When the ship tried to flee, the North Koreans opened fire, killing one crewman and wounding three others, including Commander Lloyd M. Bucher. As the crew attempted to destroy highly classified intelligence machinery and documents, ten armed North Korean sailors boarded the Pueblo and took its surviving 82 crewmen prisoner. The North Koreans towed the ship into Wonsan harbor and proceeded to hold the men captive for eleven months, forcing them to sign numerous confessions and savagely brutalizing them. After months of negotiations the US government agreed to sign a statement of guilt and accept sole responsibility for the incident. On December 23, 1968, as the document was signed, the 82 crew members were released.

21 February	A Delta Airlines DC8 was forced to fly to Havana, Cuba, in the first successful hijacking of a US commercial airliner since 1961. The hijacker was granted political asylum. (T)
4 April	Black civil rights activist Rev Martin Luther King shot dead in a hotel in Memphis. Large scale rioting erupted in many cities across America. (T)
5 June	American presidential candidate Robert Kennedy murdered by Jordanian, Sirhan Bishara Sirhan, in Los Angeles. His killer was arrested and became the cause of further terrorist attacks, as Arab groups demanded his release. (T)
22 July	Popular Front for the Liberation of Palestine carried out its first ever aircraft hijacking, seizing an El Al Boeing 707 in Rome and diverting it to Algeria. The first and only successful skyjack of an El Al plane and the first political hostage taking of the post-war era. 32 Jewish passengers held hostages for five weeks. (H)
28 August	John Gordon Meir, US ambassador to Guatemala is murdered by a rebel. He is the first ever American ambassador to be assassinated by terrorists. (T)
26 December	One Israeli killed in Popular Front for the Liberation of Palestine machine gun attack on El Al aircraft at Athens airport. Two terrorists were captured but later released by the Greek government after a Greek aircraft was hijacked to Beirut. (T)
28 December	For this and the El Al hijacking Israel retaliated by destroying 13 Arab aircraft at Beirut airport. (T)

1969

18 February	Palestinian terrorists attacked El Al Boeing 707 on runway at Zurich airport, raking the fuselage with gunfire, killing the pilot and three passengers. An Israeli skymarshall returned fire killing one of the terrorists and drove off the reminder. (T)
29 August	TWA flight 840 from Rome hijacked by Popular Front for the Liberation of Palestine led by Leila Khalid and forced to fly to Damascus. All the passengers and crew were released unharmed but the terrorists exploded a bomb in the cockpit of the aircraft. (H)
3 September	American ambassador Charles Elbrick kidnapped in Rio de Janeiro, Brazil, by left wing terrorists and freed after 15 terrorists were released from jail. (H)

1970

10 February   Three Arab terrorists attempted to hijack an El Al Boeing 707 at Munich airport but were thwarted by the pilot who grappled with a terrorist in the terminal lounge. One Israeli was killed and 11 others wounded. (T)

4 March   Five members of the Turkish People's Liberation Army (TPLA) kidnapped four US Air Force personnel outside Ankara. Demanded a $400,000 ransom and the release of all political prisoners in Turkey. The Ankara government refused to negotiate, and Turkish police arrested a suspect the same day. The four Americans were released unharmed on March 8. (H)

6 March   Members of the FAR kidnapped US labour attaché Sean M. Holly in Guatemala City. He was released two days later, after the government had freed three political prisoners. (H)

11 March   Brazil. Japanese Consul seized; released for prisoners. (H)

24 March   Terrorists kidnapped Lieutenant Colonel Donald J. Crowley, the US air attaché, in Santo Domingo. He was released two days later, after the Dominican government had freed twenty political prisoners and flown them to Mexico. (H)

14 May   German left–wing terrorist leader Andreas Baader freed in rescue raid on West Berlin jail led by fellow terrorist Ulrike Meinhof. (T)

9 June   The PFLP seized 60 hostages, among them American, British, Canadian, and German citizens, at the Inter-Continental and Philadelphia hotels in Amman in response to the bombardment of Palestinian refugee camps by the Jordanian army. The hostages were released on June 12, the day after a cease-fire was arranged in Amman between the army and the Palestinian guerrillas. They then joined 500 foreigners who were being evacuated to Beirut in an airlift by the International Red Cross. (H)

11 June   Brazil. West German ambassador seized; released for prisoners. (H)

22 July   PFLP hijacks Olympic flight Beirut to Athens and secures release of a terrorist held by Greece who subsequently became a Jordanian MP. Possible prototype for Skyjack Sunday. (H)

31 July   US Agency for International Development (AID) official Dan A. Mitrione was kidnapped by Tupamaro guerrillas, who demanded the release of all political prisoners in Uruguay. The government refused to negotiate, and Mitrione was found dead in Montevideo on August 10. (H)

7 August   Claude L. Fly, an AID agricultural expert, was kidnapped by

Tupamaros. The Uruguayan government refused the terrorists' demands to publish the text of a revolutionary manifesto, but Fly was released on March 2, 1971, after suffering a heart attack. (H)

31 August 32 armed Amboinese youths killed guard and seized Hague residence of Indonesian ambassador; demanded independence for S Molucca. Family held, but captors surrendered next day. (H)

*6 September** "Skyjack Sunday". TWA, Swissair, and Pan Am aircraft, with more than 400 passengers, were hijacked by the Popular Front for the Liberation of Palestine and ordered to Dawson Field (a former RAF military airfield in Jordan). The Pan American plane with 177 aboard, landed safely in Cairo, but was blown up moments after the evacuation of all the passengers. Another terrorist team tried to hijack an El Al Boeing over London, but security staff foiled the attempt and killed one and captured the other, Leila Khaled. The hijackers demanded the release of Palestinian prisoners held in Israeli, Swiss, British, and West German jails. (H)

*9 September** A British airliner was also hijacked and flown to Dawson Field. Although these three aircraft were destroyed by the hijackers, the hostages were released unharmed between September 25 and 29.

27 September King Hussein drove Yasser Arafat and his PLO militants out of Jordan. They fled to Lebanon.

30 September Seven terrorists, including Khaled, were released in Germany, Switzerland, and England, while Israel released some prisoners for "humanitarian" reasons. (H)

10 October Quebec separatists kidnapped state government minister Pierre LaPorte and later murdered him. The same group kidnapped British trade commissioner James Cross but released him unharmed. (H)

7 December Brazil. Swiss Ambassador taken hostage and released for prisoners. (H)

1971

*8 January** British ambassador to Uruguay Sir Geoffrey Jackson kidnapped and held for eight months by Tupamaros guerrillas demanding the release of political prisoners. Released 9 September. (H)

10 February Two Croats seized Yugoslav consulate in Gothenberg, Sweden. Surrendered without concessions. Sent to prison. (H)

September	Black September, amalgamation of Palestinian terror groups, formed after heated debate between moderates and militants. Arafat abstains.
28 November	Black September's first murder (of Jordanian PM) assassin licked blood from pavement. (T)

1972

10 February	Croats seized aircraft and hostages in Sweden who were exchanged for seven Croat prisoners flown to Madrid. (H)
	PLO raids into Israel prompted incursion into Lebanon and attack on Syria. Syria responded and war narrowly avoided.
22 February	Irish Republican Army bomb attack on the British Parachute Regiment Officers Mess in Aldershot, England, killed seven people. (T)
4 March	Two killed and 131 people injured when Protestants bomb the Abercorn restaurant in Belfast. (T)
8 May	Israeli commandos stormed hijacked Belgian Sabena airliner at Ben Gurion airport, Israel, killing the four Palestinian Black September terrorists aboard the aircraft and freeing the hostages. One passenger and five Israeli soldiers were killed. (H)
11 May	US Army headquarters in Frankfurt attacked by Red Army Faction car bomb killing one American officer and injuring 13 people. Three more US servicemen injured in another Red Army Faction car bomb attack on the US Army headquarters at Heidelberg later in the month. (T)
30 May	Popular Front for the Liberation of Palestine and Japanese Red Army terrorists opened fire in passenger terminal of Lod Airport, Israel, killing 26 civilians and wounding 78 others. Japanese terrorist Kozo Okamoto survived and was captured by the Israelis. (T)
21 July	Bloody Friday Irish Republican Army bombing attacks on Belfast killed 11 people and injured 136. Three IRA car bomb attacks in the village of Claudy left six dead. (T)
5 September★	Eight Palestinian Black September members killed two Israeli athletes and seized nine others in the Olympic Village in Munich. In a bungled rescue attempt by the West German authorities all the hostages and five terrorists were killed. (H)
5 September	Three Croatians hijacked Scandinavian airliner. Seven Croatians released and flown to Madrid. (H)
6 October	Palestinian students seized W German consulate in Algeria. Demanded release of Munich Olympic compatriots. Freed

hostages and surrendered an hour later. (H)

1973

23 January   Three Haitians kidnapped US ambassador Clinton E. Knox in Port-au-Prince. Demanded release of 31 political prisoners and $500,000 ransom. Consul General Ward L. Christensen voluntarily joined Knox in captivity during the negotiations. The terrorists later reduced their demands to the release of 16 political prisoners, a ransom of $70,000, and safe conduct to Mexico. Knox and Christensen were released after the Haitian government met the reduced demands. The terrorists and the released prisoners, accompanied by the Mexican ambassador, were flown to Mexico, where the ransom money was taken from them and returned to Haiti. Mexico refused to accept the political prisoners, who then went on to Chile. (H)

20 January   Black December, (not to be confused with Black September,) had only three members who briefly took hostages in the Indian High Commission in London. (H)

1 March   Eight members of Black September seized the Saudi embassy in Khartoum during a farewell reception for the American chargé d'affaires, George Moore. They took ten hostages, including Moore, incoming US ambassador Cleo A. Noel, Jr., the Saudi ambassador and his family, and the Belgian and Jordanian charges. They demanded the release of al-Fatah leader Abu Daoud, Sirhan Sirhan (Kennedy's assassin) and other Palestinians held by Western Europe/Israel/Egypt/Jordan and members of the Baader-Meinhof gang imprisoned in Germany. Sudan refused to negotiate and the terrorists reduced their demands to Abou Daoud and 16 Palestinians held in Jordan. All the hostages except Noel, Moore and the Belgian Charge were released. Nixon publicly refused to negotiate, The Sudanese government did not budge and the three diplomats were killed. The Palestinians surrendered on March 6 and were tried and sentenced to life imprisonment. However they were released by the Sudanese President to the PLO the next day and eventually imprisoned in Egypt. The PLO was expelled from Sudan. Israel claimed Arafat issued direct orders for the attack but there is no evidence of this, however, Black September ceased to be operationally effective after this date. (H)

4 May   Members of the People's Revolutionary Armed Forces kidnapped Terrence G. Leonhardy, the American consul general in Guadalajara, Mexico. They demanded freedom for 30 political prisoners, passage to Cuba, publication of a communiqué, and suspension of a police search for them. Leonhardy was freed on May 7 after the Mexican government met the demands and Mrs. Leonhardy paid $80,000. Five people were later arrested in connection with the case. (H)

4 August   Twelve people killed and 48 injured when neo-fascists explode bomb on a train near Bologna. (T)

23 August★   Jan Olsson and Clark Olofsson held three women and a man hostage in a Stockholm bank for six days during which time a close bond developed between captors and captives. This type of mutual dependence later came to be known as the Stockholm Syndrome. (H)

28 September   Three Jewish emigres and an Austrian seized aboard a train by two Arabs of the Eagles of the Palestinian Revolution,. Austrian government gives in and closes Schoenau Castle, a transit camp for Jewish emigres. Hostages released, captors flown to Libya. (H)

17 December   Palestinians bomb Pan Am office at Fiumicino airport, Rome, Italy killing 32 and injuring 50. They took seven Italian policemen hostage and hijacked an aircraft to Athens before flying on to Kuwait after killing one of the hostages. They then surrendered. (H)

20 December   Basque Fatherland and Liberty (ETA) killed Spanish Prime Minister Admiral Luis Carrero Blanco, in a spectacular bomb attack in Madrid. (T)

1974

2 February   Moslem gunmen seized Greek ship and two hostages in Karachi. Threatened to blow up ship and kill hostages unless Greek government freed two Arabs under sentence of death. Greeks commuted sentences to Life, gunmen flown to Libya. (H)

4 February★   American heiress Patricia Hearst kidnapped by Symbionese Liberation Army. She later joined the group, participating in a raid on the Hibernia Bank in San Francisco. (H)

6 February   PFL P. seized Japanese embassy in Kuwait. Four prisoners released and flown from Singapore to Yemen. (H)

11 April   Popular Front for the Liberation of Palestine-General Command seized part of the Qirayt Shemona settlement in northern Israel. Eighteen Israelis killed after the terrorists

	detonated explosives during a rescue attempt. (H)

*24 April** Armed Forces of Chadian Revolution seized a German doctor and two Frenchmen inc Pierre Claustre. They were held for three years and eventually released when their governments paid substantial ransoms and published the rebel manifesto. (H)

Red Brigades kidnapped Mario Sossi an Italian Public Prosecutor, but were tricked into releasing him. (H)

*15 May** 90 children were held hostage by Popular Front for the Liberation of Palestine in a school at Ma'alot, Israel. 21 people are killed and 78 wounded during a bungled rescue attempt by Israeli special forces troops. (H)

26 June Al Fatah Palestinians landed by boat near Nahariya, Israel, and attempt to take civilians hostage. Three Israelis and all the Palestinians were killed in a firefight. (T)

27 September Members of the January 12 Liberation Movement kidnapped USIA director Barbara Hutchison in Santo Domingo. The terrorists demanded the release of 38 political prisoners and a ransom of $1 million. The Dominican government refused to comply with the demands. Hutchison was freed on October 9 in return for safe conduct to Panama for her captors. (H)

September Japanese Red Army seized French embassy in Netherlands took hostage French ambassador plus ten. Ransom of $1m, release of a member in French prison and safe passage to Middle East secured. (H)

*26 October** Two Palestinian terrorists and two others took the congregation in the prison church Schveningen hostage. The Dutch authorities pretended to negotiate for 106 hours until the BBE staged a rescue in which no one was hurt. (H)

21 November Irish Republican Army sets off bombs in bars in Birmingham, England, killing 21 civilians, as part of major bombing campaign on the British mainland.

22 November British DC-10 airliner hijacked at Dubai, UAE, by Palestinian Rejectionist Front and eventually flown to Tunisia where a German passenger was killed. (T)

5 December 23rd of September Communist League member held two French diplomats in their embassy for five hours. Gunman was tricked into believing that his demand for political asylum in France would be met. Captured on his way to the airport. Diplomats were released unharmed. (H)

27 December Nicaragua: Sandinista rebels raided a Christmas party, seized hostages and demanded release of imprisoned comrades. Those freed include Daniel Ortega, one of the leaders of a rebellion that toppled the Anastasio Somoza dictatorship in 1979. The raiders and freed prisoners were flown to Cuba. (H)

1975

19 January   Arab terrorists attacked Orly airport, Paris, seizing ten hostages in a terminal bathroom. Eventually the French provided them with a plane to fly them to Baghdad. (H)

27 January★   Politician Peter Lorenz kidnapped in West Berlin by June the Second Movement (Baader-Meinhof link). Four days later the German government gave in to the captors' demands and five jailed terrorists were allowed to fly to freedom in South Yemen. Lorenz released. (H)

25 February   Montoneros guerrillas kidnapped John P. Egan, a retired businessman serving as the American honorary consul in Córdoba. They demanded that four captured guerrillas be shown on national television or Egan would be killed. He was found dead the next day. (H)

5 March   Guests and staff at Savoy Hotel, Tel Aviv, taken hostage in Palestinian raid from the sea. eight hostages murdered before rescue. seven Captors killed one captured. (H)

13 April   Civil war breaks out in Lebanon.

24 April★   German left wingers seized the German embassy in Stockholm and took 12 staff hostage to force the release of Baader-Meinhof gang members. One hostage was murdered and a terrorist killed when explosives went off by accident. (H)

12 May   USS *Mayaguez* seized 41 Marines killed in misdirected rescue. (H)

15 June   Four members of the Arab Liberation Front attacked cooperative farm village of Kfar Yuval, holding a family hostage. Demanded the release of 12 prisoners. Israelis refused and stormed the house, killing all four guerrillas and a hostage. (H)

29 June   Palestinian guerrillas captured Army colonel Ernest R. Morgan in Beirut. They demanded that the US embassy donate food, clothing, and building materials to a Muslim district of Beirut that had been heavily damaged in the Lebanese civil war. Both the PLO and the PFLP denied responsibility for the kidnapping. Colonel Morgan was released on July 12, after the Lebanese government had distributed free rice and sugar in a poor quarter of Beirut. (H)

4 August   Japanese Red Army took 52 hostages in US and Swedish embassies in Kuala Lumpur. Four JRA members in Japanese prisons released. (H)

28 September Spaghetti House restaurant London nine Italian waiters taken hostage by three Nigerians of Black Liberation Front. Released unharmed by negotiation after six days. (H)

3 October★ Irish Republican Army terrorists kidnapped Dutch industrialist Teide Herrema in Dublin. After a month long hunt the Irish police surrounded the terrorists' hide out, forcing his release. (H)

22 October Beirut, members of the PFLP captured Charles Gallagher and William Dykes of the USIA. They were released on 25 February 1976, at the home of Kemal Jumblatt. Demanded ransom and release of Palestinian guerrillas held in Lebanon or in Israel. Lebanese sources claimed that Israel had released two Palestinians in exchange for Gallagher and Dykes, but US and Israel denied, rather unconvincingly, any connection between the two releases. (H)

2 December★ South Moluccans seized train at Beilen, Netherlands, for twelve days. Three hostages were shot before the terrorists surrendered on 14th. (H)

4 December Seven South Moluccan terrorist seized the Indonesian embassy in Amsterdam beginning a two week long siege. One of the thirty six hostages died jumping from a window to escape.

6 December★ Four members of Irish Republican Army seized two hostages in Balcombe Street, London, England for six days before surrendering to police; hostages released unharmed. (H)

21 December★ As proxy for the PFLP, Carlos "The Jackal" seized 11 oil ministers and 59 civilians hostage during the OPEC meeting in Vienna. After flying to Algeria and taking delivery of several hundred million dollars in ransom money, Carlos and his team escaped. (H)

1976

3 February★ Six members of the Front for the Liberation of the Somali Coast seized a bus carrying 31 children of French military. Demanded independence for the Afars and Issas regions of Somalia, release of all political prisoners, and the departure of all French troops from Djibouti. Threatened to slit the throats of hostages. French troops in shoot out with the terrorists, kill five capture one. Captors fire on children, kill two and wound three and two adults. The attack touched off a firefight with Somali soldiers. One Somali killed, French officer wounded. One seven year old hostage taken over Somali border was released in

Mogadishu to the French embassy on February 7. (H)

27 June★ An Air France airliner was hijacked by a joint German Baader-Meinhof/Popular Front for the Liberation of Palestine terrorist group and its crew were forced to fly to Entebbe airport in Uganda. 258 passengers and crew were held hostage. All non-Israeli passengers are eventually released. On 4 July Israeli commandos flew to Uganda and rescued the remaining hostages. All the hostage takers were killed in the rescue, as were two passengers and the commando leader. One elderly hostage died (murdered by Amin?) in Ugandan hospital. 39 Ugandan soldiers killed. (H)

10 September★ A TWA flight 355 New York to Paris and 93 hostages hijacked by Croatians seeking independence from Yugoslavia. The captors surrendered in Paris and released their hostages. A New York policeman was killed defusing a bomb left in a locker in Grand Central Station. (H)

26 September Argentinian El Condor nationalists hijacked a plane en route for Port Stanley to draw attention to Argentina's claim to the Falklands. Hostages released and hijackers sent back to Argentina. (H)

26 September Four Palestinian guerrillas of "Black June" seized Hotel Semiramis in Damascus held 90 hostages until Syrian troops stormed hotel in a three-hour battle, killed one terrorist and four hostages, wounded 34. Other three terrorists captured by Syrian military police; hanged within twenty four hours in front of the hotel. (H)

1977

9 March★ Hanafi Muslim gunmen seized three buildings and 134 hostages in Washington, DC. The gunmen surrendered two days later, after their propaganda communiqué was aired. (H)

23 May★ 13 South Moluccan terrorists seized 85 hostages on a train at Assen, Netherlands. Two hostages were killed when Dutch Marines stormed the train to end a 19 day siege. (H)

5 September★ West German business leader Hanns-Martin Schleyer kidnapped by the Baader-Meinhof gang. (H)

13 October★ Four Palestinian terrorists hijack a German Lufthansa Boeing 737 and order it to fly around a number of Middle East destinations for four days. After the plane's pilot is killed, it is stormed by German GSG9 counter-terrorist troops, assisted by two British Special Air Service men, when it puts down at

Mogadishu, Somalia. All the 90 hostages are rescued and three terrorists killed. (H)

18 October   Schleyer was murdered in reprisal for Mogadishu rescue and the suicides in prison of three Baader-Meinhof leaders the previous day. (H)

1978

*18 February**   Airliner hijacked at Larnaca, Cyprus, airport by Arabs who had just murdered a leading Egyptian publisher at a nearby hotel. After being refused permission to land at a number of Arab capitals the hijackers return to Larnaca. Egyptian commandos landed and tried to attack the plane, but ended up in gun battle with Cypriot troops. Fifteen Egyptian troops, seven Cypriot soldiers and a German cameraman were killed.(H)

11 March   A nine strong Al Fatah Palestinian seaborne raiding party landed in Israel and hijacked a bus, killing 26 civilians and wounding 70. All the terrorists were killed by Israeli security forces. (T)

13 March   `Three Moluccans seized the Town Hall at Assen,Netherlands, killed two hostages and held 72 other civil servants. They wanted the relase of 21 prisoners by 2.0.pm the following day and their unstable psychological profile prompted the Dutch to send in the by now well prepared BBE straight away. All hostages released with no casualties. (H)

14 March   The Israelis invaded southern Lebanon, under codename Operation Litani.

16 March   Former Italian Premiere and Christian Democrat President, Aldo Moro kidnapped by the Red Brigades terrorist group and later murdered after fifty five days (May 9)in captivity. (H)

13 April   Revelli–Beaumont of Fiat taken in Argentina by Committee for Revolutionary Socialist Unity for 91 days. Longest European captivity up to that time. (H)

18 June   Two members of the Royal Ulster Constabulary acting as Ulster Freedom Fighters kidnapped Father Hugh Murphy in Ulster. (H)

4 July   Four "Independentistas", took four hostages in Chilean consular office in San Juan. Demanded freedom for four Puerto Rican nationalists imprisoned in the United States. Surrendered and released their hostages after 17 hours of negotiation. (H)

17 August   Two Croations took eight hostages in West German consulate in Chicago. Demanded to communicate with Stjepan Bilandzic, founder of Croatian People's Resistance seeking independence for Croatia from Yugoslavia, held in Cologne. Bilandzic persuaded captors to surrender after ten hour siege. Acquitted of kidnap charges, but convicted of imprisoning West German Vice Consul. (H)

August　　　Nicaragua: Sandinistas took over Congress to demand freedom for jailed comrades. After botched attempt to retake the building in which 14 people die, government gives in. One freed was Tomas Borge, who later became the Sandinistas' interior minister and by some accounts most powerful man in the country. Captors and prisoners were flown to Cuba. (H)

1979

14 January　　Three Palestinian killed in abortive seizure of hotel and 230 guests in Ma'alot in north-central Israel. Palestinians demanded release of others held in Israel jails. (H)

16 January　　Shah of Iran overthrown and left the country. Ayatollah Khomeini assumed power a week later.

14 February　　Four Islamic fundamentalists opposed to the Afghan government kidnapped US ambassador Adolph Dubs in Kabul and demanded the release of various "religious figures" held by the government. Dubs was killed when Afghan police stormed the hotel room where he was being held. Washington criticized Kabul for not having tried to secure Dubs's release peaceably. (H)

14 February　　200 militants occupied the US embassy in Tehran for two hours before Iranian government forces persuaded them to leave. An Iranian employee of the embassy and the son of another local employee were killed.

13 July　　　Four "Eagles of the Palestinian Revolution" took over Egyptian embassy and 20 hostages in Ankara in an attempt to get the Israeli-Egyptian peace agreement annulled. They failed and were captured and sentenced to death. (H)

4 November★　Iranian radicals seized the US embassy in Tehran, taking 66 American diplomats hostage. The crisis continued until 20 January 1981 when the hostages were released by diplomatic means. A US rescue effort led by the Delta Force counter terrorist unit failed on 25 April 1980 when a Marine Corps CH-53 helicopter crashed into a USAF C-130 transport aircraft at forward refuelling site in central Iran, killing eight Americans and injuring five. (H)

20 November★ 200 Islamic terrorists seized Grand Mosque in Mecca taking hundreds of pilgrims hostage. Saudi and French security forces retake the Islamic world's most holy shrine after a intense battle, in which some 300 people were killed and 600 wounded. (H)

18 December   Signing of International Convention Against the Taking of Hostages

---

1980

11 January   Popular League of 28 February seized Panamanian embassy in El Salvador, ambassadors of Panama and Costa Rica and five others. Secured release of prisoners. January 14. Hostages also released. (H)

31 January   Guatemala: Peasants and student activists seized Spanish embassy demanding investigation into murders and disappearances. Government of Gen. Fernando Romeo Lucas Garcia refuses to negotiate. 37 burn to death, including the father of Rigoberta Menchu, 1992 Nobel Peace Prize. Spain broke off diplomatic relations. (H)

1 February   Six Spanish policemen killed in an ambush by Basque terrorists, near Bilbao, Spain. (T)

5 February   El Salvador Spanish Ambassador and 11 hostages exchanged for prisoners. (H)

27 February★   M-19 guerrillas raided reception at the Dominican Republic embassy in Bogota and took 54 hostages including 15 ambassadors, notably Diego Ascencio of the United States. They demanded freedom for 311 jailed comrades and $50 million. After 61 days, they settled for $1 million and flight to Cuba. A decade later the M-19 disarmed. (H)

24 March   Archbishop Oscar Romero was killed in his San Salvador cathedral, El Salvador, by right wing terrorists while holding a mass. (T)

4 April   During Passover five Arab Liberation Front guerrillas slipped across Lebanese border and seized nine children from kibbutz dormitory. Wanted to disrupt Middle East peace talks and free prisoners Two rescue attempts; in first a civilian and an Israeli soldier killed. In second a small boy killed four other children wounded. All Palestinians killed. (H)

21 April★   Operation Eagle Claw to rescue US hostages in embassy in Tehran began. It ended in total failure. (H)

30 April★   Six Iraqi-backed Iranians stormed the Iranian embassy in Princess Gate, London, taking 20 hostages. Six days later British Special Air Service anti-terrorist troops re-captured the

	embassy, killed five captors and freed the hostages. Two hostages were killed and two more wounded by the captors. (H)
1 June	African National Congress bombed strategic oil-from-coal plants in South Africa causing $7 million worth of damage. (T)
19 June	Three Iraqis took over British embassy in Baghdad on the eve of Iraq's first parliamentary election in 22 years. British ambassador allowed government forces to storm building. The three Iraqis killed, embassy staff unharmed. (H)
June	Afghan students seized their own embassies in Bonn, New Delhi, Tehran to highlight Soviet invasion. Hostages released after a few hours. (H)
27 July	Shah of Iran died.
1 August	Bologna railway station, Italy, devastated by a massive bomb, believed planted by right wing terrorists linked to rogue elements in the country's intelligence services. 85 people killed and 300 injured. (T)
13 August	Air Florida flight from Key West to Miami hijacked by seven Cubans and flown to Cuba, where they released their hostages and were then taken into custody. Six further US airliners were hijacked to Cuba over the next month. All the passengers were freed without harm. Three passengers were killed when Cubans hijacked an aircraft in Peru and demanded to be flown to the United States. (T)
12 September	Iraq invaded Iran
17 September	Revolutionary Democratic Front led by woman seized Organisation American States offices and 11 hostages in El Salvador. Guard killed. RDF commando surrendered on promise to investigate murders and disappearances. (H)
13 October	Four Iranian hijackers killed when Turkish security forces stormed a hijacked Turkish Airlines aircraft after it landed in eastern Turkey. One of 155 hostages killed by captors. (H)

1981

20 January	Carter ordered unfreezing of Iranian assets as his last executive act. US hostages in Tehran released after 444 days.
3 March	Swedish prime minister Olof Palme shot by lone gunman as he leaves a cinema in Stockholm. (T)
2 May	Bolivian Socialist Falange (right wing) led by former Presidential candidate Carlos Barbery seized oil refinery and 52 hostages demanding resignation of President. Refinery stormed. No hostages hurt. (H)

13 May	Pope John Paul II seriously wounded in assassination attempt in Rome by Turkish "Grey Wolves" terrorist Mehmet Ali Agca. (T)
6 October	Egyptian president Anwar Sadat shot dead by rebel troops in Cairo. Seven other people killed and 28 wounded. (T)
17 December★	US General Dozier kidnapped in Verona by Red Brigades. Rescued after 42 days. (H)

1982

3 June	The Israeli ambassador in London, Shlomo Argov, shot and seriously injured by the Abu Nidal group. The attack was used to justify an Israeli invasion of Lebanon. (T)
6 June	Israel invaded Lebanon
19 July	David Dodge American University of Beirut first Western hostage seized. (H) NB For complete list of all Western hostages in Lebanon to June 1992 see appendix 2
7 August	Two gunmen of Secret Army for the Liberation of Armenia bombed, machine gunned and took hostages in Esenboga Airport in Ankara. Both killed also nine hostages and 71 injured when Turkish police attack. (H)
September	Honduras: Cinchonero guerrillas in San Pedro seized Chamber of Commerce and Industry and 105 hostages, including some of country's richest entrepreneurs. Freed them for 20 jailed rebels, ransom and safe passage to Cuba. (H)
5 September	"Colonel Wysocki" and Polish Revolutionary Home Army (anti-Communist) seized Polish embassy and 13 diplomatic hostages in Bern. Threatened to blow up embassy and everyone in it unless martial law was abolished in Poland, all political prisoners released, all prison camps in Poland shut down, and repression against the Polish people halted. (H)
14 September	Lebanese President Bashir Gemayel assassinated by a massive car bomb at a Beirut political meeting by a pro-Syrian Lebanese group. Scores of civilians were injured in the blast. (T)
16 September	Two days later with the support of Israeli defence minister Arial Sharon, Phalange Christian militiamen occupied the Sabra/Shatilla Palestinian refugee camps in Beirut Lebanon and massacred 460 men, women and children while nearby Israeli troops watched. (T)
5 November	Nine members of Turkish Devrimici Sol (revolutionary Left) organization seized Turkish Consulate and 80 hostages in Cologne in a storm of gunfire. An hour later a red banner was unfurled emblazoned with a hammer and sickle, a white star and

the slogan "No to the Junta constitution in Turkey" in German and Turkish. (Junta of generals seized power in Ankara in September 1980. (H)

11 November Israeli military headquarters in Tyre, Lebanon, destroyed by Islamic suicide bomber leaving 75 Israeli soldiers dead, along with 15 Lebanese and Palestinian prisoners. (T)

12 December Anti–nuclear protestor held eight tourists hostage in the Washington Monument, in Washington DC before he was shot dead by a police sniper. (H)

1983

18 April 63 people, including the CIA's Middle East Director, were killed and 120 injured in a 400 lb suicide truck bomb attack on the US embassy in Beirut. The driver was killed. Responsibility was claimed by Islamic Jihad. (T)

4 June UN Hostage Convention comes into force

27 July Armenian terrorists seized the Turkish embassy and staff in Lisbon. Five terrorists, a Portuguese policemen and Turkish woman were killed when a terrorist bomb prematurely exploded. (H)

9 October The Martyr's Mausoleum bombing in Rangoon, Burma, (Myanmar) left five South Korean cabinet ministers and 15 other people dead. South Korea's President Chun survived the attack which was blamed on North Korean intelligence agents. (T)

23 October Italian right wing terrorists exploded a bomb on a train killing fifteen people and injuring 115. (T)

Simultaneous suicide truck bombs on American and French compounds in Beirut. A 12,000 lb bomb destroyed a US Marine Corps base killing 241 Americans; 58 Frenchmen were killed when a 400 lb device destroyed one of their bases. Islamic Jihad claimed responsibility. US and French aircraft struck suspected terrorist bases in the Baka'a valley in retaliation. (T)

3 December US naval pilot Robert Goodman shot down over Lebanon and held in Syria until released on January 3 1984 following an appeal from Rev Jesse Jackson to Syrian President. (H)

14 December USS *New Jersey* began shelling civilians in Beirut. (T)

17 December The climax of an Irish Republican Army Christmas bombing campaign in London saw three policemen and three civilians killed during a car bomb attack on Harrods department store. (T)

1984

17 April British security forces including Special Air Service laid siege to Libyan People's Bureau (embassy) in London after a British policewomen was killed by small arms fire originating from inside the building. After threats were made to UK citizens living in Libya, the British government decided to respect the diplomatic immunity of the staff of the People's Bureau and allowed them to leave for Tripoli. No one was arrested for the murder. Hostages taken by Libya released in October. (T)

18 April 18 US servicemen killed and 83 people injured in bomb attack on restaurant near USAF base in Torrejon, Spain. Hizbollah claimed responsibility as revenge for March bombing in Beirut. (T)

22 April Four Palestinians hijacked bus carrying Israelis in Gaza, occupied territories. Israeli special forces stormed the bus and killed two of the terrorist after they had been captured. (H)

5 June Sikh militants seized Golden Temple in Amritsar. Over a hundred died when Indian Security Forces recaptured. (T)

20 September Suicide bomb attack on US embassy in East Beirut killed 23 people and injured 21 others. The US and British ambassadors were slightly injured in the explosion attributed to Hezbollah. (T)

12 October British Prime Minister Margaret Thatcher and her cabinet escaped death during an Irish Republican Army bomb attack on the Grand Hotel Brighton during the Conservative Party Conference. Five people killed and 30 injured in the attack which destroyed the front of the hotel. (T)

31 October Indian Prime Minister Indira Gandhi was gunned down by her own Sikh bodyguards in Dehli,(T)

4 December Kuwaiti airliner and 162 hostages, including six Americans, hijacked by four gunmen and forced to land in Tehran. The hijackers then shot one US AID worker and released 44 women and children. They threatened to blow up the plane unless Kuwait released the "Kuwait 17". They released more hostages but killed another American and beat other Kuwaitis and Americans. On 9 December Iranian security forces stormed the plane, freed the hostages and arrested the hijackers who were probably connected with Hizbollah, al Dawa or a Shia group, but refused to extradite them to Kuwait. They were tried in Iran under islamic law, but later released. (H)

1985

8 March   Unsuccessful attempt by CIA backed Christian militia to blow up Hezbollah HQ and Fadlallah. Eighty bystanders killed. (T)

14 June★   Two members Islamic Jihad, armed with grenades and pistols, hijacked TWA Flight 847 with 153 passengers and crew aboard. 122 were Americans. 23-year-old US Navy diver Robert Stethem, was brutally beaten, shot to death, and dropped on the tarmac of Beirut airport. The last 39 hostages were released in Damascus on June 30 Israel released 31 prisoners on 24 June, it insisted decision was in no way connected to the hijacking, (H)

23 June   Air India Boeing 747 is destroyed by a bomb over the Atlantic, killing all 329 people aboard the aircraft in the worst single terrorist incident to date. Sikh terrorists are blamed. (T)

9 July   Industrialist Karl-Heinz Beckurte killed in car bomb attack in Munich, Germany. Red Army Faction claim responsibility. (T)

10 July   French DSGE secret agents planted bomb on Green Peace ship *Rainbow Warrior* in Auckland harbour, New Zealand that killed one protest group member. (T)

8 August   Three US servicemen killed and 17injured in Red Army Faction bomb and gun attack on Rhein-Main airbase, Germany. (T)

25 September   Three members of the PLO elite Force-17, seized an Israeli yacht in Cyprus and three hostages on Yom Kippur. Demanded release of 20 Palestinian prisoners held in Israel. Accused hostages of being Israeli spies, killed them and surrendered to police after ten hours. Israel retaliated with air strike on Tunisia that killed more than 70 people. (H)

7 October★   Four Palestinian Liberation Front members seized the Italian cruise liner, *Achille Lauro*, during a cruise in the eastern Mediterranean, taking more than 700 people hostage. One US passenger was murdered before the Egyptian government offered the terrorists safe haven in return for the hostages' freedom. US Navy fighters incepted the Egyptian aircraft flying the terrorists to safety in Tunis and forced it to land at the NATO airbase in Italy, where the terrorists were arrested. (H)

6 November   Palace of Justice in Bogota and over 100 hostages including several judges seized by M-19 When the Colombian army stormed the building most of the hostages, including eleven Supreme Court justices, and all the terrorists were killed. (H)

23 November★   98 passengers and crew of an Egyptair aircraft were held hostage by Palestinians at Luqa, Malta. Five passengers were shot by the terrorists and two died. An ill-planned assault by Egyptian Force

777 commandos resulted in some 57 passengers being killed when the attackers set off explosives to enter the aircraft. (H)

1986

5 April   Two US soldiers were killed and 79 American servicemen wounded in Libyan backed bomb attack on a night club in West Berlin. (T)

15 April   US bombed Tripoli and Benghazi from British bases. One USAF F-111 was shot down in the raid killing its two crew. 93 Libya civilians were killed in raids. (T)

16 April   Three British hostages held in the Lebanon were killed in response to the raid. (H)

1 May   Cargese holiday camp, Corsica, seized by separatist rebels, who killed two hostages and injured three.(H)

19 May   Four members United Popular Action Movement seized United Press International office in Santiago and forced staff to transmit a statement on air and to four Chilean newspapers calling for an uprising against Pinochet and condemning United States for the "tragedy that Chile is living through". (H)

6 September   Pan American Boeing 747 seized by Arab terrorists in Pakistan. They kill seventeen hostages and wound another one hundred and twenty seven after panicking and thinking they were under attack. Pakistani security forces then stormed aircraft and freed the hostages. (H)

5 October   One of Oliver North's Iran contra arms planes shot down by Sandanistas over Nicaragua

1987

August and November PKK students took over own embassies and airline offices in various Western countries

10 September   11 People's Commandos stormed Iranian embassy in Oslo. Released hostages, three wounded, after reading statements to the media demanding overthrow of Iranian government. (H)

1988

16 March   4,000 Kurdish civilians killed during Iraqi nerve gas attack against Halabja in northern Iraq, after Iraqi dictator Saddam Hussein ordered chemical weapons to be used to put down Kurdish revolt. (T)

5 April	122 people were held hostage after a Kuwaiti Boeing 747 was hijacked and diverted to Meshed, Iran, before flying on to Cyprus. The Kuwait government refused requests by the Iranian backed Shia hijackers to release the "Dawa 17". After 15 days the hijackers were granted asylum in Algeria and released their hostages unharmed. (H)
28 June	US Naval Attache killed in Athens by Nov 17th terrorist group. (T)
20 August	Iran Iraq war ended
14 September	Lebanese gunman armed with an AK-47 Soviet assault rifle held nine military and two civilian hostages at a recruiting centre in Richmond, Virginia for five hours. Surrendered peacefully after being allowed to read statement seeking peace in Lebanon over local radio. (H)
13 November	After failed attack on Israel five Fatah Palestinians seized U.N. observation post, a Lebanese technician and five Finnish soldiers in Lebanon. Four Palestinians surrendered. The one who refused killed the Lebanese and after eighteen hours was overpowered by the Finns. (H)
21 December	Pan Am Boeing 747 blown up over Lockerbie, Scotland, by a bomb believed to have been placed on the aircraft at Frankfurt Airport, Germany. All 259 people on the aircraft were killed. Two Libyan intelligence operatives have been tried in connection with this attack. (T)

1989

28 July	Israel abducted Sheikh Obeid. (H)

1991

26 March	Four Pakistanis seized a Singapore Air A310 Airbus on a 45-minute flight to Singapore to demand the release of the husband of Benazir Bhutto, Asif Ali Zardari. Singaporean commandos shot hijackers dead. (T)
1 April	Red Army Faction terrorists killed German industrial chief Detlev Rohwedder at his home in Dusseldorf, Germany, in their last reported action. (T)
4 September	Eight members of Alfaro Vive took over British embassy in Ecuador. Demanded release of their imprisoned leader, Patrio Baquerizo. Left after thirty hours on being promised his trial would be fair and held soon. (H)

24 April   Indian Airlines plane was hijacked by a lone hostage taker who managed to conceal his weapons in a leg cast. After eleven hours of unproductive negotiations, Indian authorities planned a rescue operation. The SCTU (Special Counter Terrorist Unit), forced the emergency doors, surprised the hijacker and killed him. No other casualties. (H)

1992

17 January   Michael Barnes seized in Philippines by New Peoples Army which collected ransom to overthrow the government. Police located the apartment where Barnes was held. The Philippine Light Reaction Force stormed the apartment and freed Barnes. Fourteen hostage takers were killed. No other casualties. (H)

25 February   Six Azerbaidzhani, women and children, taken hostage while fleeing the fighting in Nagorno-Karabakh. Frequent hostage taking over the following three years by Azerbaidzhanis and Armenians alike, each other and Turkish minority inhabitants. Similar actions by Georgians and Abkhazis. (H)

20 April   A gunman seized Saudi Ambassador and colleague in embassy in Yemen. Demanded $1m ransom. Troops storm embassy, hostages unharmed. (H)

June   Last Western hostages, two Germans, in Lebanon released. See appendix two.

June–August   According to Amnesty many civilians appear to have been held for the purpose of exchange and are effectively hostages in Bosnia-Herzegovina. (H)

1993

26 February   World Trade Centre bombing in New York by followers of Egyptian cleric Umar Abd al-Rahman. Six killed 1000+ injured. (T)

8 March   Five Nicaraguans of Yolaina Command took over their embassy in Costa Rica and 25 hostages, including ambassador. Demanded removal of Sandanistas from Nicaraguan government and $6m. Get $250,000 and flown out. Hostages released unharmed. (H)

8 March   Costa Rica: Five members of so-called Command of Death took over Costa Rican Supreme Court and held 19 justices for four days, demanding $20 million. Received $250,000 and promise of a flight to Guatemala. Told to disarm before boarding plane, they did so, leading to their capture seconds later. (H)

24 June   Kurdish PKK members took over Turkish consulates throughout Europe, but surrendered though no concessions made. No one hurt. (H)

5 July   PKK (Kurdish Workers Party founded by Abdullah Ocalan 1978) kidnapped 19 Western Tourists in W Turkey. Released unharmed in August. (H)

25 November   The head of the USIA, Haynes Mahoney, was kidnapped by rebel tribesmen. Five gunmen intercepted his car in San' a and held him for several days in the desert region of Gahm. Mahoney was returned unharmed within a week after Yemen's interior minister negotiated with the kidnappers' chieftains for the diplomat's release. (H)

1994

January   Amnesty visit to India and Maharastra State reported unrecorded police detentions, and detention of people as "hostages" to force the surrender of wanted suspects. (H)

25 February   Jewish extremists killed 29 Muslims and wound 150 in Hebron Mosque. This triggered wave of suicide bombings which have continued to present day as have Israeli murder strikes in Palestine. Most of these episodes are not recorded here. (T)

6 April   Rwandan president Juvenel Habyarimana killed when his aircraft shot down by surface-to-air missile while approaching Kigali airport, Rwanda. The incident sparked massive outbreak of ethnic violence that resulted in some three quarters of a million people being killed. Ten Belgian paratroopers serving with the United Nations in Kigali were hacked to death by rebels. (T)

26 July   Khmer Rogue kidnapped Australian, British and French tourists in Cambodia. Along with two other western tourists they were all killed later in the year. (H)

24 December   Air France Airbus seized by Algerian Islamists and forced to fly to Marseilles airport. All the Algerians were killed when French CIGN counter-terrorist troops stormed the aircraft and rescued the 170 passengers and crew, 16 of whom suffered minor injuries. (H)

1995

4 February   Fourteen UN aid workers of the World Food Program held in

Mogadishu by gunmen demanding money owed by WFP. Release of hostages negotiated by Aidid's Somali National Alliance. (H)

18 March   Ethiopian aircraft and 92 passengers seized in Sudan, freed by threat-backed negotiation. (H)

20 March   Twelve killed nearly six thousand injured in Sarin attack on Tokyo underground. (T)

26 May   More than 360 United Nations peacekeepers held hostage by the Bosnian Serb army as "human shields" after NATO air strikes on their capital Pale. The UN personnel are tied to key military targets for several days until released during June. (H)

14 June   Chechens seized hospital and 2000 hostages in Budyonnovsk S Russia. Failed rescue attempt, 100+ dead gunmen allowed to escape in exchange for freeing remaining hostages. (H)

26 June   Assassination attempt made against Egyptian President Honsi Mubarak in Addis Abbaba by Islamic radicals who ambushed his motorcade. (T)

7 July   Five British, German, Norwegian and American tourists kidnapped by Kashmiri rebels in north Kashmir. One was found beheaded in October and the other four were never seen again. In May 1996 it emerged that they had been shot and buried by their captors, as they tried to escape from pursuing Indian security forces. No confirmation has yet been found to support these claims. (H)

24 July   Left wing Turks seized Social Democrat Party office in Frankfurt and four SDP hostages. Demanded SDP investigate prison conditions in Turkey. Police infiltrated building and arrested captors. No one hurt. (H)

4 November   Israeli Prime Minister Yitzak Rabin assassinated by right wing Jewish radical Yigal Amir when leaving a peace rally in Tel Aviv. (T)

19 November   Islamic Movement of Change bombed military compound in Riyadh killing some fifty Saudis and foreigners. (T)

1996

Numerous hostages taken during the year in West Papua Central Highlands as Idonesian army supresses independence movement. (H)

9 January   Chechens seized hospital and 3000 hostages in Kizlyar S Russia. Most released. Captors fled with 100 hostages. 78 killed in ensuing week long gun battle. Other Chechen rebels seized a

	ship in Turkey, taking 118 Russians and 4 Turks hostage before they surrendered to the Turkish authorities. No loss of life. (H)
Chechnya:	From when the conflict broke out in December 1994 to December 1996, 20,000 to 30,000 civilians have been killed, many as a result of indiscriminate attacks by Russian Federation federal forces on densely populated, residential areas. Men, women and children have been the victims of extrajudicial executions, hostage-taking, torture and ill-treatment in detention, particularly in so-called "filtration camps".
31 January	Tamil Tigers detonated truck bomb in Colombo killing 90 wounding 1400. (T)
19 April	Eighteen Greek tourists were gunned down near the historic Pyramids in Egypt by Islamic terrorists aiming to destroy the country's tourist industry. (T)
15 June	Irish Republican Army devastated the centre of Manchester with a truck bomb that injured hundreds of civilians and cause several hundred million pounds worth of damage. (T)
25 June	Islamic radical terrorists opposed to the western military presence in the Gulf region, exploded a truck bomb next to a USAF housing area at Dhahran, Saudi Arabia, killing 19 and wounding over 500 mostly American servicemen. (T)
26 August	Six Iraqi dissidents hijacked a Sudan Airways A310 Airbus airliner en route from Khartoum to Jordan and diverted it to Stansted, England. After eight and a half hours negotiating with British authorities the hijackers released all the 13 crew and 180 passengers unharmed. (H)
23 November	Ethopian Airways Boeing 767 hijacked enroute from Addis Adaba to Niarobi and diverted to Australia. It ran out of fuel and crashed into the Indian Ocean near Comoros Islands killing 123 people, 52 people including two hijackers survive. (H)
17 December*	14 members of MRTA (Tupac Amaru Revolutionary Movement) captured Japanese embassy in Lima. Released most of the guests except 72 or 73 senior judges, military men, prominent business men and Ambassadors. The hostages were well treated and unharmed even when Peruvian commandos stormed the embassy on April 22 1997 and killed all the captors. Demands were for the release of 400 prisoners, economic changes and free passage. (H) One hostage and two soldiers killed.
24 December	21 UN observers taken hostage by Tajik guerillas loyal to warlord Rizvon Sadirov. They were all eventually freed unharmed. (H)

1997

13 October Nine PKK terrorists kidnapped two Bulgarian and one Turkish engineers from a coal mine. The Turkish engineer was found dead, but the Bulgarians were released unharmed on 16 October. (H)

17 November Al–Gama–at al Islamiyya gunmen killed 62 and 26, mostly tourists, at Hatshepsut Temple in Egypt's Valley of the Kings. (T)

1998

30 July Revolutionary Armed Forces of Columbia (FARC) took seven hostages who were forced to help take over US embassy public concourse. All hostages released by negotiation. (H)

7 August US Embassies in Nairobi and Dar-es-Salem heavily damaged by massive bomb attacks. In the Nairobi attack 247 people were killed, including 12 Americans, and 4,000 injured. Ten people were killed and 74 injured in Tanzania incident. US intelligence blames Islamic groups linked to Saudi dissident Osama Bin Laden. (T)

15 August IRA car bomb in Omagh killed 29 and wounded 330. (T)

20 August US President Bill Clinton ordered reprisal strikes for embassy bombings against "terrorist" bases in Afghanistan and Sudan. Attacks coincided with Congressional questioning of Monica Lewinsky. No other nation was able to confirm terrorist links of targets. (T)

28 December★ Yemini militants kidnapped a group of western tourists, including 12 Britons, 2 Americans, and 2 Australians on the main road to Aden. Four victims were killed during a rescue attempt the next day. It was suspected that the seizure was instigated by the British Muslim cleric, Abu Hamza, in an attempt to exchange them for nine recently arrested Islamic militants in Briutish jails. The largest kidnapping in Yemen's recent history, it was the first in which hostages died. (H)

1999

Afghanistan: Children held hostage by Taliban in place of their fathers. (H)

15 January Abdulah Ocalan, leader of PKK arrested in Kenya.

16 February 21 embassies throughout the world seized briefly by Kurds of PKK supporting Oclan.(H)

21 August Kyrgyz rebels seized 13 hostages; seven released after six weeks and four Japanese geologists two weeks later. One hostage killed trying to escape. (H)

31 December   Kashmiri rebels hijacked Indian Airlines plane to Kandahar. A week later passengers and crew released in exchange for Indian release of three other rebels.

2000

*23 April**   Abu Sayyaf seized 21 tourists from Sipadam Island Malaysia and took them to its Jolo hideout. They were released and ransom paid via intercession of Libya as Gadafi tried to re-establish himself as part of the international community. (H)

21 May   Ministers and MPs held hostage in Fiji Parliament freed and forced to resign. (H)

21 June   Israel introduced Bill to make hostage taking by Israel retrospectively legal; became law on March 1 2002.

17 July   Indian led UN troops liberated over 200 peacekeepers , who had been surrounded for two and a half months by the Revolutionary United Front (RUF), and held hostage in Kailahun, Sierra Leone. One UN sergeant was killed and several peacekeeping soldiers were wounded in the action. (H)

28 July   16 Brazilian tourists seized by Indians; released after government agreed to enforce reserved areas. (H)

29 July   18 Thai and Kenyan hostages released after visit by Francois Lumumba. Eight of the hostages had been released in June in return for medicines and a truck. The demand for the withdrawal of Rwandan and Ugandan troops from Democratic Republic of Congo not conceded. (H)

12 October   USS *Cole* attacked by boat killing 17 wounding 39. Al Qaida suspected. (T)

2001

14 January   Four Chinese taken hostage by Abu Sayyaf. Two later killed in bungled rescue. (H)

5 March   Three Chechens seized Russian plane and 166 hostages. Demanded end to fighting in Chechnya. One hostage and one hijacker killed in rescue assault. (H)

27 April   Ethiopian aircraft and 51 passengers hijacked in Sudan; released by negotiation backed by threats.(H)

27 July   Islamic Jihad Yemeni tribesmen seized German Commercial attache. Yemeni MP negotiated release on September 24. (H)

11 September   Simultaneous aircraft highjacking and suicide attacks on twin towers of World Trade Centre New York and Pentagon in Washington. Hostages struggled with their captors in fourth plane which crashes in Pennsylvania field. President Bush declared "war on terrorism" with fateful consequences. (T)

16 September   A West African Professor abducted from a university in Mindanao escaped from Abu Sayyaf kidnapping. (H)

October   Letters containing Anthrax posted to various prominent Americans. (T)

2002

23 February   Ingrid Betancourt, former presidential candidate in Columbia, kidnapped by FARC. (H)

2 April   Palestinian gunmen took sanctuary in the Church of the Nativity in Jerusalem and were fed by the Franciscan brothers. The Israelis claimed the Franciscans were being held hostage. Four brothers who escaped confirmed this but the remainder and the head of the order denied it and declared that the Israelis were looking for an excuse to attack.

11 April   FARC detonated bomb in Cali, Columbia, and took nine Departmental Assembly members hostage in ensuing panic. Hostages still held December 31. (H)

15 May   Mai-Mai abducted a Kenyan, Swede and 24 Thai nationals in the Democratic republic of Congo. Negotiations for release of the hostages broke down when the Mai-Mai insisted on the pullback of soldiers from the occupying Ugandan army and from the local Ugandan ally, the Front for the Liberation of Congo (FLC). (H)

5 June   Bungled rescue of three hostages (2US) at Zamboanga Phillipines. Two hostages and several soldiers and terrorists killed.(H)

22 August   Discovery of severed heads of two of six Jehovas Witness hostages taken by Abu Sayyaf. (T)

23 October★   40 heavily armed Chechens wired with explosives took hostage over 700 of audience and actors during a performance of the musical Nord-Ost in Moscow. Demand end to war in Chechnya, removal of Russian troops and large sum of money. All non-Russians (nearly 60) were released. After two days negotiations Russian Special Forces stormed the building after filling it with narcotic gas. All Chechens were killed, and 129 hostages, the majority by the gas. Movsar Barayev Gang claimed responsibility. (H)

Appendix Two

The Lebanon Hostages

6 June 1982		Israeli army under Ariel Sharon invades Lebanon.		
July 1982		Two Iranian advisers to militia abducted.		

82/7	David Dodge	American	19 July 1982	21 July 1983

16 September 1982	Sabra and Chatila massacre.
11 November 1982	Israeli military HQ in Tyre destroyed by Islamic suicide bomber leaving 75 dead.
18 April 1983	Truck bomb at US embassy leaves 63 dead. Buckley takes over as CIA chief.

83/7	Christian Joubert	French	21 July 1983	15 April 1984

September 1983	Two thousand US, French and Italian plus 100 British troops arrive in Lebanon.
23 October 1983	Truck bombs on American and French Beirut military compounds leave 240 US marines and 58 French dead.
December 1983	Bomb attack in Kuwait. Seventeen Shia of Dawa jailed.

84/2	Frank Regier	American	10 February 1984	15 April 1984
84/3	Jeremy Levin	American	6 March 1984	
84/3	William Buckley	American	16 March 1984	Killed in captivity June 85
84/5	Ben Weir	American	8 May 1984	14 September 1985
84/8	Jonathan Wright	British	August 1984	Escaped Sept 1984

20 September 1984   Suicide bomb at US embassy in east Beirut leaves 23 dead.

85/1	Eric Wehril	Swiss	3 January 1985	Less than a week
85/1	Rev. Lawrence Jenko	American	8 January 1985	26 July 1986

8 March 1985   Unsuccessful CIA attempt to blow up Fadallah. Eighty bystanders killed.

85/3	Nicholas Kluiters	Dutch	14 March 1985	Unknown
85/3	Terry Anderson	American	16 March 1985	4 December 1991
85/3	G-S Peyrolles	French	24 March 1985	2 April 1985
85/3	Marcel Carton	French	March 1985	4 May 1988
85/3	Marcel Fontaine	French	March 1985	4 May 1988
85/3	Brian Levick	British	Abducted and released in March 1985	
85/3	Geoffrey Nash	British	Abducted and released in March 1985	
85/5	Michel Seurat	French	22 May 1985	Died in captivity
85/5	J-P Kauffmann	French	22 May 1985	4 May 1988
85/5	Dennis Hill	British	27 May 1985	Killed 29 May 1985
85/5	David Jacobsen	American	28 May 1985	2 November 1986
85/6	Thomas Sutherland	American	9 June 1985	18 November 1991

14 June 1985   TWA847 skyjacking by Hizbollah.
20 August 1985   First Irangate missiles delivered to Iran by Oliver North.

85/9	Alberto Molinari	Italian	11 Sept 1985	Killed, date unknown

14 September 1985		Remaining US missiles delivered.		
85/10	Arkady Katkov	Russian	1 October 1985	Killed
85/10	ANON	Russian	1 October 1985	Freed
85/10	ANON	Russian	1 October 1985	Freed
85/10	ANON	Russian	1 October 1985	Freed

---

7 October 1985   *Achille Lauro* seizure.

86/1	Do Chae Sung	South Korean	31 January 1986	26 October 1987
86/2	Marcel Coudari	French	2 February 1986	10 November 1986
86/2	Camille Sontag	French	2 February 1986	10 November 1986
86/3	Leigh Douglas	British	March 1986	Killed in captivity 16 April 1994
86/3	Philip Padfield	British	March 1986	Killed in captivity 16 April 1994
86/3	Alec Collett	British	26 March 1986	Killed in captivity in April 1994
86/3	Aurel Cornea	French	9 March 1986	24 December 1986
86/3	George Hansen	French	9 March 1986	20 June 1986
86/3	J-L Normandin	French	March 1986	November 1987
86/4	Michael Brian	French	8 April 1986	12 April 1986

---

15 April 1986   US bombs Tripoli and 93 civilians are killed.

86/4	John McCarthy	British	17 April 1986	August 1991
86/4	Brian Keenan	Irish	11 April 1986	August 24, 1990
86/9	Joseph Cicippio	American	12 Sept 1986	December 1991
86/9	Frank Reed	American	9 Sept 1986	30 April 1990
86/10	Edward Tracy	American	21 October 1986	11 August 1991

---

7 and 14 January 1987   Capture of Hamadi brothers (responsible for TWA847) in Germany.

87/1	Roger Auque	French	January 1987	November 1987
87/1	Rudolf Cordes	German	January 1987	7 September 1988
87/1	Alfred Schmidt	German	20 January 1987	7 September 1987

87/1	Alan Steen	American	24 January 1987	4 December 1991
87/1	Terry Waite	British	20 January 1987	18 November 1991
87/1	Robert Polhill	American	24 January 1987	22 April 1990
87/1	Jesse Turner	American	24 January 1987	21 October 1991
87/1	Mitheleshwar Singh	Indian	24 January 1987	October 1988
88/1	Ralph Schray	German	27 January 1988	Five weeks later
88/2	William Jorgensen	Norwegian	5 February 1988	One month later
88/2	Jan Stening	Swiss	5 February 1988	One month later
88/2	William Higgins	American	17 February 1988	Killed in captivity in July 1989
88/5	Jan Cools	Belgian	21 May 1988	15 June 1989

20 August 1988	Iran-Iraq war ends

88/11	Peter Winkler	Swiss	November 1988	One month later

February 1989	Khomeini's *Satanic Verses* Fatwa. Britain breaks diplomatic relations.
14 March 1989	General Aoun starts another civil war in Lebanon.
28 July 1989	Sheikh Obeid kidnapped by Israel.

89/5	Jackie Mann	British	12 May 1989	September 1991
89/5	Thomas Kemptner	German	16 May 1989	June 1992
89/5	Heinrich Struebig	German	16 May 1989	June 1992
89/10	Emmanuel Christen	Swiss	6 October 1989	8 August 1990
89/10	Elio Erriquez	Swiss	6 October 1989	14 August 1990

Notes to Chapters

Chapter One

(1) *Genesis* Chapter 14, verses 12 to 16.

(2) *The Greek Myths*, Robert Graves, Folio Society, 1996, p.312 seq.

(3) *Captives and Hostages in the Peloponnesian War*, Andreas Panog-oupolos, Grigoris Athens, 1989.

(4) Jenny Straus Clay of the University of Virginia in a paper posted on the Internet.

(5) *Alexander the Great*, Robin Lane Fox, Penguin 1986.

(6) Levi Straus in *Hostage Taking*, ed. Ronald D. Crelinsten and Dennis Szabo, Lexington 1979.

(7) *The Itinerarium Peregrionorum et Gesta Regis Ricardi*, Longmans, 1864, transl. James Brundage, Marquette University Press, 1962 pp. 183–84.

(8) Ibid.

(9) *Fortune's Hostages*, Caroline Moorhead, Hamish Hamilton, 1980.

(10) I am indebted to my friend the Icelandic scholar and folklorist Jennifer Westwood for the information in these two paragraphs.

(11) Moorhead, p.5.

(12) *Lives at Risk*, Russel D. Buhite, Scholarly Resources, 1995, p.16.

(13) For a riveting account of this expedition see Alan Moorhead's *The Blue Nile*, Four Square, 1964, p.211 seq.

(14) Buhite pp. 150–52.

(15) Buhite pp. 66–83 and an article in french by Christophe Choelet on the Internet.

(16) *Cardinal Mercier, Pastorals, Letters, Allocutions, 1914–17*, P.J. Kennedy & Sons, New York, 1917, p.86.

(17) For a detailed account of hostage taking in France during WWII see *Le Livre des Otages*, Serge Klarsfeld, Les Editeurs Francais Réunis, 1979.

(18) For a lucid and detailed analysis of the Nuremberg Trials see *Terrorism & Hostages in International Law*, Joseph J. Lambert, CUP, 1990, on which the preceding paragraphs draw heavily and *The Nuremberg Trials*, John and Anne Tusa, OUP, 1990. Also *UN War Crimes Commission Trials of War Criminals Vol. VIII*

(19) Thomas Schelling quoted by Aston in *Perspectives on Terrorism*, Lawrence Freedman/Yonah Alexander, ed. Scholarly Resources Inc, 1983

(20) *Inside Terrorism,* Bruce Hoffman, Gollancz 1998, p.68.

Chapter Two

(1) R Thackrah in *Terrorism and the Liberal State*, Paul Wilkinson, NY Univ. Press, 1979, p.26.

(2) *Crusaders, Criminals and Crazies*, F.G. Hacker, Bantam, NY, 1978.

(3) Kissane quoted in *Practical, Tactical & Legal Perspectives on Hostage-Taking*, J M Poland & M J McCrystle, Edwin Mellen Press,

1999, pp. 39–44.

(4) Freedman.

(5) *Hostage*, M.S. Miron and A.P. Goldstein, Pergamon NY, 1979.

(6) Ibid p.20.

(7) *No One a Neutral*, Mayer Nudell and Norman Antokol, Alpha Publications, USA, 1990, p.150.

(8) Paul Wilkinson essay in *Kidnap and Ransom*, Richard Clutterbuck, Faber, 1978.

(9) Crelensten in *Contemporary Research on Terrorism*, ed. Paul Wilkinson and A.M.Stewart, Aberdeen 1987.

(10) Crelensten p.20.

(11) Jacques Leaute, Sorbonne Institute of Criminology.

Chapter Three

(1) *No One* ... Nudell, p.87.

(2) Web article by Jeremy A. Sierra, *The Cuban Revolution*, Hugh Thomas, Addison-Wesley, paperback, 1977.

(3) *Lovers and Madmen*, Julie Busic, Writers Club, 2000, p.334.

(4) Ibid p.347.

(5) *No One* ... Nudell, and *Triumph and Terror*, Capt. John Testrake, Kingsway, 1988.

(6) Testrake p.132.

(7) Testrake p.140.

(8) Testrake p.200.

(9) *Hijacking & Hostages*, J Paul de B Taillon and Ulrich K. Wegener, Praeger, 2002, p22

(10) David Davis, *Jersey Post* 02/01/01.

(11) See Cabinet papers for 1970 released under the 30-year rule.

(12) BBC *UK Confidential* 01/01/01.

(13) In an interview with Philip Baum, Aviation Security, October 2000.

(14) BBC *UK Confidential* 01/01/01.

(15) For a longer account see *Carlos the Jackal: Trail of Terror*, Patrick Bellamy, from his book of that title and various other web sites.

Chapter Four

(1) Hoffman p.145.

(2) Tupamaros communiqué February, 1971.

(3) *People's Prisoner*, Sir Geoffrey Jackson, Faber, 1973, p.212.

(4) Leo Ettinger in *Victims of Terror*, Frank Ochberg, David Soskis ed., Westview, 1982, p.74.

(5) Jackson p.57.

(6) Ettinger in Ochberg p.77.

(7) Ettinger in Ochberg p.74.

(8) Jackson p.32.

(9) Jackson p.143.

(10) Jackson p.110.

(11) Jackson pp. 173–74.

(12) Jackson quoted in *Terrorism & Hostage Negotiations*, Abraham Miller, Westview, 1980, p.56.

(13) *Pity the Nation*, Robert Fisk, OUP, 1991, p.435.

(14) Fisk p.617.

(15) Fisk pp. 598–99.

(16) *No One* ... Nudell.

(17) *Hostage*, Con Coughlin, Little Brown, 1992.

(18) Quoted in an article in *The Independent* by Gerry Feehily, Feb 2003.

(19) In an interview with the author.

(20) Quoted in *At Your Own Risk*, Tom and Jean Sutherland, Fulcrum, 1996, p.83.

(21) *Man Without a Gun*, Giandomenico Picco, Times Books, 1999.

Chapter Five

(1) *Our Man Inside*, Diego & Nancy Ascencio, Little Brown, 1983.

(2) Asencio p.35.

(3) Denise Noe on the Court TV crime library website.
(4) Ibid.
(5) Ibid.
(6) *The Ultimate Weapon: Terrorists and World Order*, Jan Edward Schreiber, Morrow NY, 1978, pp. 188–89.
(7) *Every Secret Thing*, Patty Hearst, Methuen, 1982.
(8) Ibid.
(9) Ibid.
(10) Flyn in *Contemporary Research on Terrorism*, ed. P. Wilkinson and A. M. Stuart, Aberdeen, 1987, p.346.

Chapter Six

(1) *No One ... Nuddell.*
(2) *In the Shadow of the Ayatollah,* William J.Daugherty, Naval Institute Press, 2001, p.53.
(3) *Freeing the Hostages,* Russell Moses, Pittsburgh 1996, p53.
(4) International Court of Justice, 1980, Report No. 3.
(5) Daugherty, p.93.
(6) Moses, p.333.
(7) *Afghanistan: A History of Conflict,* John C. Griffiths, André Deutsch, 2002, p.173.
(8) Moses, p.342.
(9) *The Iranian Rescue Mission,* Paul B. Ryan, Naval Institute Press, USA, 1985, p.3.
(10) Daugherty, pp. 64 and 93.
(11) Ryan, p.11.
(12) Nowruz, 25/5/02.
(13) Article by Alfred Lilienthal, Washington Report on Middle Eastern Affairs.
(14) *bin Laden,* Yossef Bodansky, Random House, 2001.
(15) Interviews on various television channels.
(16) *Vengeance: The True Story of an Israeli Counter-Terrorism Team,*

George Jonas, Collins, 1984.
(17) *Memoirs of a Palestinian Terrorist,* Abu Daoud, 1999.

Chapter Seven

(1) *Anderson Valley Advertiser,* 30/04/97.
(2) Ibid.
(3) Ibid.

Chapter Eight

(1) Of the many accounts of this event I found the one by Major Louis Williams of the Israel Defence Force published on the internet the most useful.
(2) Ochberg p.28.
(3) Ibid p.33.

Chapter Nine

(1) *Crisis Negotiations: Managing Critical Incidents and Hostage Situations etc.,* Michael J. McMains & Wayman C. Mullins, Anderson Publishing, USA, 2003, pp. 8–9, and Internet
(2) Schreiber pp. 105–08, for a full and graphic account of this incident. Also Poland, p.45.
(3) Schreiber.
(4) Miller, p.22.
(5) Poland, p.45.
(6) *Terrorism: Interdisciplinary Perspectives*, Burr Eichelman, David A Soskis, William H Reid, [eds.], American Psychiatric Association, 1983, p.145.
(7) Quoted in Ochberg, p.11.
(8) Ibid.
(9) For fuller accounts see Crelinsten pp. 116–18 and Ochberg pp. 9–25.

Chapter Ten

(1) Kaplan quoted in Eichelman p.16.

(2) See Hacker in Freedman.
(3) Warren Christopher in *American Hostages in Iran,* ed. Paul Kreisberg, Yale, 1985, p.20.
(4) Miller, p.29, Taillon, p.73.
(5) McMains, p.26.
(6) Miller, p.350.
(7) Rogan, Hammer, VanZandt, ed., p.65 (see biblio).
(8) Miller, p.32.
(9) *Areopagitica,* John Milton, Nonesuch edition, 1948, p.696.
(10) *Effective Emergency...,* Nudell (see biblio).
(11) Rogan, p.34 and Hammer in Rogan, p.115.
(12) Picco, p.119.
(13) Donohue in Rogan, p.69.
(14) McMains, p.11.
(15) Dwayne Fischer and Gary Noesner FBI web article *The Law Enforcement and Response.*
(16) Hacker in Freedman.
(17) Interview with the author.
(18) Rogan, p.39.
(19) Picco, p.136.
(20) Waite interview with the author.
(21) Donohue in Rogan, pp. 30–1.
(22) Picco, pp. 5 and 114.
(23) Picco, p.241.
(24) Quoted in McMains, p.11.
(25) *Effective Emergency...,* Nudell.
(26) Waite interview with the author.
(27) Mullany in Crelinsten, p.51.
(28) Womack and Walsh in Rogan, p.66.
(29) Moses, p.350.
(30) Chapter Four in Rogan.
(31) Quoting William Zartman in Moses, p.340.
(32) *Effective Emergency..,* Nudell, p.73.
(33) Rogan, Introduction.
(34) Christopher, p.21.

Chapter Eleven
(1) Dwayne Fischer and Gary Noesner, FBI web article *The Law Enforcement and Response.*
(2) Hacker in Freedman.
(3) Eichelman, pp.172–73, and Russell and Millar.
(4) *Some Other Rainbow,* John McCarthy and Jill Morrell, BCA, 1993.
(5) Hoffman, Preface.
(6) See Eichelman and hostage autobiographies.
(7) *Flying Hero Class,* Thomas. Keneally, Hodder, 1991, p.73.
(8) Jackson, p.179.
(9) See Hacker.
(10) Miller, p.24.
(11) *Effective Emergency,* Nudell.
(12) Frank Ochberg in *Terrorism, Vol. 1, No. 2,* 1978, p.350.
(13) Schreiber.
(14) Aston in Freedman.
(15) Moorhead, p.98.
(16) Crelinsten, p.23.
(17) Buhite, p.198 and Miller, p.27.
(18) Jackson, p.108.
(19) Sutherland, p.93.
(20) Schreiber, pp. 141–42.
(21) Marighella quoted in Aston.
(22) Keneally, p.179.
(23) See Freedman, Miller, Aston, Zawodny et al., and autobiographies.
(24) F.J. Hacker in Freedman.

Chapter Twelve
(1) Miller, p.11.
(2) Hoffman, p.149.
(3) Ascencio, p.3.
(4) B.M. Jenkins, Rand Corporation report, 1976.
(5) See Crelinsten, p.134 seq.
(6) Asencio, p.174.
(7) McCarthy.
(8) Quoted by Symmonds in Eichelman, p.84.
(9) Crelinsten, p.135.

(10) Ettinger in Ochberg.
(11) *Taken on Trust,* Terry Waite, Hodder, 1993, p.139.
(12) Jackson, p.103.
(13) Interview with the author.
(14) Thomas Keneally.
(15) Moorhead in an interview with Dr Ferdinando Imposimato.
(16) Moorhead.
(17) Robert Hauber in Freedman.
(18) Asencio, p.106.
(19) *L'Affaire Claustre.*
(20) Bourgeois, Diaries on the Internet.
(21) Crayton in Freedman.
(22) *No One ...,* Nuddell, p.149.
(23) Linda Laushway quoted in Crelinsten, p.22.
(24) Thomas Strenz, *Use of Ego Defence Mechanisms,* on the Internet.
(25) McCarthy.
(26) Waite interview with the author.
(27) Paraphrased from the author's discussion with Waite.
(28) *Yours Till the End,* Sunnie and Jackie Mann, Heineman, 1992.
(29) *L'Affaire Claustre,* p.431, author's translation – with help!
(30) *An Evil Cradling,* Brian Keenan, Hutchinson, 1992.
(31) Crayton in Freedman.
(32) Symmonds in Eichelman, p.73.
(33) Crelinsten, p.142.
(34) Interview with the author.
(35) Eric Shaw in Freedman.
(36) Miller, p.26.
(37) Flynn, Campbell, Hillman et al.
(38) Quoted in Moorhead.
(39) Flynn.
(40) Interview with the author.
(41) Full account Dr Gordon J. Turnbull, *NCP Clinical Quarterly 4(1),* Winter, 1994.
(42) Sutherland, p.387.
(43) Article in *Newsweek,* May 1980.

Chapter Thirteen
(1) Hoffman.
(2) Crelensten, p.20.
(3) Poland, p.29.
(4) Schreiber, p.150.
(5) Lambert, p.50.
(6) Joshua Black, Martin Sldadany Jr., a paper at Houston University, April, 2000.
(7) Ibid.
(8) Khalil Osman, Crescent International, July 16-30, 2000.
(9) Uri Lubrani quoted in Coughlin
(10) Wilkinson, *Terrorism and the Liberal State* (see biblio).
(11) Robert Friedlander quoted Miller, p.7.
(12) Miller, p.18.
(13) Buhite, p.200.
(14) Claustre, p.432.
(15) Taillon.
(16) *The Human Shield,* Tim Lewis, Leomansley, 1993.
(17) Buhite, p.197, Miller, p.19, etc
(18) Osman (see 8).
(19) I am indebted to Dr Philip Towle of the Department of International Studies, Cambridge University for this anecdote.
(20) Aston in Freedman.
(21) Ibid.

Chapter Fourteen
(1) For a detailed analysis of these trends see US State Department, Taillon, Aston in Freedman et al.
(2) Chamberlain on Hitler's annexation of the Sudetenland.
(3) Schreiber, p.13.
(4) William Reid in Eichelman, p.165.
(5) Taillon, p.30.
(6) Eg Schreiber, p.73.
(7) Karl Marcus quoted in Schreiber.
(8) ABTA figures.
(9) Schreiber, p.198.

Reading List

Autobiography and Biography

Anderson, Terry A. *Den of Lions.* Hodder, 1994
Asencio, Diego and Nancy. *Our Man Inside.* Little Brown, 1983
Busic, Julie. *Lovers and Madmen.* Writers Club, 2000
Daugherty, William J. *In the Shadow of the Ayatollah.* Naval Inst Press, 2001
Hearst, Patty. *Every Secret Thing.* Methuen, 1982
Jackson, Sir Geoffrey. *People's Prison.* Faber, 1973
Keenan, Brian. *An Evil Cradling.* Hutchison, 1992
Kelly, Terina. *Terina: Diary of a hostage in Ethiopia.* Wolfhound, 1984
Lewis, Tim. *The Human Shield.* Leomansley, 1993
Mann, Sunnie and Jackie. *Yours till the End.* Heineman, 1992
McCarthy John & Morrell Jill. *Some Other Rainbow.* BCA, 1993
Pflug, Jackie Nink. *Miles to go Before I sleep.* Hazelden USA, 1996
Picco, Giandomenico. *Man Without a Gun.* Times Books, 1999
Say, Peggy and Knobler, Peter. *Forgotten.* Simon & Schuster, 1991
Sutherland, Tom and Jean. *At Your Own Risk.* Fulcrum, 1996
Svirskii, Grigori. *Hostages: The Personal Testimony of a Soviet Jew.* Bodley, 1976
Testrake, Capt John. *Triumph over Terror.* Kingsway (British edn),1988
Waite, Terry. *Taken on Trust.* Hodder, 1993

Non-fiction

Bolz, Frank, A. Jnr. *Hostage Cop.* Simon & Schuster, 1980
Buhite, D. *Lives at Risk.* Scholarly Resources, 1995
Campbell, James F. *Hostage: Terror and Triumph.* Contributions in Psychology, 1992
Claustre, Pierre. *L'Affaire Claustre: autopsie d'un prize d'otages*, Karthala 1990
Clutterbuck, Richard. *Kidnap and Ransom.* Faber, 1978
Coughlin, Con. *Hostage.* Little Brown, 1992
Crelinsten, Ronald D. and Szabo, Denis. *Hostage Taking.* Lexington, 1979
Davidson, A.J. *Kidnapped.* Gill and MacMillan, 2003
Eichelman, Burr, Soskis, David, A. and Reid, William, H.
    Terrorism: Interdisciplinary Perspectives. American Psychiatric Association, 1983
Fisk, Robert. *Pity The Nation.* OUP, 1991
Freedman, Lawrence and Yonah, Alexander ed. *Perspectives on Terrorism.*
    Scholarly Resources Inc, 1983
Hoffman, Bruce. *Inside Terrorism.* Gollancz, 1998
Jenkins, B.M. et al. *Numbered Lives.* Rand Corporation, 1977

Jonas, G. *Vengeance: The True Story of an Israeli Counter-Terrorist Team.* Collins, 1984

Kaam, Ben van. *The South Moluccans.* Hurst, 1980

Klarsfeld, Serge. *Le Livre des Otages.* Les Editeurs France Réunis, 1979

Kreisberg, Paul, ed. *American Hostages in Iran.* Yale, 1985

Lambert, Joseph J. *Terrorism and Hostages in International Law.* CUP, 1990

McKnight, Gerald. *The Mind of the Terrorist.* Indianapolis, 1974

McMains, Michael, J. and Mullins, Wayman, C. *Crisis Negotiations: Managing Critical Incidents and Hostage Situations.* Andesron Publishing USA, 2003

Miller, Abraham. *Terrorism and Hostage Negotiations.* Westview, 1980

Moorhead, Caroline. *Fortune's Hostages.* Hamish Hamilton, 1980

Moses, Russell Leigh. *Freeing the Hostages.* Univ. Pittsburgh, 1996

Nudell, Meyer and Antokol, Norman. *Effective Emergency and Crisis Management.* Lexington, 1988

Nudell, Meyer and Antokol, Norman. *No One a Neutral.* Alpha USA, 1990

Ochberg, Frank and Soskis, David, ed. *Victims of Terror.* Westview, 1982

Poland, J.M. and McCrystle, M.J. Political, *Legal and Tactical Perspectives on Hostage Taking.* Edwin Mellen Press, 199

Rogan, Hammer, VanZandt, eds. *Dynamic Processes of Crisis Negotiation.* Praeger, 1997

Ryan, Paul B. *The Iranian Rescue Mission.* Naval Institute Press USA, 1985

Schmid, Alex P. and Jongman, Albert J, et. al. *Political terrorism a New Guide.* North-Holland, 1988

Schreiber, Jan Edward. *The Ultimate Weapon: terrorists and World Order.* Morrow New York, 1978

Taillon, J Paul de B. and Wegener, Ulrich K. *Hijacking & Hostages.* Praeger, 2002

Thompson, L. *Rescuers: The World's Top Anti-Terrorist Units.* David & Charles, 1986

Wilkinson, Paul. *Terrorism and the Liberal State.* New York University Press, 1979

Wilkinson, Paul and Stuart A.M, eds. *Contemporary Research on Terrorism.* Aberdeen, 1987

Fiction

Keneally, Thomas. *Flying Hero Class.* Hodder, 1991

History

Connell, Thomas. *America's Japanese Hostages.* Praeger, 2002

Fox, Robin Lane. *Alexander the Great.* Penguin, 1986

Panogoupolos, A. *Captives and Hostages in the Peloponnesian War.* Grigoris Athens, 1989

Runciman, Sir Steven. *History of the Crusades.* CUP, 1951

Tusa, John and Anne. *The Nuremberg Trials.* Macmillan, 1983

Webb, B. Garrison. *Civil War Hostages.* White Mane USA, 2000

Index